3 BETTER ENGLISH EVERY DAY

Language for Living

PAUL J. HAMEL

Los Angeles Unified School District
Santa Monica City College

D0225146

THOMSON

HEINLE

Australia Canada Mexico Singapore Spain United Kingdom United States

THOMSON

HEINLE

Better English Every Day
Volume III
Paul J. Hamel

Copyright © 1984 Heinle, a part of Thomson Learning, Inc.
Thomson Learning™ is a trademark used herein under license.

Printed in the United States of America
  18 19 20 21 22 23   06 05 04

For more information contact Heinle, 25 Thomson Place, Boston, MA 02210 USA,
or you can visit our Internet site at http://www.heinle.com

For permission to use material from this text or product contact us:
Tel   1-800-730-2214
Fax   1-800-730-2215
Web   www.thomsonrights.com

ISBN: 0-0306-9604-6

Library of Congress Catalog Card Number: 83-082148

To Sister Alice Landry

ACKNOWLEDGMENTS

Grateful acknowledgments are due to the many people who have encouraged me in writing this series. In particular I am indebted to Nancy Loncke for her invaluable contributions to this series in its early stages.

Special thanks to Elaine Kirn for her sound advice, for helping develop the format and for doing detailed editing. I would especially like to thank Tim Welch, Laura Welch, and Anne Boynton-Trigg for coordinating the production of the series; Pat Campbell, Nancy Cook, Linda Mrowicki, and Jean Zukowski/Faust for editing; Larry Layton for the book design; Frank Ridgeway and Betty Darwin for the art; Shelah Harris and Online Graphics for the typesetting; Becky Evans and Penny Yost for layout; and Bill Riling for lettering.

Special thanks also goes to the administrators, teachers, and students of Fairfax Community Adult School, Santa Monica City College, Jewish Vocational Service, and the Refugee Employment Training Project for their comments, suggestions, and assistance in developing the lessons.

I am especially grateful to David Chaille for his valuable ideas, insights, and for introducing me to publishing.

Last but not least, I am very grateful to George Gati for his editing, patience, understanding, and putting up with me during the many long hours it took to complete this series.

CONTENTS

INTRODUCTION
TO THE TEACHER

This series of three books is designed for adult students of English as a Second Language. It presents the grammar, vocabulary, and survival skills required in a basic ESL program. In addition, it supplies students with ample opportunity to practice the four language skills in the context of interesting and varied activities.

The major aim of this series is to present survival English so that newcomers can move more quickly into the labor market and function successfully on the job. The series covers critical survival skills needed to deal with real-life situations. The books emphasize finding and keeping a job, and the grammar program is highly integrated into prevocational materials and activities. Lessons carefully integrate survival skills, grammatical structures, and vocabulary to present practical and meaningful activities for the students. Grammatical structures are not presented and then forgotten. They reappear in multiple varied contexts throughout the series. The vocabulary, although often used in what appears to be nonvocational areas, represents common job-related words and are easily transferable to a work environment.

By the time students finish the series, they will have been exposed to enough English and job-related information to successfully begin work at an entry-level position or enter a technical English program.

TEACHING NOTES

These teaching notes detail some effective ways of teaching language skills. The basic techniques in these notes offer guidelines and suggestions to help the teacher present lessons in an effective and interesting way. We hope that these suggestions will inspire other, more creative techniques.

Listening Comprehension

The teacher may want to use the following techniques to develop effective listening comprehension skills.

1. After introducing key vocabulary words at the beginning of a reading lesson or dialog, slowly read the text aloud to your students before having them open their books. Then ask general comprehension questions. At the end of the reading lesson, dialog, or follow-up review exercise, read the text again at normal speed. The students should not be allowed to read along; they should concentrate on listening.
2. Give frequent short dictations. (See the section on dictation.)
3. When doing drills or question-and-answer exercises,

have students cue one another whenever possible. This forces them to listen to each other and become accustomed to different accents.
4. Have students work in pairs and groups so that they can listen and respond to one another on a more personal level. (See the section on pairing and grouping.)
5. When practicing dialogs or role-playing, occasionally have pairs of students stand back-to-back so that they must understand each other without the aid of nonverbal cues.
6. Invite a guest speaker, the principal, the school nurse, a police officer, etc., to be interviewed in class so that the students can hear other accents and intonation. Before allowing the students to interview the speaker, prime the class by discussing the kinds of questions they will ask. By practicing the questions beforehand, students will be less embarrassed about asking questions or making mistakes.
7. Give the students the opportunity to listen to different examples of spoken English through music, games, movies, slide presentations, etc.

Dictation

Do not underestimate the usefulness of dictation. It can be a very effective tool for practicing the four language skills. It is especially useful as a warm-up exercise at the beginning of the class period to review previously covered materials. Frequent short dictations focusing on commonly used words and expressions used in simple sentences repeatedly stressing function words, such as articles, prepositions, pronouns, and auxiliary verbs, will do much to improve students' writing and spelling. Once students become accustomed to simple dictations presented in this series, you may want to vary the dictation format to keep interest high. As an example, try the following:

1. Dictate six questions.
2. After the students have written all six questions in their notebooks, have six volunteers write the questions on the chalkboard.
3. Have six other students read and correct the questions.
4. Have six more volunteers go up to the chalkboard and write the answers to the questions.
5. Have students read and correct the answers.
6. Discuss additional possible answers to the questions.

Other Suggestions:

1. Dictate the answers, and then have students write the questions.

2. Dictate single words that students must use in complete sentences.
3. Dictate jumbled sentences that students must put into correct word order.
4. Dictate sentences that students must change from affirmative to negative, interrogative to affirmative, etc.

Pronunciation, Spelling, and Word Building

Although teaching pronunciation and spelling should play a very important role in the beginning English class, it has too often been ignored. Despite many irregularly spelled words, some basic pronunciation and spelling rules can be taught early on to improve reading and writing skills. Keep such lessons short, introduce them frequently, and review them repeatedly.

Suggestions:

1. Use visuals, objects, pictures, and gestures as much as possible for constant reinforcement.
2. Do not overburden the students with too much pronunciation or spelling material at once. Do not teach more than one pronunciation lesson per day.
3. Irregularly spelled words should be taught separately from words that follow rules. A good way to teach them is through constant and frequent dictation.

Vocabulary

The following suggestions are only a few of those to be kept in mind when teaching vocabulary.

1. Use as many flash cards, objects (realia), and pictures as possible in order to reinforce the words visually. This will help hold interest and aid students in remembering new vocabulary.
2. Define the words and give many contextual examples in sentences, expressions, and situations. Also help define and contrast the new vocabulary with synonyms, antonyms, and homonyms.
3. When selecting vocabulary, concentrate on practical, high frequency, functional vocabulary and expressions.
4. Do not overburden your students with too many vocabulary items at any one time. Introduce ten or so new words per lesson.

Suggested Activities:

1. Flash Cards: Write new words on 5" x 8" index cards and use them in your lessons. Daily add a few new words. Mix them up and use them for review. Continually add to them until you have developed a valuable word bank. Use the cards for pronunciation practice, drills, recognition (i.e., have students make complete sentences with the words), dictation, spelling bees, and other word games.
2. Conversation Practice: Cut out pictures describing everyday life from newspapers and magazines and paste them on construction paper. Then, on the back of each picture, write four or five vocabulary words represented in the picture (a noun, a verb, an adjective, and a preposition). Even if many more words could be added, limit the number. Divide the class into pairs or small groups and distribute the pictures. (See the section on pairing and grouping.) Tell the students to use the vocabulary on the back of the pictures to identify the objects and discuss what is happening. As a variation, write a list of question words on the chalkboard and have students use them in asking one another questions. Walk around the classroom, listening, and correcting errors and spending time with the weaker students. Let groups exchange pictures to continue the exercise.
3. Tic-tac-toe: Draw a tic-tac-toe grid and fill it in with vocabulary. Divide the class into two teams, each team assigned the symbol "X" or "O." Then flip a coin to determine which team begins. Have the students take turns in an orderly fashion by going down the rows. Tell the first student of the first team to use any word from the grid in a sentence. If the sentence is correct, replace the word with the team's symbol, X or O. Otherwise, leave the word. Go on to the first person on the other team. Continue in this manner until one team wins by having three consecutive X's or O's in a row vertically, horizontally, or diagonally. Keep score by giving one point for each game won. After each game, replace all the words in the grid with a different category of words such as all prepositions, all verbs, all antonym pairs, etc.
4. Crossword Puzzle: Draw a grid and words on the chalkboard. Divide the class into two teams and flip a coin to determine which team goes first. Have the first student of the first team go to the chalkboard and write a word that uses one letter of an existing word in the crossword. If the word fits and is correctly spelled, give one point for every letter of the new word. Then, go on to the first student of the other team. If the word is incorrect, erase it and go to the opposite team.

Pair Practice and Grouping

Pairing and grouping exercises give the students time, especially in large classes, to practice important speaking skills. Organizing students to work together can be somewhat frustrating at the start, but once they clearly understand what you expect of them, subsequent pairing or grouping activities usually proceed smoothly. Most pair practice exercises consist of simple substitution or transformation drills that you can also use for drilling the class as a whole.

Pair Practice:

1. Explain that this kind of exercise is to allow students to practice their *speaking* skills, not their writing skills. Tell students to put away all writing materials.
2. Have each student choose a partner. You will probably have to go around the classroom and pair students up the first few times you do this type of activity. Encourage students to pair up with different partners each time.
3. Indicate the material you want the students to practice.
4. Walk around the classroom, listening to individual students and correcting any errors that you hear. This provides an excellent opportunity to spend time with your weaker students.

Grouping:

In more advanced classes, dividing students into small groups for conversation practice is especially effective.

1. Divide the class into groups of four or five.
2. Present a problem, values clarification, for example, and tell the students that they must come up with a solution to the problem that all members of the group support unanimously.
3. While the groups are discussing, compromising, and agreeing on solutions, walk around the classroom to answer questions or correct any mistakes you hear.
4. Bring the whole class together for a general discussion to compare the various answers.

Reading

Some suggestions:

1. Before reading the dialog or passage, introduce the new vocabulary and grammatical structures. For effective visual reinforcement, use the chalkboard, flash cards, and pictures. Give many contextual examples of new words.
2. Read the text. The students should not see the text at this point. Use this time as a listening comprehension exercise. (See the section on listening comprehension.)
3. Ask general comprehension questions.
4. Read the text a second time, with the students reading along. As you read, tell the students to underline any unfamiliar vocabulary and expressions.
5. Discuss the vocabulary and expressions the students have underlined.
6. Ask more detailed comprehension questions.
7. Have volunteers read the passage aloud. (optional)

Other Suggestions:

1. Have students read the text silently. Then ask basic comprehension questions.
2. Have students retell the story in their own words.
3. After asking detailed comprehension questions, have students ask their own detailed questions of each other.
4. On another day, give a short dictation based on part of the text. (See section on dictation.)
5. Prepare a handout of the text with some of the vocabulary items missing (cloze-type exercise). Have students supply the words.
6. Have students write a story modeled on the text or dialog.
7. If possible, have students change the story from dialog to text or vice versa.
8. Do a read-and-look-up exercise: have students read a sentence silently, then try to repeat as much of the sentence as they can without looking at the book.
9. Prepare a handout of a text or dialog with some of the words missing. Read the text aloud and have students fill in the missing words as they read along.

Dialogs

Some suggestions:

1. Before presenting the dialog to the class, select and introduce any vocabulary items and structures that the students are not familiar with.
2. Read the dialog once for general comprehension. You may want to let the students read along.
3. Have students close their books.
4. Read the first line aloud, and then have the students repeat it. If necessary, have them repeat it several times for correct pronunciation and intonation.
5. Teach the second line (rejoinder) in the same manner. If the line is too long, present it in segments.
6. Repeat the first line, having a student respond with the rejoinder. Then reverse roles.
7. Select two students to repeat the two lines.
8. Teach the next two lines in the same manner.
9. Return to the beginning of the dialog and review it to the point where you left off.
10. Continue to the end of the dialog. (If the dialog is very long, select only one part. Do not try to teach dialogs which are more than eight or ten lines.)

Other Suggestions:

1. Write the first part of the rejoinder on the chalkboard and have students come up to write the second part.
2. Give part of the dialog as a dictation on a subsequent day.
3. As a written quiz, prepare a handout of the dialog with some of the key vocabulary items missing. Have students fill in the blanks from memory.

4. Have students write their own dialog modeled on the text.
5. Have students rewrite the dialog as a narrative.
6. Adapt the dialog to be used as the basis of a role-playing exercise. (See the section on role-playing.)

Writing

Expose students through short frequent exercises to writing that is closely related to the vocabulary, structures, and topics you have already taught. Exercises should also be varied, practical, and related to students' daily lives.

Be careful not to overwhelm students. Begin this program with simple exercises such as addressing envelopes and writing postcards, notes, and shopping lists. Such initial practice will give students time to learn the most commonly used words, which are also the most irregularly spelled, such as pronouns, articles, prepositions, and auxiliary verbs. Once students have learned the basics, gradually build up to longer and more complex exercises.

Other Suggestions:

1. Assign writing exercises that reinforce or review previously learned material.
2. When giving a writing assignment as homework, reserve the last part of the class period for writing. This will allow you to walk around the classroom to make sure everyone understands the assignment.
3. When correcting the students' papers, correct only serious mistakes in structure and spelling. Praise the correct use of recently taught vocabulary and structures.
4. If you find mistakes that several students are making, note them and teach a special lesson based on these mistakes.
5. Include the entire class in the correcting process by copying the incorrect sentences taken from their papers onto the chalkboard or on a handout. Have a class discussion on how best to correct the mistakes.
6. Have students rewrite their corrected exercises in their notebooks.
7. Keep a list of spelling errors to be used in a future dictation.

Grammar

Some Suggestions:

1. Present grammar sequenced in order of increasing difficulty. For example, introduce the simple past tense before teaching the present perfect. With major grammatical structures, such as the use of the simple past, introduce structures in well-spaced segments. Don't try to teach all the irregular verbs at once. It is more appropriate to teach a few at a time over a long period.

2. In introducing grammar, use situations, visuals, and graphics to give students several different ways of understanding the structure.
3. Present and reinforce grammar in the context of survival skills, situations, activities, stories, and games. For example, when teaching the possessive *of,* also teach the names of food containers (carton *of* milk, can *of* soup, etc.).
4. End all lessons, or do follow-up reviews, with communicative activities, such as role-playing, incorporating the grammatical structure. For example, after teaching *some* and *any,* role-play ordering food in a restaurant. For teaching prepositions, set up an obstacle course in the classroom and have students direct each other through it. (See the section on role-playing.)
5. When presenting drills, vary them whenever possible. Cue responses with gestures, objects, pictures, and flash cards.
6. In nonacademic courses, minimize the use of grammatical terms. For instance, most students are interested in learning how to *use* the structures rather than in knowing the differences between transitive and intransitive verbs.
7. Constantly review previously taught grammar. Reintroduce it in another context, contrast it with another grammatical structure, or build it into another lesson.

Role-Playing

Use role-playing to expand your lessons and reinforce vocabulary and structures. Before expecting students to perform successfully in role-playing exercises, consider the following:

1. Discuss the situation beforehand so that students can familiarize themselves with the topic as well as with necessary vocabulary and structure.
2. Teach a dialog as a primer, or allow students to prepare themselves in pairs or small groups. (See the section on pair practice.)
3. Have students do each role-playing exercise twice, the first time with teacher participation and the second time without.
4. Encourage students to vary situations and be creative.
5. Don't over-correct. Note major mistakes; discuss and correct them later. To practice active listening, have the class note errors, too.
6. Discuss the role-playing exercise afterward for students' reaction and interpretations.

Some Basic Situations:

Asking and giving street directions; looking at and asking questions about a new apartment; calling the telephone operator for information; buying an item in a store; going on a job interview; speaking to a doctor, dentist, or pharmacist; getting a driver's license; introducing and meeting people at a party; making or canceling an appointment; leaving a message; asking a postal clerk about correct postage; cashing a check; opening a checking or savings account at a bank; ordering food at a restaurant; etc.

General Suggestions

1. Create an atmosphere where students are not afraid to make mistakes. Simple communication is more important than speaking perfectly.
2. Encourage students to use what they have learned in class in their speech. Encourage them to speak to one another in English during their breaks and free time. You might even reserve a special "English table" or area in your classroom where students can practice while having a snack or a cup of coffee.
3. Be eclectic. Use any method, technique, or combination of methods that work for you and your students.
4. Use as much variety in your lessons as possible.
5. Space your best lessons and activities throughout the course to keep interest high. Don't empty your entire "bag of tricks" early on.
6. Make and collect as many teaching aids (visuals, objects, handouts) as possible. Store them for future use.
7. Require that your students bring dictionaries to school and use them often.

1

A NEW SEMESTER

- Review of Books 1 and 2

LISTEN

David Fernandez and Sami Hamati meet at the beginning of a new semester.

Sami: Hi, David. How are you?

David: Oh, hi, Sami. I'm fine. What about you?

Sami: OK. What class are you taking this semester?

David: I'm taking the radio and T.V. repair course. I hope that it will help me find a job. What are you taking?

Sami: ESL 3. Did you have a good vacation?

David: Not really. I looked for a job, but without any luck.

Sami: Did you look at the notices on the bulletin board in the hall?

David: No, I didn't, but I will before I go home.

Sami: Where is everybody?

David: I think that they're all next to the catering truck.

Sami: Come on. Let's go over there and say, "Hi."

UNDERSTAND   *Circle **True**, **False**, or **We don't know**.*

1. It's a new semester.	(True)	False	We don't know.
2. David has a job.	True	False	We don't know.
3. Sami has a job.	True	False	We don't know.
4. You can buy food at a catering truck.	True	False	We don't know.
5. "Over there" means "over here."	True	False	We don't know.
6. "ESL" means "English as a Second Language."	True	False	We don't know.

READ

The students are talking at the catering truck.

1. Wanda/Joanne

2. Stephen/Paul

3. Sami/Rita

4. Li and Yen Chu

5. Mr. Barns/Mr. Fuller

6. Caterer/Tan

7. Lan/Mona

8. Raymond/Roberto

9. Carmen/Mario

PAIR PRACTICE

Talk with another student in the present continuous. Use the pictures and phrases above.

Student 1: What's .... saying?
            or
            What's .... telling ....?
Student 2: He/She's saying/telling ....

PAIR PRACTICE

Talk in the past tense. Use the pictures and phrases above.

Student 1: What did .... say?
            or
            What did .... tell ....?
Student 2: He/She said/told ....

READ

Roberto and Raymond are twins. They're talking with Joanne Yates.

PAIR PRACTICE   *Talk with another student. Use the phrases below in the present continuous.*

Student 1: Are you ....ing ....?
Student 2: I'm not ....ing ...., but he is.

1. use this chair
2. sit here
3. read this book
4. drink this coffee
5. eat this sandwich
6. wait for Mr. Fuller

PAIR PRACTICE   *Use the phrases below in the simple present tense.*

Student 1: Do you ....?
Student 2: I don't ...., but he does.

1. live near here
2. know everybody here
3. want a cup of coffee
4. work near here
5. feel OK
6. have a car

PAIR PRACTICE   *Use the phrases below in the past tense.*

Student 1: Did your brother ....?
Student 2: Yes, he ...., but I didn't.

1. take a vacation
2. take a trip
3. have a good time
4. practice his English
5. rest
6. spend a lot of money

PAIR PRACTICE   *Use the phrases below in the future tense.*

Student 1: Will your brother ....?
Student 2: Maybe he will ...., but I won't.

1. repeat this class
2. take a typing class
3. look for a new job
4. fix his car
5. wash his car
6. stay home next weekend

WRITE   *Change the verbs under the line to the past tense.*

David Fernandez and Rita Landry are talking.

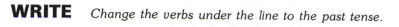

Rita: How was your vacation, David?

David: I **didn't have** much of a vacation. Every day **was** _____
          <u>don't have</u>   <u>is</u>

the same for me. I _____ up, _____ breakfast, and
                      <u>get</u>   <u>make</u>

_____ ready as usual, but I _____ to work because I
   <u>get</u>   <u>don't go</u>

_____ my job. I _____ in a furniture factory for about
   <u>lose</u>   <u>work</u>

a year before I _____. The boss _____ me that I
                  <u>leave</u>   <u>tell</u>

_____ a very good employee, but the company
   <u>am</u>

_____ enough work to employ all their workers, so they
   <u>doesn't have</u>

_____ let me go. I _____ for a job last month. I
   <u>have to</u>   <u>look</u>

_____ the newspaper ads, _____ some letters,
   <u>read</u>   <u>write</u>

_____ some appointments, _____ a lot of application
   <u>make</u>   <u>fill out</u>

forms, and _____ a few interviews.
              <u>have</u>

Rita: Well, what _____?
                      <u>happen</u>

David: Nothing. I _____ a job. I'll continue to look. I'm sure that
                      <u>don't get</u>

I'll find a job soon.

READ

Now David's asking Rita about her vacation.

AND WHAT ABOUT YOU, RITA, WHAT DID YOU DO LAST MONTH?

WHEN WERE YOU IN SAN FRANCISCO?

I WENT TO NEW YORK AND SAN FRANCISCO.

I DON'T REMEMBER. LET ME LOOK AT MY CALENDAR.

JULY

1 visit the museum	2 attend exercise class	3 begin to read new book	4 play tennis	5 rain, stay home	6 have lunch with Joanne	7 attend exercise class
8 Call parents	9 watch special program on T.V.	10 go to library	11 lunch with Judy	12 rain, stay home	13 shop for food	14 have dinner at 7:00 with Bob
15 go to the airport	16 arrive in New York	17 stay in New York	18 stay in New York	19 stay in New York	20 stay in New York	21 go to San Francisco
22 stay in S.F.	23 stay in S.F.	24 return home	25 attend exercise class	26 finish book	27 shop for food	28 go to movie at 7:30 with Bob
29 call Mom and Dad	30 visit Uncle John	31 go to the dentist				

PAIR PRACTICE   *Ask and answer questions about Rita's calendar.*

Student 1: When was Rita ....?
Student 2: She was ....

WHEN WAS RITA IN SAN FRANCISCO?

SHE WAS THERE FROM JULY TWENTY-FIRST TO JULY TWENTY-FOURTH.

PAIR PRACTICE   *Use the calendar above.*

Student 1: What did Rita do on ....?
Student 2: She ....

WHAT DID RITA DO ON JULY SIXTH?

SHE HAD LUNCH WITH JOANNE.

WRITE   *Help Maria Corral ask Yen Chu questions about her vacation. The answers will help you figure out the questions. Use some of the question words in the box.*

| how much   how   what   why   how long   when   where |

Maria Corral and Yen Chu are talking.

Maria: *Where did you go?*

Yen: We went to San Francisco.

Maria: *How long...*

Yen: We stayed only one week.

Maria: _____

Yen: We saw the Golden Gate Bridge, the Financial District, and other interesting places.

Maria: _____

Yen: Because San Francisco isn't too far from here and because we didn't have a lot of money.

Maria: _____

Yen: We went by car.

Maria: _____

Yen: The weather was horrible. It was cold and foggy.

Maria: _____

Yen: We didn't spend a lot of money.

Maria: _____

Yen: We came back home last Sunday evening.

READ

Carmen Martinez and Mario Corral are talking about the schedule of classes.

WHAT DO YOU HAVE IN YOUR HAND?

CAN I LOOK AT IT?

OH, THIS? IT'S THE NEW SCHEDULE OF CLASSES.

SURE. HERE YOU ARE.

SCHEDULE OF CLASSES

From September 12 to December 20

CLASS	LEVEL	ROOM	TIME	DAY	INSTRUCTOR
Typing	1	109	6:30-9:30	M + W	Mr. Welch
Typing	2	110	6:30-9:30	T + Th	Mr. Welch
Wood Shop	1 + 2	106	6:30-9:30	M + W	Mr. Fuller
Auto Mechanics	1 + 2	107	6:30-9:30	T + Th	Ms. Kirn
Radio and T.V. Repair	1	108	6:30-9:30	M + W	Mr. Craig
ESL	1	123	2:30-5:00	M-Th	Mrs. Rose
ESL	1	204	7:00-9:30	M-Th	Ms. Childs
ESL	2	315	2:30-5:00	M-Th	Mr. Barns
ESL	2	210	7:00-9:30	M-Th	Miss Sumner
ESL	3	303	7:00-9:30	M-Th	Mr. Barns
ESL	4	202	7:00-9:30	M-Th	Mr. Thompson

WRITE   *Fill in the spaces below with the words in the box.*

do	does	is	are	will	did

Mario: 1. When *does* the auto mechanics class meet?

2. What room *is* the radio and T.V. repair class in?

3. How long _____ the students study in the evening?

4. How many days _____ the ESL classes meet?

5. When _____ the classes begin?

6. When _____ the courses end?

7. How many classes _____ Mr. Barns teach?

8. How many teachers _____ working this semester?

9. How many levels of ESL classes _____ there this semester?

10. _____ Mrs. Rose teaching ESL 1 this semester?

CHALLENGE   *Answer the questions above. Use the schedule of classes.*

WRITE

Put the sentences below in the correct order from 1 to 9. Use the pictures to find the correct order.

Miko Takahashi enters the classroom. Mr. Barns, the teacher, is putting some maps and posters on the wall before the lesson begins.

_____ Put it up on the wall.

_____ Cut four pieces of tape and stick them to your fingers.

_____ Take the roll of tape out of the drawer.

___*1*___ Pick up the map from the table.

_____ Unfold the map.

_____ Walk to the bulletin board.

_____ Finally, tape the corners of the map.

_____ Open the drawer.

_____ Make sure the map's straight.

READ

It's seven o'clock and the ESL class is beginning.

Mr. Barns: Welcome back, everybody. I hope that you all had a nice vacation. Before we begin our first lesson, I have to take the roll.
Are there any new students with registration slips?

Alex Brotski: I'm a new student. Here's my registration card.

Mr. Barns: Thank you.

REGISTRATION CARD

NAME: _Alex Brotski_

ADDRESS: _1607 Curson Avenue_

CITY: _Los Angeles_   STATE: _CA_   ZIP: _90038_

DATE OF BIRTH: _1959_   PLACE OF BIRTH: _Russia_

CLASS: _E S L_   LEVEL: _3_

TELEPHONE: _494-6943_   SIGNATURE: _Alex Brotski_

ROLL BOOK

CLASS: _ESL_   TIME: _7:00-9:30_ DAY: _M-Th_ ROOM: _303_ TEACHER: _Roy Barns_

	NAME OF STUDENT	ADDRESS	TELEPHONE	SEX	DATE AND PLACE OF BIRTH
1.	Maria Corral	396 Ship Street	787-6935	F	4/6/52 Mexico
2.	Mario Corral	396 Ship Street	787-6935	M	6/9/53 Mexico
3.	Tan Tran	469 Western Ave.	963-0421	M	3/4/42 Vietnam
4.	Yen Chu	16 4th Ave #103	499-5264	F	1/6/34 China
5.	Stephen Bratko	1160 Fairfax St. #3	765-4012	M	7/14/48 Poland
6.	Wanda Bratko	1160 Fairfax St #3	765-4012	F	4/23/51 Poland
7.	Sami Hamati	2347 Third Blvd.	946-5210	M	2/10/37 Egypt
8.	Miko Takahashi	69 Valerio St	499-1236	F	11/29/64 Japan
9.					

UNDERSTAND   *Circle **True**, **False**, or **We don't know**.*

1. Mr. Barns had a nice vacation.	True	False	We don't know.
2. "Take the roll" means "call the names."	True	False	We don't know.
3. Alex is a new student.	True	False	We don't know.
4. "Slip" means "piece of paper."	True	False	We don't know.

WRITE   *Add the information from the registration card to the roll book.*

READ

Here are the roll books for a few of the adult classes.

ROLL BOOK

CLASS: *Wood Shop*   TIME: 6:30-9:30 DAY: M+W ROOM: *106* TEACHER: *James Fuller*

NAME OF STUDENT	ADDRESS	TELEPHONE	SEX	DATE AND PLACE OF BIRTH
1. Paul Green	23 Chain St.	253-7461	M	12/3/36 New York
2. Raymond Monte	19 6th St.	996-8301	M	4/3/60 Italy
3. Roberto Monte	4369 Ocean Ave.	434-0101	M	4/3/60 Italy
4. Hans Hausmann	32½ Seaside Ct.	736-4934	F	6/9/34 Germany

ROLL BOOK

CLASS: *Auto Mechanics*   TIME: 6:30-9:30 DAY: T+Th ROOM: *107* TEACHER: *Ms. Kirn*

NAME OF STUDENT	ADDRESS	TELEPHONE	SEX	DATE AND PLACE OF BIRTH
1. Rita Landry	19 Warren St.	378-0411	F	9/26/58 Quebec
2. Joanne Yates	65 Church St.	643-0571	F	3/13/55 Boston
3. Kim Lee	93 St. James St.	472-8126	F	
4.				

ROLL BOOK

CLASS: *Typing 2*   TIME: 6:30-9:30 DAY: T+Th ROOM: *110* TEACHER: *Mr. Welch*

NAME OF STUDENT	ADDRESS	TELEPHONE	SEX	DATE AND PLACE OF BIRTH
1. Frank Jenkins	1961 Main St.	463-1109	M	6/1/47 Canada
2. Mona Boulos	23 Shell St.	643-9821	F	11/29/29 Lebanon
	1st Street	546-1943	M	10/31/28 Hawaii

ROLL BOOK

CLASS: *Radio and T.V. Repair*   TIME: 6:30-9:30 DAY: M+W ROOM: *108* TEACHER: *Mr. Craig*

NAME OF STUDENT	ADDRESS	TELEPHONE	SEX	DATE AND PLACE OF BIRTH
1. David Fernandez	13 Theater Dr. #1	421-9605	M	4/3/61 Puerto Rico
2. Laura Speek	2488 Hilltop Dr.	433-0607	F	6/28/52 Estonia
3. Ray Lee	632 Los Feliz Dr.	499-8039	M	3/26/55 Hong Kong
4. Tim Canet	120 Orange Ave.	889-1201	M	4/4/50 Argentina

PAIR PRACTICE   *Ask and answer questions about the people in the roll books.*

Student 1:   What class is .... in?
              or
         Where does .... live?
              or
         Where's .... from?
              or
         Who's the teacher for ....?

Student 2: ....

WHAT CLASS IS DAVID IN?

HE'S IN THE RADIO AND T.V. REPAIR CLASS.

READ

Sami Hamati is giving you a note.

DICTATION

Cover the sentences under each line. Write the dictation on the line as your teacher reads it to you. Then uncover the sentences and correct your writing.

1. _____

   Hi, I'm Sami. I'm a student in this class.

2. _____

   Are you a new student in this school?

3. _____

   What's your name?

4. _____

   Where are you from?

5. _____

   Where do you live?

6. _____

   When did you arrive here?

7. _____

   How do you like our class?

8. _____

   Welcome to this class.

   Sami

WRITE   *Answer Sami's note.*

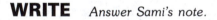

Dear Sami,

_____

_____

_____

_____

_____

_____

PAIR PRACTICE   *Interview a student in your class. Then let him or her interview you.*

Directions: 1. Before the interview, think about and write some interview questions on the question lines below.
2. Find a partner and ask your questions.
3. Write your partner's answers on the lines below your questions.
4. Then answer your partner's questions.
5. Give a short report about your partner to your class.
6. Use some of the question words in the box.

how many	what	how	where	how often	what kind of
how much	what time	who	whose	how long	when ·

INTERVIEW QUESTIONS

1. Question: *What's your name?*

   Answer: _____

2. Question: _____

   Answer: _____

3. Question: _____

   Answer: _____

4. Question: _____

   Answer: _____

5. Question: _____

   Answer: _____

6. Question: _____

   Answer: _____

7. Question: _____

   Answer: _____

8. Question: _____

   Answer: _____

9. Question: _____

   Answer: _____

10. Question: _____

    Answer: _____

11. Question: _____

    Answer: _____

WORD BUILDING   Prefixes and Suffixes

- *Most of the answers for the crossword puzzle contain a prefix or suffix. Listed below are some prefixes and suffixes.*

  Prefixes: un-   re-

  Suffixes: -or   -er   -y   -ist   -ish   -ward   -tion

ACROSS

1. A .... works in a hospital.

5. Policemen and .... work together.

6. do again

8. not important

11. A banana usually has a .... color.

12. A .... fixes teeth.

13. wash again

14. I don't know how to get to your home. Please give me ....

DOWN

1. A .... drives a car.

2. This road is .... in the winter in New York.

3. opposite of "upward"

4. opposite of "did"

7. paint again

9. .... use typewriters.

10. tell again

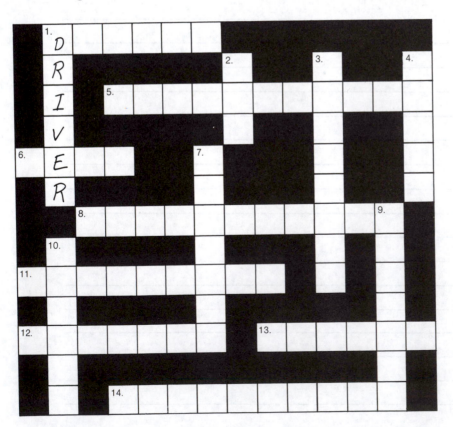

2

A TRIP TO THE POST OFFICE

COMPETENCIES	• Using the Post Office
	• Understanding Postal Terms
	• Filling Out Change-of-Address Forms
GRAMMAR	• Definite and Indefinite Object Pronouns
	• Position of Object Pronouns
	• *one/the other*
	• *one/another*
VOCABULARY	• Common Post Office Terms
WORD BUILDING	• The Suffixes *-al* and *-ical*

LISTEN

James Fuller is asking his wife for envelopes and a stamp.

James: I need envelopes. Do we have any?
Betty: Look in the desk drawer. I saw some yesterday.
James: There's a whole box of envelopes, but I don't see any stamps. I need a stamp for this last letter.
Betty: Look in my purse. I always keep one there.
James: What time does the letter carrier deliver the mail?
Betty: About this time.

A few minutes later James is talking to the letter carrier.

Carrier: Hi, Mr. Fuller. Here's your mail.
James: Thanks a lot. Can you mail these letters for me?
Carrier: Sure I can. I'll be happy to mail them for you. By the way, there's a large package at the post office for you.
James: When can I get it?
Carrier: You can pick it up at the post office between 8:30 and 5.
James: Thanks again.
Carrier: Take care. See you tomorrow.

UNDERSTAND   *Circle True, False, or We don't know.*

1. Mr. Fuller's paying his monthly bills.	True	False	We don't know.
2. "A whole box" means "a full box."	True	False	We don't know.
3. There are many stamps in Betty's purse.	True	False	We don't know.
4. "By the way" means "changing the subject."	True	False	We don't know.
5. The post office opens at 8 in the morning.	True	False	We don't know.
6. The mail carrier is delivering a package.	True	False	We don't know.
7. "Take care" means "Good-bye."	True	False	We don't know.

GRAMMAR   Definite and Indefinite Object Pronouns

- *It* and *them* are definite pronouns.
- *We use them to replace nouns with the definite article* **the**.
- *We use them to refer to specific persons or things.*
- *Other definite pronouns are* **me**, **him**, **her**, **you**, *and* **us**.

EXAMPLES

I'll be happy to mail   **the letters**   for you.
I'll be happy to mail   **them**   for you.

When can I get   **the package?**
When can I get   **it?**

- *One*, *some*, *and* **any** *are indefinite pronouns.*

- *We use the indefinite pronouns to replace nouns with the indefinite article* **a** *and* **an** *in the singular and without articles in the plural.*

- *We use indefinite pronouns when we aren't referring to any specific person or thing. We use them to mean* **one of many**.

- *We usually use* **any** *in questions and in the negative.*

EXAMPLES

There are   **envelopes**   in the desk drawer.
There are   **some**   in the desk drawer.

I think there's   **a stamp**   in my purse.
I think there's   **one**   in my purse.

Do we have   **envelopes?**
Do we have   **any?**

There aren't   **stamps**   in the desk drawer.
There aren't   **any**   in the desk drawer.

READ   *Make logical complete sentences with the words in the boxes.*

Do you	want / need / have	envelopes? / a stamp? / a package? / letters? / the envelopes? / the stamp? / the package? / the letters?

Yes, / No,	I	want / don't want / need / don't need / have / don't have	one. / some. / any. / it. / them.

PAIR PRACTICE

Talk with another student using the words and pictures below. Use **one** *or* **some** *in the answers.*

Student 1: I need ....

Student 2: There is/are .... in/on ....

> I NEED A STAMP.

> THERE'S ONE IN MY PURSE.

1. a stamp/purse
2. envelopes/drawer
3. a book/shelf
4. a calendar/wall

5. a pen/desk
6. an empty box/closet
7. a calculator/table
8. money/wallet

PAIR PRACTICE

Ask and answer questions with the words and pictures below. Use **it** *or* **them** *in the answers.*

Student 1: Did you see ....?

Student 2: Yes, I saw .... on/in ....

> DID YOU SEE MY PEN?

> YES, I SAW IT ON THE TABLE.

1. my pen/table
2. the notebooks/desk
3. my watch/bedroom
4. my shoes/closet

5. the calculator/drawer
6. these photos/album
7. my glasses/your head
8. my keys/your hand

WRITE   *Fill in the spaces with definite or indefinite articles.*

1. Did you pay the electric bill?

   No, I didn't pay *it*_____.

2. Do you want me to pay the bills?

   Yes, please pay _____.

3. Where did you put the checkbook?

   I put _____ in the top drawer.

4. Where are the bills?

   I put _____ in the bottom drawer.

5. Do you want to send a check to your niece for her birthday?

   No, don't send her _____. I'll send her a present.

6. We need stamps.

   I'll buy _____ tomorrow.

7. Do we have small envelopes?

   No, we don't have _____.

8. Do we have big envelopes?

   Yes, I think that we have _____.

9. Do you have letters to mail?

   Yes, there's _____ near the phone.

10. Do you want me to mail these letters?

    Yes, please mail _____ for me.

11. Do you want me to pick up the package at the post office?

    No, don't pick _____ up. I'll do that tomorrow.

PAIR PRACTICE   *Ask and answer questions about the items in the picture above. Use* **one,** **some,** *or* **any.**

Student 1: Is/Are there .... on the desk?
Student 2: Yes, there is one.
or
Yes, there are some.
or
No, there aren't any.

READ

Betty Fuller and Nancy Barns are talking on the telephone.

Betty: I'm going to go to the post office this morning. Then, I plan to have lunch. Do you want to come?

Nancy: Sure, I have to send two packages to my mother.

Betty: Good. I have to buy some stamps, pick up a package, and get a change-of-address form for my daughter. She's moving, you know. After we finish our business at the post office, I'll buy you lunch. Are you sending gifts to your mother?

Nancy: Yes, I am. I'm sending her some clothes for her birthday. I can't describe them to you, so I'll show them to you before I wrap them.

Betty: Didn't you give your mother clothes for her birthday last year?

Nancy: No, I didn't. I gave clothes to my father and I gave my mother money.

Betty: Oh, that's right. Now I remember. I'll be at your place at 10 o'clock, OK?

Nancy: OK. See you then.

UNDERSTAND   *Circle **True**, **False**, or **We don't know***.

1. Nancy's sending her mother two sweaters.	True	False	We don't know.
2. Betty's daughter needs a change-of-address form because she's moving.	True	False	We don't know.
3. Betty lives with her daughter.	True	False	We don't know.
4. Nancy didn't send her mother clothes last year.	True	False	We don't know.
5. Nancy sent her parents gifts last year.	True	False	We don't know.
6. Betty can't see the clothes because Nancy wrapped them.	True	False	We don't know.

GRAMMAR   Indirect Object Position

- *When the indirect object follows the direct object, we usually use the prepositions* **to** *or* **for**.

EXAMPLES	Direct Object	Indirect Object
I have to send	two packages	to my mother.
I have to get	a form	for my daughter.
Are you sending	gifts	to your mother?
I gave	clothes	to my father.

- *The indirect object usually comes first when the direct object is a long one.*

- *The following verbs take indirect objects:* **buy, give, write, sell, throw, tell, ask, show**.

- *If the indirect object comes before the direct object, we do not use a preposition.*

EXAMPLES	Indirect Object	Direct Object	
I'll buy	you	lunch.	
I'm sending	her	some clothes.	
I'll show	them	to you.	
Didn't you give	her	clothes	last year?
I gave	my mother	money.	

- *The indirect object never comes before the direct object after the following verbs:* **say, explain, describe**.

EXAMPLE	Direct Object	Indirect Object
I can't describe	them	to you.

READ   *Make logical complete sentences with the words in the boxes.*

Nancy	is sending	packages		Betty.
	will get	lunch	to	her mother.
	will buy	a form		her father.
Betty	will show	some money	for	her daughter.
	gave	some clothes		Nancy.

Nancy	is sending	Betty	packages.
	will get	her mother	lunch.
	will buy	her father	a form.
	will show	her daughter	some money.
Betty	gave	Nancy	some clothes.
	sent		

READ

This is what Betty will give for birthdays this year.

BIRTHDAY PRESENTS

Person	Birthday	Gift
Mother	July 26	clothes
Father	March 16	radio
Daughter	January 30	lamp
Brothers	November 1	record
	September 6	record
Sister	June 15	perfume
Nancy Barns	May 25	sweater
Grandchildren	February 17	toys
	December 10	toys
	April 12	toys
Uncle	August 22	card
Aunt	October 3	card
Cousin	April 11	tie

PAIR PRACTICE   *Talk with another student. Use the list above.*

Student 1: What will Betty give her ....?
Student 2: She'll give him/her/them ....

WHAT WILL BETTY GIVE HER MOTHER?

SHE'LL GIVE HER CLOTHES.

PAIR PRACTICE   *Use the list above.*

Student 1: When will Betty send her .... the ....?
Student 2: She'll send him/her/them the .... in ....

SHE'LL SEND HIM THE RADIO IN MARCH.

WHEN WILL BETTY SEND HER FATHER THE RADIO?

PAIR PRACTICE   *Use the list above.*

Student 1: What will Betty give to her ....?
Student 2: She'll give .... to her ....

WHAT WILL BETTY GIVE TO HER BROTHERS?

SHE'LL GIVE RECORDS TO HER BROTHERS.

PAIR PRACTICE   *Use the list above.*

Student 1: What will Betty buy for her ....?
Student 2: She'll buy .... for her ....

WHAT WILL BETTY BUY FOR HER COUSIN?

SHE'LL BUY A TIE FOR HER COUSIN.

READ

Nancy and Betty are at the post office. Nancy's talking to the postal clerk.

Nancy: I'd like to send these two packages to Seattle, Washington.
 Clerk: By first or third class?
Nancy: Send them by third class.
 Clerk: That'll be $6.49 for the first and $5.52 for the other package.
Nancy: Here's a twenty-dollar bill.
 Clerk: And here's your change.

Now it's Betty's turn.

Betty: Please give me a change-of-address form and a sheet of twenty-cent stamps.
Clerk: Is that all?
Betty: Give me another sheet. We never have enough stamps at home.
Clerk: That'll be forty dollars and here's a change-of-address form.
Betty: Here you are.
Clerk: Will that be all?
Betty: No, I also want to pick up a package.
Clerk: Your name, please?
Betty: Betty Fuller.
Clerk: Here it is.
Betty: Thank you.

UNDERSTAND   *Circle True, False, or We don't know.*

1. Nancy sent the packages by first class.	True	False	We don't know.
2. Nancy's change was $3.50.	True	False	We don't know.
3. "I'd like" means "I want."	True	False	We don't know.

CHALLENGE   *Find Seattle, Washington on a map.*

READ

Nancy and Betty are looking at the rate schedule on the wall.

FIRST CLASS: Letters, personal mail, packages under 12 ounces

SECOND CLASS: Magazines

THIRD CLASS: Packages under one pound, ads, calendars

BOOK CLASS: Books

AEROGRAMMES: Light overseas letters

AIRMAIL: By airplane

REGULAR MAIL: First class domestic letters and packages

CERTIFIED MAIL: Packages under one pound, ads

REGISTERED MAIL: Insured or valuable letters and packages

SPECIAL DELIVERY: Fast delivery

OVERSEAS MAIL: By boat or airplane

 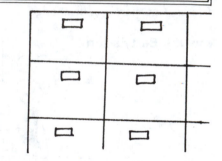

PAIR PRACTICE   *Talk with another student about the schedule above. Use the phrases below.*

Student 1: How can I send ....?
Student 2: You can send .... by ....

1. a letter
2. an expensive gift
3. a magazine
4. a letter to England
5. a book
6. a fast letter
7. a light package
8. ....

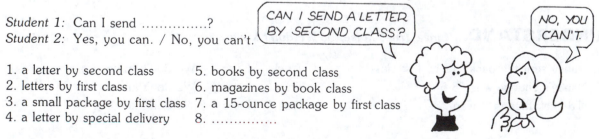

HOW CAN I SEND A LETTER?

YOU CAN SEND A LETTER BY FIRST CLASS.

PAIR PRACTICE   *Talk about the schedule above. Use the phrases below.*

Student 1: Can I send ....?
Student 2: Yes, you can. / No, you can't.

1. a letter by second class
2. letters by first class
3. a small package by first class
4. a letter by special delivery
5. books by second class
6. magazines by book class
7. a 15-ounce package by first class
8. ....

CAN I SEND A LETTER BY SECOND CLASS?

NO, YOU CAN'T.

GRAMMAR *the other/another*

- *We use* **the other/the others** *to show that there are additional, alternate, or remaining objects in a set.*

EXAMPLES

It'll cost $6.49 for **the first package** and $5.52 for **the other package**.
There are two packages, **one** is big and **the other** is small.
This package is light, **the others** are heavy.

- *We use* **another** *to show* **one more** *of the same kind.*

EXAMPLES

There are five postcards. **One** is from Japan, **another** is from Mexico, and **another** is from China.

READ   *Make logical complete sentences with the words in the boxes.*

There are	two three four five	packages, one is	heavy, big, small, light,	the other the others	isn't. aren't.

I have only	one two three four	of the	packages. letters. postcards. stamps.

Do you have	the other	one?
	another	ones?

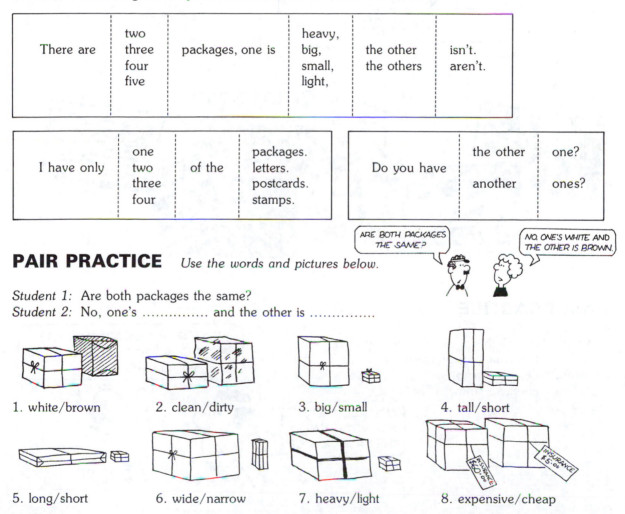

ARE BOTH PACKAGES THE SAME?

NO, ONE'S WHITE AND THE OTHER IS BROWN.

PAIR PRACTICE   *Use the words and pictures below.*

Student 1: Are both packages the same?
Student 2: No, one's .... and the other is ....

1. white/brown
2. clean/dirty
3. big/small
4. tall/short

5. long/short
6. wide/narrow
7. heavy/light
8. expensive/cheap

POSTCARDS

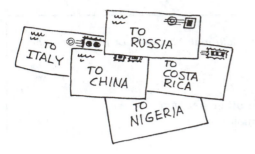

PACKAGES

STAMPS

PAIR PRACTICE   *Use the pictures above.*

Student 1: Are all the .... from/to/for
the same person/place?

Student 2: One's from/to/for ....,
another's from/to/for ....

PAIR PRACTICE   *Ask questions using the words below. Answer in your own words.*

Student 1: Are both of your .... the same?
Student 2: Yes, they are.
              or
        No, one's .... and the other is ....

1. shoes
2. eyes
3. parents
4. ears

5. feet
6. socks
7. hands
8. ....

WRITE   *Complete the dialog with your own words.*

Clerk: *May I help you?* _____?

Customer: I want to mail this package.

Clerk: Where are you sending it?

Customer: _____.

Clerk: Please write on this custom's declaration what's in the box.

Customer: _____.

Clerk: _____?

Customer: I want to send it by first class mail.

Clerk: That'll be $7.02.

Customer: _____.

Clerk: Will that be all?

Customer: _____.

WRITE   *Substitute the words below the lines with the object pronouns in the box.*

me   you   him   her   it   us   them   one   the other

Nancy and Roy are having dinner.

Roy: How was your day?

Nancy: Not very exciting. Betty didn't want to go to the post office alone today, so

she asked _*me*___ to go with _*her*___. When she came here, I
      Nancy   Betty

showed _____ the clothes I bought for my mother. I wrapped the
      Betty

clothes in two packages. I carried _____ and Betty carried _____. We
                                    a package   the second package

went to the bus stop and waited ten minutes. We saw the bus down the

street, and finally _____ came and the doors opened for
                    the bus

_____, but all the seats were full. We were very surprised when two
Betty and me

very nice men got up and gave _____ their seats. We thanked _____.
                              Betty and me   the two men

    When we arrived at the post office, we stood in line a short time. When it

was our turn, we gave the clerk our packages. We put _____ on the counter.
                                                     the packages

"I want to send _____ to Seattle," I said.
                the packages

"How do you want to send _____?" he asked _____.
                         the packages   Nancy

"'By regular mail," I told _____.
                          the clerk

He said that the cost was $12.01. I thanked _____ and left. Then Betty and I
                                            the clerk

went to lunch.

READ

Betty's helping her daughter, Carol Miller, fill out a change-of-address form.

Betty: What's your old address? I forgot.
Carol: It's twenty-four sixty-five Eighth Street, Apartment one-oh-six, Los Angeles, California. The zip code is nine-oh-oh-three-eight.
Betty: What's your new address?
Carol: It's two-three-four-six Palms Avenue, Apartment A, Santa Monica, California. The zip code is nine-oh-four-oh-five.
Betty: When are you moving?
Carol: On the first of November.

WRITE   *Help Betty fill out the change-of-address form. Use the information in the dialog above.*

THIS ORDER PROVIDES for the forwarding of First-Class Mail for a period not to exceed 18 months. All parcels of obvious value will be forwarded for a period not to exceed one year.		**Print or Type** *(Last Name, First Name, Middle Initial)*	
CHANGE OF ADDRESS IS FOR: ☐ Firm ☐ **Entire Family** *(When last name of family members differ, separate orders for each last name must be filed.)* ☐ **Individual Signer Only**	**OLD ADDRESS**	No. and St., Apt., Suite P.O. Box R.D. No. Box	
		Post Office State ZIP Code	
I agree to pay forwarding postage for newspapers and magazines for 90 days. ☐ No ☐ Yes	**NEW ADDRESS**	No. and St., Apt., Suite P.O. Box R.D. No. Box	
USPS USE ONLY Clerk/Carrier Endorsement		Post Office State ZIP Code	
Carrier Route Number	**Effective Date**		**If Temporary, Expiration Date**
Date Entered	**Sign Here** X		**Date Signed**

PS FORM 3575, JAN. 1984   *Signature & title of person authorizing address change. (DO NOT print or type.)*

WRITE   *Here is a form from the post office. Fill it out.*

CHANGE OF ADDRESS ORDER

PRIVACY ACT: Filing this form is voluntary, but your mail cannot be forwarded without an order. If filed, your new address will be given to others. Use Form 3576 to tell correspondents and publishers of address changes.

OFFICIAL BUSINESS
PENALTY FOR PRIVATE
USE S300

BUSINESS REPLY CARD
FIRST CLASS PERMIT NO 73026, WASHINGTON, DC

NO POS
NECES
IF M
IN
UNITE

POSTMASTER
Post Office   State   ZIP Code

THIS ORDER PROVIDES for the forwarding of First-Class Mail for a period not to exceed 18 months. All parcels of obvious value will be forwarded for a period not to exceed one year.

CHANGE OF ADDRESS IS FOR:

☐ Firm

☐ Entire Family *(When last name of family members differ, separate orders for each last name must be filed.)*

☐ Individual Signer Only

I agree to pay forwarding postage for newspapers and magazines for 90 days.

☐ No   ☐ Yes

USPS USE ONLY
Clerk/Carrier Endorsement

Carrier Route Number

Date Entered

PS FORM 3575. JAN. 1984

Print or Type *(Last Name, First Name, Middle Initial)*

OLD ADDRESS

No. and St.,
Apt., Suite
P.O. Box
R.D. No. Box

Post Office
State
ZIP Code

NEW ADDRESS

No. and St.,
Apt., Suite
P.O. Box
R.D. No. Box

Post Office
State
ZIP Code

Effective Date   If Temporary, Expiration Date

Sign Here
X   Date Signed

Signature & title of person authorizing address change. (DO NOT print or type.)

DICTATION   *Cover the sentences under each line. Write the dictation on the line as your teacher reads it to you. Then uncover the sentences and correct your writing.*

A letter from Nancy's mother.

Dear Nancy,

1. _____

This is only a short note to thank you for the packages.

2. _____

One came yesterday and the other one arrived today.

3. _____

The blouse and skirt are beautiful, and they fit fine.

4. _____

I received four sweaters this year for my birthday.

5. _____

One was from your father, and another one was from your brother.

6. _____

The other ones were from friends.

7. _____

All the clothes are nice and I can't wait to wear them all.

8. _____

Your father sends his love. Take care.

Love, Mom

PAIR PRACTICE   *Fold the page on the dotted line. Look at your side only. Do the exercise orally.*

Student 1	**Student 2**

Student 1

Listen to your partner's questions and find the answers on the form below.

THIS ORDER PROVIDES for the forwarding of First-Class Mail for a period not to exceed 18 months. All parcels of obvious value will be forwarded for a period not to exceed one year.	Print or Type *(Last Name, First Name, Middle Initial)* RANALDI, JOSEPH
CHANGE OF ADDRESS IS FOR: ☐ Firm ☐ Entire Family *(When last name of family members differ, separate orders for each last name must be filed.)* ☒ Individual Signer Only	**OLD ADDRESS** — No. and St., Apt., Suite P.O. Box R.D. No. Box 6541 DENTON ST. Post Office State ZIP Code LOS ANGELES, CA 90038
I agree to pay forwarding postage for newspapers and magazines for 90 days. ☐ No ☒ Yes	**NEW ADDRESS** — No. and St., Apt., Suite P.O. Box R.D. No. Box 169 BOSTON AVE. Post Office State ZIP Code LOS ANGELES, CA 91406
USPS USE ONLY Clerk/Carrier Endorsement	
Carrier Route Number	Effective Date Nov. 1	If Temporary, Expiration Date
Date Entered	Sign Here X Joseph Ranaldi	Date Signed Oct. 25

Now ask your partner these questions.

1. What kind of list do you see?
2. How many Christmas presents will Nancy buy?
3. What will Nancy buy Roy?
4. What will Nancy buy Betty?
5. What will James receive from Nancy?
6. Who will get presents from Nancy?
7. What kind of presents will Nancy buy?

Student 2

Ask your partner these questions.

1. What kind of form do you see?
2. Whose name is on the form?
3. What's the old address?
4. Is there a telephone number on the form?
5. Is there a signature on the form?
6. When did he fill out this form?
7. When does he want the post office to deliver his mail to his new address?

Listen to your partner's questions and find the answers on the list below.

> Buy these presents for Christmas,
>
> Roy — aftershave lotion
> Patty — books
> Bobby — toys
> Mom — bath soap
> Dad — wallet
> Betty — plant
> James — tie

FOLD HERE

WORD BUILDING The Suffixes *-al* and *-ical*

- *We use the suffixes* **-al** *and* **-ical** *to make adjectives from nouns.*

EXAMPLES

1. In this <u>nation</u>, baseball is a <u>national</u> sport.

2. This <u>person</u> has a <u>personal</u> computer.

3. She loved <u>music</u>, so she learned to play a <u>musical</u> instrument.

WRITE *Fill in the spaces with the suffixes* **-al** *or* **-ical**.

1. The delegates spoke about gener*al* soci____, leg____, polit____, and nation____ problems at the internation____ meeting in the capit____ city of a trop____ country.

2. Many hospital patients have dent____, phys____, ment____, and person____ problems.

3. The musician played some origin____ class____ music on her mus____ instrument.

4. Students in adult schools can sometimes learn pract____ electr____, techn____, mechan____, and industri____ skills.

3

LET ME BUY YOU LUNCH

COMPETENCIES	• Ordering Food in a Restaurant • Reading a Menu • Discussing Home Security
GRAMMAR	• *some/any* • *something/anything/nothing* • *somebody/anybody/nobody*
VOCABULARY	• Common Food Items • Restaurant Vocabulary
PRONUNCIATION	• Homophones

LISTEN

Betty Fuller and Nancy Barns are going to have lunch.

COME ON, BETTY. LET ME BUY YOU SOME LUNCH. I'M STARVED. I KNOW A NICE LITTLE FRENCH RESTAURANT AROUND THE CORNER.

Betty and Nancy are at the restaurant.

WELCOME, LADIES. HERE ARE SOME MENUS. I'LL GIVE YOU SOME TIME TO DECIDE. I'LL BE BACK IN A FEW MINUTES.

Betty and Nancy are deciding on the food.

Betty: I think I'll order some chicken. It's today's special. Maybe I'll have some dessert later. Are you going to have any chicken?

Nancy: No chicken for me today. We had chicken for dinner last night. Do they have any hamburgers?

Betty: This is a French restaurant. They don't have any hamburgers!

Nancy: Then, maybe I'll have eggs.

Betty: The chef makes a terrific omelet.

Nancy: Good. I'll have that, but I won't have any dessert. I'm on a diet!

UNDERSTAND   *Circle **True**, **False**, or **We don't know**.*

1. "I'm starved" means "I'm very hungry."	True	False	We don't know.
2. The waiter is French.	True	False	We don't know.
3. Betty's on a diet.	True	False	We don't know.
4. Omelets are the special of the day.	True	False	We don't know.
5. It's evening.	True	False	We don't know.

WRITE   *Underline the words **some** and **any** each place they appear in the dialog above.*

GRAMMAR   *some/any*

- *Use **some** as an indefinite article or pronoun in the affirmative. **Some** can often be omitted.*

EXAMPLES   ***Affirmative***

Let's stop for	**some**	lunch.
Let me buy you	**some**	lunch.
Here are	**some**	menus.
I'll give you	**some**	time to decide.
I think I'll order	**some**	chicken.
Maybe I'll have	**some**	eggs.

- *We usually use **any** in questions and in negative sentences. **Any** can often be omitted.*

EXAMPLES   ***Questions***

Do you need	**any**	help?
Are you going to order	**any**	chicken?
Do they have	**any**	hamburgers?

Negative

They don't have	**any**	hamburgers!
I won't get	**any**	dessert.

- *We can also use **no** as an adjective to express the negative. We normally use **no** in short answers.*

EXAMPLE   **No**   chicken for me today.

READ   *Make logical complete sentences with the words in the boxes.*

Would you like	chicken?
	eggs?
Do you want	coffee?
	dessert?
Will you order	soup?
	salad?

Yes,	I'll order	some.
	I won't order	
	I'd like	
No,	I want	any.
	I don't want	

	coffee?
	butter?
Would you like	sugar?
	salt?
	pepper?
	ketchup?

I don't want any	coffee,	
	butter,	
	sugar,	thank you.
	salt,	
No	pepper,	
	ketchup,	

READ   *Here is a menu.*

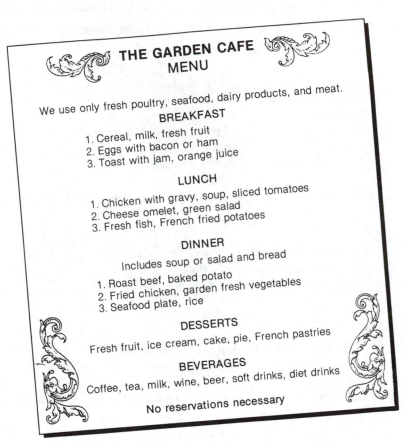

**THE GARDEN CAFE
MENU**

We use only fresh poultry, seafood, dairy products, and meat.

BREAKFAST

1. Cereal, milk, fresh fruit
2. Eggs with bacon or ham
3. Toast with jam, orange juice

LUNCH

1. Chicken with gravy, soup, sliced tomatoes
2. Cheese omelet, green salad
3. Fresh fish, French fried potatoes

DINNER

Includes soup or salad and bread

1. Roast beef, baked potato
2. Fried chicken, garden fresh vegetables
3. Seafood plate, rice

DESSERTS

Fresh fruit, ice cream, cake, pie, French pastries

BEVERAGES

Coffee, tea, milk, wine, beer, soft drinks, diet drinks

No reservations necessary

PAIR PRACTICE   *Ask about the items below. Use the menu above.*

Student 1: Does the restaurant have any ....?
Student 2: Yes, it has some ....
            or
         No, it doesn't have any ....

1. hamburgers
2. omelets
3. hot dogs
4. fish
5. salad
6. turkey
7. ice cream
8. cookies
9. milk
10. carrots
11. soft drinks
12. ....

PAIR PRACTICE   *Use the menu above.*

Student 1: What would you like to order?
Student 2: I'd like some ....

WRITE   *Fill in the spaces below with **some** or **any**.*

Betty and Nancy are ordering lunch.

Waiter: Are you ready to order?

Betty: Yes, I'd like *Some* chicken with soup and _____ sliced tomatoes.

Waiter: Would you like _____ wine with your lunch?

Betty: No, I don't want _____ wine, but I will have _____ coffee.

Waiter: Do you want _____ milk and sugar for your coffee?

Betty: Please bring me _____ milk, but I don't want _____ sugar.

Waiter: Would you like _____ dessert?

Betty: Maybe later.

Nancy: I'd like a cheese omelet.

Waiter: I'm sorry, but we don't have _____ eggs today.

Nancy: That's too bad. Do you have _____ fish today?

Waiter: Oh, yes, we have _____ very fresh fish.

Nancy: Good, I'll have that with _____ green vegetables. I don't want _____ fried potatoes. Also bring me a diet soft drink.

Waiter: Very well, ma'am. Would you like to try _____ of our pastries for dessert?

Nancy: I'd like very much to have _____ pastries, but I won't have _____. I'm trying to stay on my diet.

Waiter: Thank you, ladies. Your orders will be ready soon.

WRITE   *Complete the dialog with answers in the negative.*

Betty: Don't you want any dessert?

Nancy: <u>No, I don't want any dessert.</u>

Betty: Do you want any butter for your bread?

Nancy: _____

Betty: Do you use any salt and pepper on your food?

Nancy: _____

Do people need reservations at this restaurant?

Betty: _____

Nancy: Is there any music here in the afternoons?

Betty: _____

Oh no! Nancy, I forgot to go to the bank.

Nancy: Don't you have any money?

Betty: _____

Nancy: That's OK. I have enough money to pay the bill.

WRITE   *Match the questions with their answers. Write the letters of the answers on the lines after the questions.*

1. Do you often have chicken? __e__
2. Do you eat cake? ____
3. Do you like pepper? ____
4. Do you like tomatoes? ____
5. Do you like oranges? ____
6. Do you eat cheese? ____
7. Do you like to eat fish? ____
8. Do you only drink diet drinks? ____
9. Do you eat a lot of beef? ____

a. No, I don't eat a lot of meat.
b. No, I don't like many spices.
c. Yes, I love all kinds of fruit.
d. No, I drink all kinds of beverages.
e. Yes, we often eat poultry at home.
f. Yes, I like all vegetables.
g. No, I don't eat desserts very often.
h. Yes, I sometimes eat dairy products.
i. Yes, I love seafood.

WRITE   *Complete the sentences. Use* **some** *or* **any**.

The restaurant is busy.

1.

Do you have any pie?

Yes, we have *some pie.*

2.

Do you have any pizza?

No, I'm sorry, but
_____
_____

3.

Can I order wine here?

Of course, you can _____
_____

4.

Please bring me a hot dog.

I'm sorry, sir, but
_____
_____

5.

I'd like an ice cream omelet!

I don't think that we _____
_____

READ

Nancy and Betty are leaving the restaurant.

I'LL LEAVE THE TIP. LET'S HAVE LUNCH AGAIN SOON.

NEXT TIME, I'LL REMEMBER TO BRING ENOUGH MONEY.

GROUP DISCUSSION   *When and where do people give tips? How much?*

PAIR PRACTICE   *Fold this page on the dotted line. Look at your side only.*

Student 1	Student 2

Student 1

Listen to your partner's order, and then write it on the order form.

COFFEE SHOP ORDER	

Now give your order to your partner.

MENU
DINNER
ALL YOU CAN EAT FOR $7.99.
* Vegetable Soup, Roast Beef, Baked Potato
* Green Salad, Fried Chicken, Fresh Vegetables
* Soup, Fish, Rice, Bread

DESSERT
Ice Cream, Cake, Pie

BEVERAGES
Coffee, Tea, Milk,
Wine, Beer, Soft Drinks

Student 2

Give your order to your partner.

MENU
BREAKFAST
ALL YOU CAN EAT FOR $5.99.
* Cereal, Milk, Fruit
* Eggs, Bacon, Toast
* Toast, Jam, Orange Juice

LUNCH
* Hamburger, French Fries
* Chicken Sandwich, Green Salad
* Hot Dog, Potato Chips, Pickle

BEVERAGES
Coffee, Tea, Milk,
Wine, Beer, Soft Drinks

Now listen to your partner's order, and then write it on the order form.

COFFEE SHOP ORDER	

FOLD HERE

LISTEN

It's midnight. Betty Fuller hears something and wakes up.

Betty: James, wake up!
James: What is it?
Betty: I hear something downstairs.
James: I don't hear anything. Go back to sleep.
Betty: I know I heard somebody.
James: There isn't anybody there.
Betty: Listen. I hear it again. Don't you hear anything?
James: It's probably someone's television.
Betty: I can't sleep. I think somebody is in the house. Go and see.
James: OK! OK! I'll go, but I'm sure that nobody will be there.

A few minutes later.

Betty: Did you see anybody?
James: No, I didn't, but I saw something.
Betty: Well, what was it?
James: It was nothing. It was only the cat.
        It wanted to go outside.

UNDERSTAND   *Circle **True**, **False**, or **We don't know**.*

1. Betty's afraid.	True	False	We don't know.
2. Betty heard something.	True	False	We don't know.
3. Their bedroom is upstairs.	True	False	We don't know.
4. Betty and James have a dog.	True	False	We don't know.
5. Betty went downstairs to look.	True	False	We don't know.
6. They forgot to put the cat outside before they went to bed.	True	False	We don't know.

GRAMMAR   *something/somebody*

- We use **something** and **anything** for things or objects, and **somebody** and **anybody** (or **someone** and **anyone**) for people.

- We use **something** and **somebody** in the affirmative, and **anything** and **anybody** in questions and negative sentences.

- We usually use **nothing** or **nobody** in short answers or as the subject of the sentence.

EXAMPLES   *Affirmative*

I hear	**something**	downstairs.
I know I heard	**somebody.**	
It's probably	**someone's**	television.
I think	**somebody**	is in the house.
I saw	**something.**	

Questions   *Negative*

Don't you hear	**anything?**		I don't hear	**anything.**	
Did you see	**anybody?**		There isn't	**anybody**	there.
				Nobody	will be there.
			It was	**nothing.**	

- We use **something** and **somebody** when we don't know what the object or who the person is.

EXAMPLES

I see	**some students.**	(I know that they are students.)
I see	**somebody.**	(I don't know who the person is.)
He has	**some change.**	(I know that it's money.)
He has	**something.**	(I don't know what it is.)

READ   *Make logical complete sentences with the words in the boxes.*

Do you want to	talk to see speak to listen to eat drink read	anybody? anything?

Yes, I want to No, I don't want to	talk to see speak to listen to eat drink read	somebody. something. anybody. anything.

Would you like anything	to eat? to read? to drink?

No, I don't want anything Nothing	to eat, to read, to drink,	thanks.

WRITE   *Answer the questions below. Use some of the words in the box.*

something   somebody   anything   anybody

Betty's asking her husband, James, some questions.

Betty: Did you see anybody downstairs?

James: No, *I didn't see anybody downstairs.*

Betty: Did anybody take anything?

James: No, _____

Betty: Did you hear anything?

James: No, _____

Betty: Don't you think that somebody's trying to break into the house?

James: No, _____

Betty: Was there anybody outside?

James: No, _____

Betty: Was it somebody's television?

James: No, _____

Betty: Shhhh! Do you hear anything now?

James: Yes, _____,
          but it's only the cats in the garbage cans.

PAIR PRACTICE   *Talk with another student about the picture. Use the words below.*

Betty is having a bad dream.

Student 1: What's ....?
Student 2: There's something/somebody/nothing ....

1. under the bed
2. outside
3. on the ceiling
4. at the door

5. on the bed
6. in the bed
7. on the floor
8. ....

PAIR PRACTICE   *Use the picture above.*

Student 1: Is there anything/anybody ....?
Student 2: Yes, there's something/somebody ....
              or
    No, there isn't anything/anybody ....
              or
    No, there's nothing/nobody ....

WRITE   *Fill out the questionnaire.*

QUESTIONNAIRE

1. Do you know anything about home safety?

   _____

2. Can anybody find your address and telephone?

   _____

3. Is it possible for somebody to break into your house? How?

   _____

4. Do you know any of your neighbors?

   _____

5. Does anybody watch your house for you when you are out?

   _____

6. What can you do if you see somebody trying to break into your neighbor's home?

   _____

7. What can you do if somebody strange telephones you?

   _____

8. Do you keep anything valuable at home?

   _____

9. Can anybody see anything through your windows from the outside?

   _____

10. When you leave your home for a long time, do you tell anybody?

    _____

11. Did anybody ever steal anything from you? What? Where? When?

    _____

12. Can you do anything to stop or prevent crimes? What?

    _____

DISCUSSION   *Discuss possible answers to the questions above in class.*

PRONUNCIATION   Homophones

> • Homophones are words that sound the same, but are different in spelling and meaning.

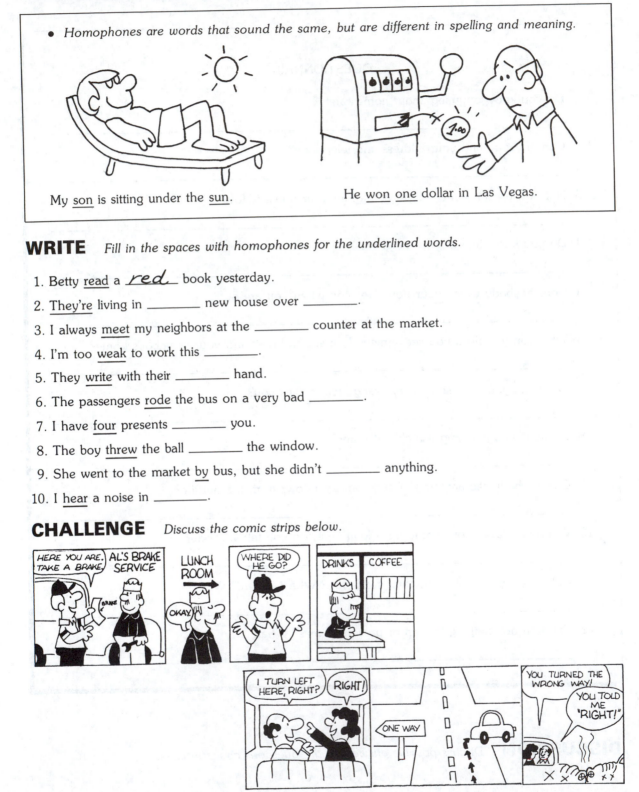

My <u>son</u> is sitting under the <u>sun</u>.

He <u>won</u> <u>one</u> dollar in Las Vegas.

WRITE   Fill in the spaces with homophones for the underlined words.

1. Betty <u>read</u> a *red* book yesterday.

2. <u>They're</u> living in _____ new house over _____.

3. I always <u>meet</u> my neighbors at the _____ counter at the market.

4. I'm too <u>weak</u> to work this _____.

5. They <u>write</u> with their _____ hand.

6. The passengers <u>rode</u> the bus on a very bad _____.

7. I have <u>four</u> presents _____ you.

8. The boy <u>threw</u> the ball _____ the window.

9. She went to the market <u>by</u> bus, but she didn't _____ anything.

10. I <u>hear</u> a noise in _____.

CHALLENGE   Discuss the comic strips below.

WHAT KIND OF JOB ARE YOU LOOKING FOR?

COMPETENCIES	• Understanding Simple Job Ads
	• Talking about Basic Skills, Qualifications, and Job Benefits
	• Making an Appointment for a Job Interview
	• Filling Out a Simple Job Application
	• Answering Simple Interview Questions
	• Leaving a Message by Phone
GRAMMAR	• Relative Pronouns: *who, which, that*
	• Position of Prepositions with Relative Pronouns and Question Words
VOCABULARY	• Basic Job Search Vocabulary
	• Application Terms
	• Common Abbreviations Used in Employment Ads
WORD BUILDING	• The Suffix *-ment*

LISTEN

David Fernandez and Joanne Yates are talking.

Joanne: Hi, David. What are you doing?

David: I'm reading the newspaper want ads.

Joanne: Are there any ads that interest you?

David: There are a lot of ads, but they're for jobs that require people who have many years of experience.

Joanne: What kind of job are you looking for?

David: I'm looking for a job as a painter, or a carpenter, or a job that's in a related area.

Joanne: Yesterday I saw a help-wanted sign that advertised for a salesperson.

David: But I'm not a salesperson.

Joanne: Well, the ad advertised for a salesperson who knows something about lumber, paint, and hardware. It looked like a nice place to work.

David: Where did you see the sign?

Joanne: At the Acme Home Improvement Center. I forgot the name of the street that it's on.

David: I'll find the address. Who do I talk to?

Joanne: I think the manager's the person who you want to speak to.

David: Thanks for the tip. I'm going there right now.

Joanne: Good luck.

UNDERSTAND   *Circle True, False, or We don't know.*

1. David has many years of experience.	True	False	We don't know.
2. David isn't a salesperson.	True	False	We don't know.
3. Carpenters know something about lumber.	True	False	We don't know.
4. The Acme Home Improvement Center needs an employee.	True	False	We don't know.
5. A job as a salesperson at the Acme Home Improvement Center is related to a job as a carpenter.	True	False	We don't know.

WRITE   *Underline the words **who** and **that** each place they appear in the dialog above.*

GRAMMAR   Relative Pronouns: *who, which, that*

- *We usually use* **who** *for people and* **that** *(or* **which***) for things.*

EXAMPLES   *Things*

Are there any	**ads**	**that**	interest you?
I'm looking for a	**job**	**that**	's in a related area.
I saw a	**sign**	**that**	advertised for a salesperson.

People

The ads require	**people**	**who**	have a lot of experience.
They're looking for a	**salesperson**	**who**	knows about lumber.

- *Relative pronouns can be used as the subect or object of a sentence, but when we use them as the object, they can be deleted.*

EXAMPLES

The manager's the person	**who**	you want to talk to.
The manager's the person	~~**who**~~	you want to talk to.
I forgot the name of the street	**that**	it's on.
I forgot the name of the street	~~**that**~~	it's on.

- *When we use relative pronouns with a preposition, we use* **which** *or* **whom***.*

- *In conversation, we often use* **that** *and* **who** *and place the preposition after the verb.*

EXAMPLES

(formal)	The manager's the person	**to whom**	you want to speak.	
(conversational)	The manager's the person	**who**	you want to speak	**to.**
(formal)	I forgot the street	**on which**	you live.	
(conversational)	I forgot the street	**that**	you live	**on.**

READ   *Make logical complete sentences with the words in the box.*

				knows something about lumber.
	needs	a job	that	interests him.
David	wants	a person		needs a salesperson.
Joanne	saw	a sign	who	can do the job.
The store	knows	a store		she told David about.
		a salesperson		advertised a job.

PAIR PRACTICE

*Talk with another student. Answer the question with a **who** clause using the pictures and phrases below.*

Student 1: What kind of person is the store looking for?

Student 2: They're looking for a person who ....

1. is honest
2. is good with numbers
3. can use a cash register
4. can sell things
5. is accurate
6. works well with people
7. handles money well
8. is bilingual

PAIR PRACTICE

*Answer the question with a **that** clause using the pictures and phrases below.*

Student 1: What kind of job do you want?

Student 2: I want a job that ....

1. pays well
2. is near my house
3. gives me the chance to advance
4. has benefits
5. isn't boring
6. has good working conditions
7. has a good schedule
8. gives training

READ

David's reading the newspaper want ads.

CARPENTER: LONG BEACH
req. no exp.
will train
gd. wages
f.t./p.t.
call Jones 357-0971

CARPENTER: LOS ANGELES
1 yr. exp.
xlnt. bene.
ref. req.
lic.
apply in per. ABC Co.

91 Main St. L.A.

CARPENTER: SANTA MONICA
3 yrs. loc. exp.
hi. sal.
med. ins. pd.
pd. vac.
write XYZ Corp.
21 8th. St. S.M.

CARPENTER: LONG BEACH
requires no experience
will train
good wages
full time or part time
call Mr. Jones at 357-0971

CARPENTER: LOS ANGELES
minimum one year experience
excellent benefits
references are required
license
apply in person at the ABC
Company
91 Main Street, Los Angeles

CARPENTER: SANTA MONICA
three years' local experience
high salary
medical insurance paid
paid vacation
write to the XYZ Corporation
21 Eighth Street, Santa Monica

WRITE   *Match the questions with their answers. Write the letters of the answers on the lines after the questions.*

1. What does "required" mean? _e_
2. What's another word for "wages"? ____
3. How long is "full time"? ____
4. What's an example of "benefits"? ____
5. What does "references" mean? ____
6. Does "local" mean "far"? ____
7. How can I "apply in person"? ____

a. You can't call, you must go there.
b. People who know how well you work.
c. Another word is "salary."
d. Insurance, for example.
e. It means "needed" or "necessary."
f. Eight hours a day or forty hours a week.
g. No, it means "in your area."

PAIR PRACTICE   *Ask and answer questions about the ads above. Use **who** or **that** in the answers.*

Student 1: What job ....?
              or
              What kind of person ....?
Student 2: The job that ....
              or
              They want a person who ....

WHAT JOB REQUIRES NO EXPERIENCE?

THE JOB THAT'S IN LONG BEACH REQUIRES NO EXPERIENCE.

WRITE   *Fill in the spaces with **who** or **that**.*

David's telling Joanne about the ads.

1. The job *that* is in Long Beach requires no experience, but it's very far.

2. A person _____ has a year of experience can apply for the job in Los Angeles.

3. The ABC Company is looking for an employee _____ has a license.

4. Mr. Jones, _____ put the ad in the newspaper, pays good wages.

5. Applicants _____ want the job in Los Angeles have to apply in person.

6. The company _____ is on 8th Street hires people _____ have 3 years' local experience.

7. The ads _____ are in the newspaper have a lot of abbreviations.

8. I don't understand all the abbreviations _____ are in the newspaper.

WRITE   *Rewrite the ad in complete words.*

CARPENTER: DOWNTOWN

exp. req.

xlnt. work cond.

f.t.

ins. pd.

hi. sal.

gd. bene.

apply in per. 23 Main St.

Carpenter: Downtown

_____
_____
_____
_____
_____
_____
_____

CHALLENGE   *Place an ad in the newspaper for a job that you want. Describe the perfect job for you.*

NEWSPAPER ADS: ONE LINE, ONE DAY, ONE DOLLAR
PLEASE PRINT CLEARLY

_____
_____
_____
_____

READ

David's calling the Acme Home Improvement Center.

Secretary: Hello, Acme Home Improvement Center. May I help you?
David: I'm calling about the ad for a salesperson.
Secretary: Do you think that you are qualified for the job?
David: Yes, I do.
Secretary: Do you have any experience as a salesperson?
David: No, I don't, but I know a lot about lumber, paint, and hardware.
Secretary: When can you come in for an interview?
David: At your convenience.
Secretary: We have an opening tomorrow at 10 a.m.
David: That'll be fine.
Secretary: Your name and telephone number, please?
David: David Fernandez. My phone number's 421-9605. What address do I go to?
Secretary: Go to 1200 26th Street. We're on the corner of 26th and Broadway.
David: Who will I ask for?
Secretary: Ask for Mrs. Doris Hirsch in the personnel department.
David: Thank you.
Secretary: You're welcome. Good-bye.

UNDERSTAND   *Circle **True**, **False**, or **We don't know**.*

1. David thinks he's qualified for the job.	True	False	We don't know.
2. "Convenience" means "early."	True	False	We don't know.
3. Mrs. Hirsch is the personnel manager.	True	False	We don't know.
4. Broadway is a street.	True	False	We don't know.

GRAMMAR   Position of Prepositions

- *When we use prepositions at the beginning of formal questions or relative clauses, we use* **which** *or* **whom**.

- *In conversation, we use* **what** *and* **who** *and place the preposition after the verb.*

EXAMPLES

(formal)	**To which**	address do I go?	
(conversational)	**What**	address do I go	**to?**
(formal)	**For whom**	will I ask?	
(conversational)	**Who**	will I ask	**for?**

PAIR PRACTICE   *Practice with another student. Change the formal questions below into conversational ones.*

Student 1:   ....?
Student 2:   What?
Student 1:   Who/What ....?
Student 2:   I don't know.

TO WHOM CAN I SPEAK?
WHO DO I SPEAK TO?
WHAT? I DON'T KNOW.

1. To whom can I speak?
2. On which street is the store?
3. In which city is the store?
4. At which address is the store?

5. At which store did you see the sign?
6. To whom can I give my application?
7. With whom did you go to the store?
8. For whom do I ask?

WRITE   *Fill in the spaces with the correct preposition.*

1. Who do you come to school *with* ?

WHO DO YOU COME TO SCHOOL WITH?

2. Who do you live _____?

3. Who do you talk _____ at break time?

4. What stores do you shop _____?

5. What street do you live _____?

6. What city do you live _____?

7. What kind of music do you like to listen _____?

8. Who do you pay your rent _____?

9. What do you use this book _____?

CHALLENGE   *Answer the questions above.*

CHAPTER 4 / Module Three 55

READ

David's talking to Mrs. Hirsch about the job.

Mrs. Hirsch: Are you David Fernandez?
     David: Yes, I am.
Mrs. Hirsch: Please come in and sit down.
     David: Thank you.

> SALESPERSON WANTED
> to sell lumber, paint, and hardware.
> Full or part time.
> We will train you.
> Inquire inside.

WRITE   *Complete the sentences. Use relative clauses with **that** or **who**.*

David's speaking to the manager.

Mrs. Hirsch: What kind of job are you looking for?

     David: I'm looking for a job *that is interesting.*

Mrs. Hirsch: Do you have any sales experience?

     David: No, I don't, but I have experience _____

Mrs. Hirsch: Who told you about this job?

     David: I have a friend _____

Mrs. Hirsch: What kind of worker are you?

     David: I'm a worker _____

Mrs. Hirsch: Do you have any friends or relatives who work here?

     David: No, I don't know anybody _____

Mrs. Hirsch: Do you go to school?

     David: Yes, I go to the adult school _____

Mrs. Hirsch: Do you have good references?

     David: Yes, I have references _____

          Are there many applicants for this job?

Mrs. Hirsch: Yes, there are a lot of people _____

     David: What kind of employee are you looking for?

Mrs. Hirsch: We need a salesperson _____

     David: I believe that I'm the kind of person _____

CHALLENGE   *Discuss other possible answers to the questions above.*

READ

Mrs. Hirsch is looking at a questionnaire that David filled out before the interview.

QUESTIONNAIRE
LIKES AND DISLIKES

Directions: Answer the questions below with a check in the boxes.

	YES	NO
1. Do you like to work with machines or tools?	✓	
2. Do you like to work with people?	✓	
3. Is it easy for you to talk to people?	✓	
4. Do you have any selling skills?		✓
5. Can you follow directions well?	✓	
6. Can you explain directions clearly?	✓	
7. Do you like to work alone?		✓
8. Can you use common tools?	✓	
9. Do you like to work outside?		✓
10. Do you like to help other people?	✓	
11. Do you ask for help when you need it?	✓	
12. Are you a quiet person?	✓	

YES	NO

WRITE   *Fill out the questionnaire next to David's.*

PAIR PRACTICE   *Change the questions in the questionnaire above. Use relative clauses with* **who**.

Student 1: Are you the kind of person who ....?
Student 2: Yes, I am. / No, I'm not.

ARE YOU THE KIND OF PERSON WHO LIKES TO WORK WITH MACHINES OR TOOLS?

YES, I AM.

READ

EMPLOYMENT APPLICATION
PLEASE PRINT

PERSONAL DATA:

Name: *Fernandez*   *David*   *Juan*   Date: *2/13/84*
Last   First   Middle   Mo./Day/Year

Address: *13*   *Theater Drive*   *#1*   *L.A.*   *CA*   *90038*
Number   Street   Apt.   City   State   Zip Code

Telephone: *(213)* *421-9605*   Social Security Number: *032-66-2526*
Area Code   Number

Place of birth: *San Juan*   *Puerto Rico*
City   State or Country

Do you have any relatives who are working for this company? *No* Name: *—*
What kind of work are you looking for? *Salesperson*   Wages expected: *Open*
Are you working now? *No* Where? *—*

Give two references:

	Name	Address	Telephone
1.	Mr. Castell	6439 River Street, L.A.	964-2301
2.	Mrs. Faber	120 South Wood St., L.A.	943-0061

Signature: *David Fernandez*

WE'LL KEEP YOUR APPLICATION AND WE'LL CALL YOU ABOUT THE JOB AFTER WE FINISH ALL THE INTERVIEWS.

THANK YOU FOR YOUR TIME.

WRITE   *Fill out an application for the job, too.*

EMPLOYMENT APPLICATION
PLEASE PRINT

PERSONAL DATA:

Name: _____   Date: _____
Last   First   Middle   Mo./Day/Year

Address: _____
Number   Street   Apt.   City   State   Zip Code

Telephone: _____   Social Security Number: _____
Area Code   Number

Place of birth: _____
City   State or Country

Do you have any relatives who are working for this company? ___ Name: _____
What kind of work are you looking for? _____   Wages expected: _____
Are you working now? ___ Where? _____

Give two references:

	Name	Address	Telephone
1.			
2.			

Signature: _____

WRITE *Change the verbs under the lines from the present to the past tense.*

Sami Hamati's asking David Fernandez about his interview.

Sami: I *heard* that you *had* a job interview. How _____ it?
hear   have   is

David: Joanne _____ me about a job opening at the Acme Home Improvement
            tell

Center. She _____ that they _____ a salesperson who _____
          say   need   know

something about lumber, paint, and hardware. I _____ and _____ an
                                        call   make

appointment to see the personnel manager. When I _____ there, the
                                            arrive

secretary _____ me an application. I _____ in the waiting room and
            give   sit

_____ it out. The personnel manager _____ out of her office and
fill   come

_____ me in. She _____ me about the company and she _____ me
invite   tell   ask

many questions. She _____ the job and I _____ that the job _____
            explain   say   interest

me very much. I _____ her about my qualifications, experience, and
            tell

education. She _____ that there _____ many applicants for the job,
        say   are

and that she _____ interview them before she _____ a decision. The
       have to   make

interview _____ and I _____ her for her time.
       end   thank

Sami: _____ you _____ the job?
   Do   get

David: I don't know. The manager never _____.
                          call

Sami: Why don't you telephone her and ask about the job?

David: OK. I will.

WRITE

Unscramble the questions. Then find the answers to the questions in the dialog on the previous page. Write the answers on the lines below.

Sami is telling Joanne about David's interview.

Joanne: What/talk/about/David/did/? *What did David talk about?*

Sami: *He talked about his interview.*

Joanne: Who/make/did/an appointment/with/he/? _____

_____

Sami: _____

Joanne: What/fill out/he/did/? _____

Sami: _____

Joanne: the application/from/Who/get/he/did/? _____

_____

Sami: _____

Joanne: give/did/Who/he/to/the application/? _____

_____

Sami: _____

Joanne: he/get/Did/the job/? _____

Sami: _____

DICTATION

Cover the sentences under each line. Write the dictation on the line as your teacher reads it to you. Then uncover the sentences and correct your writing.

It's 12:30 p.m. David's calling the Acme Home Improvement Center.

1. _____

   David: I'd like to speak to the personnel manager.

2. _____

   Secretary: May I ask who's calling?

3. _____

   David: This is David Fernandez. I had a job interview with her last week.

4. _____

   Secretary: The manager isn't here. Do you want to leave a message?

5. _____

   David: Yes, please ask her to call me. It's about the salesperson job.

6. _____

   Secretary: I'll give her your message. Thank you. Good-bye.

WRITE   *Help the secretary write a note about David to Mrs. Hirsch. Look at the example below.*

IMPORTANT MESSAGE

FOR _Mrs. Hirsch_

DATE _Nov. 21_ TIME _12:20_ A.M. P.M.

M _r. Grummer_

OF _J. V.'S. Employment Agency_

PHONE _(213)_ _655-8911_
AREA CODE   NUMBER   EXTENSION

TELEPHONED	✓	PLEASE CALL	✓
CAME TO SEE YOU		WILL CALL AGAIN	
WANTS TO SEE YOU		RUSH	
RETURNED YOUR CALL		SPECIAL ATTENTION	

MESSAGE _He has an applicant for the job as a salesperson. Call before 3 p.m._

SIGNED _Jill_

IMPORTANT MESSAGE

FOR _____

DATE _____ TIME _____ A.M. P.M.

M _____

OF _____

PHONE _____
AREA CODE   NUMBER   EXTENSION

TELEPHONED		PLEASE CALL	
CAME TO SEE YOU		WILL CALL AGAIN	
WANTS TO SEE YOU		RUSH	
RETURNED YOUR CALL		SPECIAL ATTENTION	

MESSAGE _____

SIGNED _____

READ

Mrs. Doris Hirsch is back in her office.

> *Mrs. Hirsch:* Were there any calls or messages?
> *Secretary:* Yes, I left them on your desk.

UNDERSTAND   *Circle True, False, or We don't know.*

1. "Rush" means "unimportant."   True   False   We don't know.
2. Mr. Grummer wants Mrs. Hirsch to call him back.   True   False   We don't know.
3. Mrs. Hirsch wasn't in her office at 12:20.   True   False   We don't know.
4. Mr. Grummer and Mrs. Hirsch work together.   True   False   We don't know.

PAIR PRACTICE   *Fold the page on the dotted line. Look at your side only. Do the exercise orally.*

Student 1

Listen to your partner's questions and find the answers in the ads below.

SALESPERSON

xlnt. sal.
med. ins.
1. yr. exp. req.
f.t./p.t.
call 461-0203
for appointment

SALESPERSON

no. exp. req.
will train
dent./med. ins. pd.
apply in per.
Computer Store
123 Main St.

Now ask your partner these questions.

1. What do you see in your picture?
2. What kind of jobs are they advertising?
3. What kind of experience is necessary to get the jobs?
4. How can you make appointments for interviews?
5. Are both jobs full-time?
6. Do applicants for the jobs need to have experience?
7. How much do the jobs pay?

Student 2

Ask your partner these questions.

1. What kind of ads do you see?
2. How much experience do the applicants need?
3. Do the jobs pay well?
4. Are the jobs full-time or part-time?
5. How can you make appointments for the jobs in the ads?
6. Are there any benefits? What kind?
7. Are there any abbreviations in the ads?
8. Do you understand all the abbreviations?

Listen to your partner's questions and find the answers in the signs below.

WANTED

Bilingual salesperson
who is honest and who
handles money well. No
experience necessary.
We will train. Inquire
inside.

WANTED

Experienced Carpenter
Part-time
Weekend Work
$15.00/hr.
Call 643-6654

FOLD HERE

WORD BUILDING   The Suffix *-ment*

- *We use the suffix* **-ment** *to change verbs and other words into nouns.*
- *It has the meaning of product, means, action, or state of being.*

EXAMPLES

1. enjoy ⟶ enjoy<u>ment</u>   2. agree ⟶ agree<u>ment</u>   3. move ⟶ move<u>ment</u>

WRITE   *Add the suffix* **-ment** *to the words below.*

1. David sat in his apart*ment* and read the require_____s for a job in an advertise_____ in the newspaper.

2. He went to the employ_____ develop_____ depart_____ to speak to a person in manage_____.

3. He explained that he knew how to do experi_____s, and how to use carpentry equip_____ and other kinds of instru_____s for measure_____.

4. He told them that he wanted a job because he didn't want to get unemploy_____ insurance from the govern_____.

CHALLENGE   *Discuss the comic strip below. How many meanings does the word* **graveyard** *have? Look in your dictionary.*

5

WHO'S THE BEST PERSON FOR THE JOB?

COMPETENCIES	• Evaluating Job Applicants
	• Evaluating Different Cars
	• Basic Facts about U.S. Geography
	• Discussing Reasons for Working
GRAMMAR	• The Comparative
	• The Superlative
	• *so that/in order to/for*
	• *as . . . as*
VOCABULARY	• Common Adjectives and Adverbs
	• Some Names of American States and Cities
	• Prepositions: *above* and *below*
PRONUNCIATION	• Doubling Consonants
	• The /kw/ and /ks/ Sounds

LISTEN

Mrs. Doris Hirsch, Bill, and Steve work in the personnel department of the Acme Home Improvement Center. They're talking about some job applicants.

Doris: Here are two good applicants, Bob Johnson and Gale Hope.
Bill: Let's hire Bob. He can work faster than Gale.
Steve: How do you know? Maybe Gale can work better than Bob.
Bill: I think that Bob is younger than Gale.
Steve: That's not important. Gale has more education.
Bill: Bob is stronger than Gale.
Steve: Maybe, but Gale has more experience than Bob.
Bill: Bob will be more dependable and can work for less money than Gale.
Steve: Gale has two children, and she needs the job more than Bob.
Bill: Bob has a bigger family than Gale.
Steve: Gale told me that she can come to work earlier than Bob.
Bill: But Bob can work later than Gale.
Steve: Gale speaks better English than Bob.
Bill: But Gale writes worse than Bob.
Doris: OK! OK! Enough! What about David Fernandez?
Steve: I don't know very much about him.
Doris: It's almost five o'clock. Let's talk about him tomorrow, OK? Steve, can you give me a ride home? My car's at the repair shop.
Steve: Sure, come on.

UNDERSTAND   *Circle True, False, or We don't know.*

1. Gale works better than Bob.	True	False	We don't know.
2. Bob has three children.	True	False	We don't know.
3. Gale is a woman.	True	False	We don't know.
4. Gale speaks English better than she writes it.	True	False	We don't know.
5. They gave the job to David Fernandez.	True	False	We don't know.

GRAMMAR   The Comparative

- We use the comparative to compare two objects or people.
- We use the suffix **-er** after short adjectives or adverbs with one or two syllables.
- We use **more** before long adjectives with three or more syllables.
- We always place **than** after the comparative.

EXAMPLES

He can work	**faster**		**than**	Gale.
Bob is	**younger**		**than**	Gale.
Bob is	**stronger**		**than**	Gale.
Bob has a	**bigger**	family	**than**	Gale.
Gale can begin	**earlier**		**than**	Bob.
Bob can stay	**later**		**than**	Gale.

Bob is **more** dependable **than** Gale.

- Some irregular comparative forms are as follows:

good/well	→	better than
bad	→	worse than
a little	→	less than
much/many	→	more than

EXAMPLES

Gale speaks	**better**	English	**than**	Bob.
Gale writes	**worse**		**than**	Bob.
Gale has	**more**	experience	**than**	Bob.
Bob can work for	**less**	money	**than**	Gale.

READ   *Make logical complete sentences with the words in the boxes.*

Gale	works	better		Gale.
She	speaks	worse	than	she.
Bob	writes	more		Bob.
He	needs a job	faster		he.
	is	less		

	older,		
Who's	younger,	Gale	Bob?
	more dependable,		or
	more experienced,	Bob	Gale?
	more qualified,		

PAIR PRACTICE   *Practice the comparative form. Use the suffix -er with the words below.*

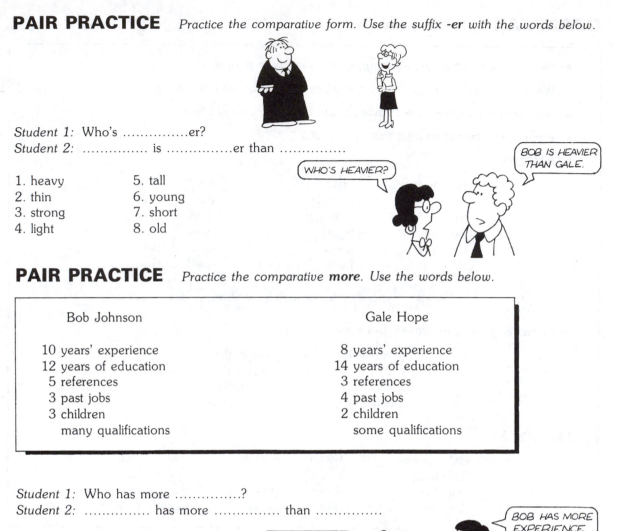

Student 1: Who's ....er?
Student 2: .... is ....er than ....

1. heavy
2. thin
3. strong
4. light
5. tall
6. young
7. short
8. old

WHO'S HEAVIER?

BOB IS HEAVIER THAN GALE.

PAIR PRACTICE   *Practice the comparative **more**. Use the words below.*

Bob Johnson	Gale Hope
10 years' experience	8 years' experience
12 years of education	14 years of education
5 references	3 references
3 past jobs	4 past jobs
3 children	2 children
many qualifications	some qualifications

Student 1: Who has more ....?
Student 2: .... has more .... than ....

1. experience
2. education
3. references
4. qualifications
5. children
6. past jobs

WHO HAS MORE EXPERIENCE?

BOB HAS MORE EXPERIENCE THAN GALE.

PAIR PRACTICE   *Ask and answer questions about the information below.*

BOB READS AND WRITES ENGLISH WELL. BOB'S A FAST WORKER. HE CAN'T BEGIN WORK EARLY BECAUSE HE HAS TO TAKE HIS KIDS TO SCHOOL IN THE MORNING, BUT HE CAN WORK OVERTIME OR STAY LATE.

GALE SPEAKS ENGLISH WELL, AND READS AND WRITES O.K. GALE DOES GOOD QUALITY WORK. GALE CAN BEGIN WORK EARLY, BUT CAN'T STAY LATER THAN 6 P.M. BECAUSE SHE HAS TWO CHILDREN.

Student 1: Who can ....?
Student 2: .... can ....

WHO CAN SPEAK ENGLISH BETTER?

GALE CAN SPEAK BETTER THAN BOB.

WRITE   *Help Mrs. Doris Hirsch answer some questions. Use the information below.*

DAVID	GALE
—knows about lumber, paint, and hardware —12 years of education —6 years' experience as a carpenter —no sales experience —2 references	—salesperson for 5 years —14 years of education —can handle money well —3 references —doesn't know anything about hardware —needs a job very badly

Bill: Who knows more about hardware?

Doris: _David knows more about hardware._

Steve: Who has more experience as a salesperson?

Doris: _____

Bill: Who has worked longer?

Doris: _____

Steve: Who can handle money better?

Doris: _____

Bill: Who has less education?

Doris: _____

Steve: Who has more references?

Doris: _____

Bill: Who needs the job more, Gale or David?

Doris: _____

READ

IT'S FIVE O'CLOCK. IT'S TIME TO GO HOME. LET'S TALK ABOUT THESE APPLICANTS TOMORROW.

SURE, I CAN GIVE YOU A RIDE. COME ON.

STEVE, CAN YOU GIVE ME A RIDE HOME? MY CAR'S AT THE REPAIR SHOP.

READ

Doris is riding in Steve's new car.

> I LIKE YOUR NEW CAR.

Doris: I like your new car. I need one, too. My car's always in the repair shop.

Steve: What kind of car do you want to buy?

Doris: I really don't know. I want a car that gets good mileage.

Steve: Then buy a Super X-100. It's the most economical car that you can find.

Doris: I need a roomy car for the kids.

Steve: No problem. It's the best car for big families. It's the roomiest and most comfortable car in the world.

Doris: I want a safe car, too.

Steve: It's the safest car of all.

Doris: Does it need much servicing?

Steve: Not at all. It has the most efficient motor of all, and it needs the least servicing or repairs of any car.

Doris: I can't pay a lot of money.

Steve: The Super X-100 is one of the cheapest cars in America, and I have a friend who can give you the best deal in town.

Doris: Thanks for the advice, but I have to speak to my husband before we decide to go out and buy a car.

Steve: Well, here's your house.

Doris: Thanks for the ride.

Steve: You're welcome. Let me know if you need a ride tomorrow. Bye.

UNDERSTAND   *Circle* **True**, **False**, *or* **We don't know.**

1. Steve has a Super X-100.	True	False	We don't know.
2. A car that gets good mileage is economical.	True	False	We don't know.
3. Doris has a son and a daughter.	True	False	We don't know.
4. Doris is divorced.	True	False	We don't know.
5. "A good deal" means "a low price."	True	False	We don't know.

GRAMMAR   The Superlative

- We use the superlative to show the superiority of one item over all the others in the same group.

- We use the suffix **-est** after short adjectives or adverbs with one or two syllables.

- We use **most** before long adjectives with three or more syllables.

- We always use **the** before the superlative.

EXAMPLES

It's **the roomiest** car in the world.
It's **the safest** car of all.
It's **the easiest** car to drive.
It's **the cheapest** car in America.

It's **the most** economical car that you can find.
It's **the most** comfortable car in the world.
It has **the most** efficient motor of all.

- The irregular superlative forms are as follows:

good/well ⟶ the best
bad ⟶ the worst
a little ⟶ the least
much/many ⟶ the most

EXAMPLES

It's **the best** car for a big family.
It needs **the least** servicing of any car.
You can get **the best** deal from a friend of mine.

READ   Make complete sentences with the words in the box.

The Super X-100	is	the	most economical		in the world.
			most expensive		of all.
			least dangerous		of any car.
			safest	car	in America.
	isn't		best		to drive.
			worst		to buy.
					to own.

PAIR PRACTICE

*Practice the superlative form. Use the suffix **-est** with the words below.*

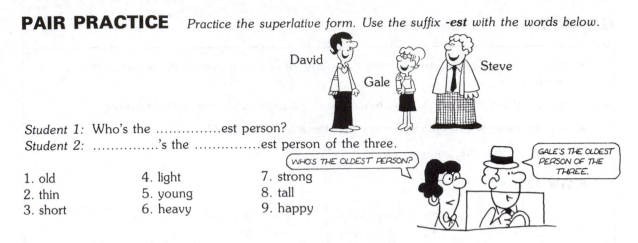

Student 1: Who's the ....est person?
Student 2: ....'s the ....est person of the three.

1. old
2. thin
3. short
4. light
5. young
6. heavy
7. strong
8. tall
9. happy

PAIR PRACTICE

*Practice the superlatives **the most** or **the least**. Use the words below. Find the answers in the chart.*

YEARLY CAR BUYERS' RATING REPORT			
A = THE MOST B = AVERAGE C = THE LEAST			
	Eagle Sports Car	Super X-100	The Tiger
economical	B	A	C
comfortable	B	A	C
efficient	C	A	B
practical	C	B	A
dangerous	A	C	B
expensive	A	C	B
popular	B	A	C
TOTAL	B	A	C

Student 1: What's the most/least .... car?
Student 2: The .... is the most/least .... car of all.

1. economical
2. comfortable
3. uncomfortable
4. dangerous
5. efficient
6. practical
7. expensive
8. inexpensive
9. popular
10. unpopular

CHALLENGE

What's the best and worst car in the graph above? Why?

WRITE   *Answer the questionnaire in your own words.*

NEW CAR CUSTOMER SURVEY

WHAT DO YOU THINK ABOUT AMERICAN AND FOREIGN CARS?

1. In your opinion, what's the most expensive American car?

_____

2. What company makes the least expensive cars?

_____

3. What's the most comfortable American car?

_____

4. What's the most beautiful car in the world?

_____

5. What's the least beautiful car of all?

_____

6. What country makes the smallest car of all?

_____

7. What country makes the biggest cars?

_____

8. What country makes the fastest cars?

_____

9. What do you think is the worst car of all?

_____

10. What is the most popular car in this country?

_____

11. What do you think is the best car?

_____

DISCUSSION   *Discuss in class other possible answers to the questions above.*

SPELLING   Rules for Adding *-er* and *-est*.

- *Most words do not change spelling when we add **-er** and **-est**.*

EXAMPLES   small → small<u>er</u> → small<u>est</u>
               cold → col<u>der</u> → cold<u>est</u>

- *We change **y** to **i** before we add the suffixes **-er** or **-est** to adjectives or adverbs.*

EXAMPLES   early → earl<u>ier</u> → earl<u>iest</u>
               heavy → heav<u>ier</u> → heav<u>iest</u>

- *When a word ends in a consonant-vowel-consonant pattern and the final vowel is stressed, we double the final consonant before adding **-er** or **-est**. We never double **w** or **y**.*

EXAMPLES   big → big<u>ger</u> → big<u>gest</u>
               thin → thin<u>ner</u> → thin<u>nest</u>

- *If the word ends in **e**, only add **-r** or **-st**.*

EXAMPLES   safe → saf<u>er</u> → saf<u>est</u>
               nice → nic<u>er</u> → nic<u>est</u>

WRITE   Add the suffixes *-er* and *-est* to the following words.

1. easy   *easier*   *easiest*
2. slow   *slower*   *slowest*
3. roomy _____   _____
4. big   _____   _____
5. dry   _____   _____
6. nice   _____   _____
7. heavy _____   _____

8. thin   _____   _____
9. large _____   _____
10. quick _____   _____
11. fast _____   _____
12. wet   _____   _____
13. late _____   _____
14. cheap _____   _____

READ

Mrs. Doris Hirsch is at home. Her son, George, is asking her for some help.

WRITE   *Fill in the spaces below with the comparative or superlative form of the word under the line.*

THE UNITED STATES

The United States is a big country, but it is not the _**biggest**_ country in the world. The Soviet
big

Union, Canada, and China are _____ than the U.S.A. The U.S.A. has fifty states. Alaska is the
large

_____ state and Rhode Island is the _____ state. Rhode Island is _____
   large   small   industrial

and has a _____ population than Alaska. Of all the fifty states, Alaska has the _____
        great   few

people. The state that has the _____ people is California. The _____ states are
many   old

Massachusetts and Virginia, and the _____ states are Hawaii and Alaska.
new

The United States has many big cities. New York City is the _____ with _____ than
big   many

eight million people. Los Angeles is the second _____ and Chicago is the third. Many people say
big

that San Francisco in Northern California is the _____ city in the country. Other people
beautiful

say that Seattle in Washington State is the _____, _____, and _____ city to
clean   safe   good

live in. The weather is not the same in all parts of the country. In general, the North is _____ than
cold

the South and the West is usually _____ than the East.
dry

WRITE   *Help George answer the questions. Find the answers on the previous page, if necessary.*

Doris is asking her son some questions about the United States.

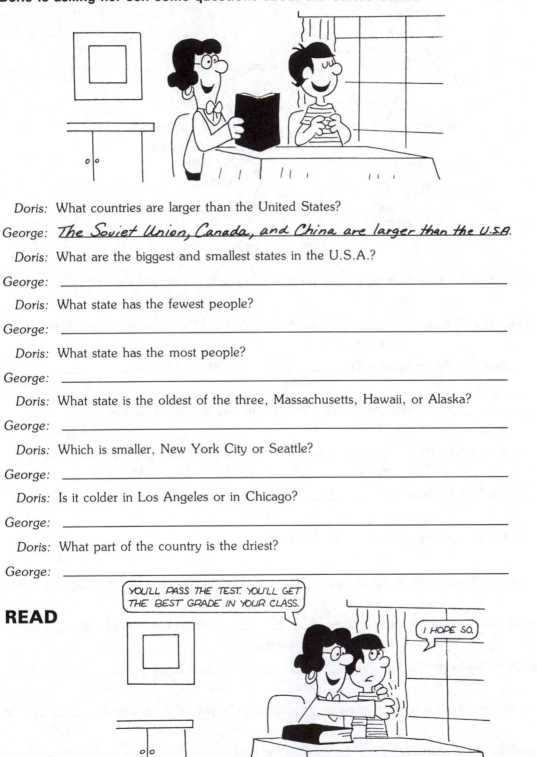

Doris: What countries are larger than the United States?

George: *The Soviet Union, Canada, and China are larger than the U.S.A.*

Doris: What are the biggest and smallest states in the U.S.A.?

George: _____

Doris: What state has the fewest people?

George: _____

Doris: What state has the most people?

George: _____

Doris: What state is the oldest of the three, Massachusetts, Hawaii, or Alaska?

George: _____

Doris: Which is smaller, New York City or Seattle?

George: _____

Doris: Is it colder in Los Angeles or in Chicago?

George: _____

Doris: What part of the country is the driest?

George: _____

YOU'LL PASS THE TEST. YOU'LL GET THE BEST GRADE IN YOUR CLASS.

I HOPE SO.

READ

READ

Doris and George are talking about work.

George: Ask me some more questions for my test.
 Doris: I can't. I have to go to work.
George: Why do you have to go to work?
 Doris: I have to work so that your father and I can buy food and pay the rent.
George: Why does everybody have to work?
 Doris: Most people work so that they can support their families.
George: Grandma doesn't work.
 Doris: She's a senior citizen. She sometimes works so that she can earn some extra
        income. Other people volunteer their time so that they can help others. Im-
        migrants sometimes work in jobs that they don't like so that they can get ex-
        perience for a better job in the future.
George: Do kids work, too?
 Doris: College students work so that they can pay for their tuition and books. Kids
        have paper routes or work on yards so that they can have pocket money.
        So, you see, there are many reasons for work.
George: When I grow up, I know the job that I want.
 Doris: And what job is that?
George: I'm going to be a millionaire.
 Doris: That's a very nice job!

UNDERSTAND   *Circle **True**, **False**, or **We don't know**.*

1. George wants to go to work with Doris.	True	False	We don't know.
2. Doris works so that she can pay the rent.	True	False	We don't know.
3. George is not old enough to work.	True	False	We don't know.
4. "Earn" means "make money."	True	False	We don't know.
5. George will be a millionaire.	True	False	We don't know.
6. "Extra" means "more."	True	False	We don't know.

GRAMMAR   *so that/in order to/for*

- *We use the expression **so that** to show purpose, reason, or results.*
- *We usually use **can** after **so that**.*

EXAMPLES

I have to work	so that	I	can	buy food and pay the rent.
Most people work	so that	they	can	support their families.
She works	so that	she	can	earn some extra money.
They work	so that	they	can	help other people.
Immigrants work	so that	they	can	get experience.
Students work	so that	they	can	pay their tuition.
Kids work	so that	they	can	have pocket money.

- *We can replace **so that** with **in order to** or **to** before verbs.*

EXAMPLES

I have to work	in order to	buy food and pay the rent.
Most people work	to	support their families.
She works	to	earn some extra money.

- *We can substitute **in order to get** with **for** only before nouns.*

EXAMPLES

Students work	for	tuition.
Kids work	for	pocket money.

- *All the expressions above are answers to **why** questions.*

EXAMPLES

	They work	so that they can support	their families.
Why do people work?	They work	in order to support	their families.
	They work	to support	their families.
	They work	for	their families.

READ   *Make logical complete sentences with the words in the box.*

People		so that they can	get	experience.
			help	
Kids	work	in order to	earn	their families.
			support	
Immigrants		to	buy	money.
			pay	
Students				tuition.
		for		
Senior citizens				food.

PAIR PRACTICE   *Use the words below. Answer with* **so that** *and your own words.*

Student 1: Why do people ....?
Student 2: People .... so that they can ....

1. exercise
2. work
3. go to school
4. sleep
5. eat

6. study
7. save money
8. read the newspaper
9. listen to the news
10. ....

WHY DO PEOPLE EXERCISE?

PEOPLE EXERCISE SO THAT THEY CAN BE HEALTHY.

PAIR PRACTICE   *Use the phrases below. Answer with* **in order to** *or* **to** *and your own words.*

Student 1: Why do ....?
Student 2: .... in order to/to ....

1. people watch T.V.
2. we need laws
3. children ask questions
4. people come to this country
5. some people wear glasses

6. people wear watches
7. some stores stay open 24 hours
8. you do this grammar exercise
9. you work
10. you ....

WHY DO PEOPLE WATCH T.V.?

PEOPLE WATCH T.V. TO GET INFORMATION AND TO RELAX.

PAIR PRACTICE   *Use the phrases below. Answer with* **for** *and your own words.*

Student 1: Why do you go to ....?
Student 2: I go to .... for ....

1. a restaurant
2. the market
3. the bank
4. the post office
5. a flower shop

6. a library
7. a barber
8. a hairdresser
9. a pharmacy or drugstore
10. ....

I GO TO A RESTAURANT FOR DINNER.

WHY DO YOU GO TO A RESTAURANT?

READ

Mrs. Hirsch is talking to Steve and Bill about the applicants.

Doris: We have to choose an applicant so that we can call him or her today.
Steve: Did you call any of the references that the applicants gave?
  Bill: Yes, I did.
Doris: What did you learn from them?
  Bill: I learned that one works as well as the other.
Doris: Well, what did they tell you?
Steve: They all gave above-average recommendations.

UNDERSTAND   *Circle **True**, **False**, or **We don't know**.*

1. David works better than Gale.	True	False	We don't know.
2. David works as well as Gale.	True	False	We don't know.
3. Gale works as hard as Bob.	True	False	We don't know.
4. Bill called all the references.	True	False	We don't know.

GRAMMAR   *as ... as*

- *We use the expression **as ... as** to show equality.*

- *We can use this expression with both adjectives and adverbs.*

EXAMPLES

One works	**as**	well	**as**	the other.
David works	**as**	well	**as**	Gale.
Gale works	**as**	hard	**as**	Bob.

READ   *Make logical complete sentences with the words in the box.*

David			carefully		David.
Gale	works	as	well	as	Gale.
Bob			fast		Bob.
			hard		

PAIR PRACTICE   *Talk with another student. Use the words below.*

Student 1: Does Gale work ....er than David?
                               or
            Does Gale work more .... than David?
Student 2: No, she works as .... as he.

1. well
2. fast
3. quickly
4. long
5. carefully

6. hard
7. safely
8. efficiently
9. regularly
10. intelligently

DOES GALE WORK BETTER THAN DAVID?

NO, SHE WORKS AS WELL AS HE.

PAIR PRACTICE   *Use the phrases below.*

Student 1: Can .... work as .... as ....?
Student 2: Yes, ... can work as .... as ....
                               or
            No, ... can't work as .... as ....

1. a woman/fast/a man
2. a man/fast/a woman
3. a woman/good/a man
4. a machine/quickly/a person
5. a person/efficiently/a machine
6. an adult/hard/a child
7. a person/long/a machine
8. an older person/carefully/a younger person

CAN A WOMAN WORK AS FAST AS A MAN?

YES, A WOMAN CAN WORK AS FAST AS A MAN.

PAIR PRACTICE   *Use the words below. Answer in your own words.*

I WORK AS WELL AS A MACHINE.

Student 1: How well do you ....?
Student 2: I .... as well as a ....

1. work
2. speak
3. drive
4. cook
5. study

6. run
7. swim
8. sleep
9. eat
10. ....

HOW WELL DO YOU WORK?

PAIR PRACTICE   *Compare David, Gale, and Bob with the average American worker. Answer with **above average**, **average**, or **below average**.*

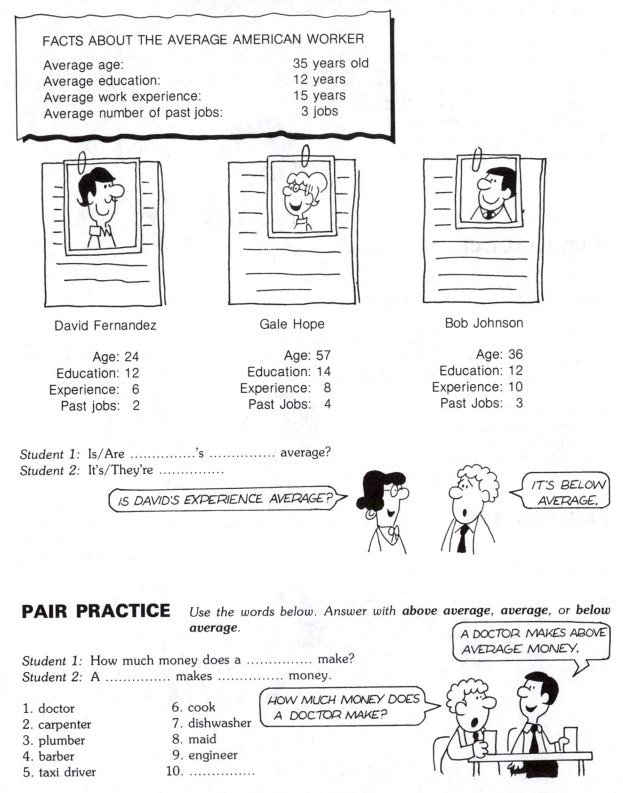

FACTS ABOUT THE AVERAGE AMERICAN WORKER

Average age:	35 years old
Average education:	12 years
Average work experience:	15 years
Average number of past jobs:	3 jobs

David Fernandez

Age: 24
Education: 12
Experience: 6
Past jobs: 2

Gale Hope

Age: 57
Education: 14
Experience: 8
Past Jobs: 4

Bob Johnson

Age: 36
Education: 12
Experience: 10
Past Jobs: 3

Student 1: Is/Are ....'s .... average?
Student 2: It's/They're ....

IS DAVID'S EXPERIENCE AVERAGE?

IT'S BELOW AVERAGE.

PAIR PRACTICE   *Use the words below. Answer with **above average**, **average**, or **below average**.*

A DOCTOR MAKES ABOVE AVERAGE MONEY.

Student 1: How much money does a .... make?
Student 2: A .... makes .... money.

HOW MUCH MONEY DOES A DOCTOR MAKE?

1. doctor
2. carpenter
3. plumber
4. barber
5. taxi driver

6. cook
7. dishwasher
8. maid
9. engineer
10. ....

DICTATION

David never received a phone call from the Acme Home Improvement Center about the job, but he did get a letter.

Dear Mr. Fernandez:

1. _____

   We filled the job for a salesperson.

2. _____

   We had many people who applied for the job.

3. _____

   It was not possible to hire all of them.

4. _____

   So, we hired the applicant with the best qualifications.

5. _____

   We will keep your application.

6. _____

   We will call you as soon as we have another job opening.

7. _____

   We're sure that with your experience, you will find employment.

8. _____

   Thank you for your interest in our company.

9. _____

   We wish you the best of luck.   Sincerely yours,

   Mrs. Doris Hirsch

DISCUSSION

Who was the better person for the job, Bob Johnson or Gale Hope? Why? Why didn't David get the job? Discuss the reasons in class, and then choose one person for the job. Write Bob's or Gale's name on the blank line below.

READ

Mrs. Doris Hirsch is calling the applicant about the job.

PAIR PRACTICE

Fold the page on the dotted line. Look at your side only. Do the exercise orally.

Student 1

Listen to your partner's questions and find the answers in the chart below.

POPULATION OF 10 OF THE 50 STATES

1980 Census

STATES	POPULATION
Alaska	400,500
California	24,000,000
Florida	9,800,000
Hawaii	970,000
Illinois	11,500,000
New York	18,000,000
Pennsylvania	12,000,000
Rhode Island	950,000
Texas	14,500,000
Washington	4,250,000

Now ask your partner these questions.

1. What kind of chart do you see?
2. How many cities are on the chart?
3. Which is the biggest city?
4. What's the average population of the ten biggest cities?
5. Is Chicago above or below average in population compared to the other ten biggest cities?
6. What cities have as many people as Houston?
7. Is Los Angeles bigger or smaller than New York?

Student 2

Ask your partner these questions.

1. What kind of chart do you see?
2. Which state has the most people?
3. What state has the fewest people?
4. How many states are there in the United States?
5. How many states are in the chart?
6. Which is bigger, New York or California?
7. Does Rhode Island have as many people as Hawaii?

Listen to your partner's questions and find the answers in the chart below.

POPULATION OF THE TEN BIGGEST CITIES IN THE UNITED STATES

(with surrounding area)

CITIES (and area)	POPULATION
Boston	2,800,000
Chicago	7,000,000
Dallas-Forth Worth	3,000,000
Detroit	4,500,000
Houston	3,000,000
Los Angeles	7,500,000
New York	9,000,000
Philadelphia	5,000,000
San Francisco-Oakland	3,500,000
Washington D.C.	3,000,000

AVERAGE: 4,800,000 people

FOLD HERE

PRONUNCIATION   The /kw/ and /ks/ Sounds

- *We usually spell the /kw/ sound as* **qu**, *and the /ks/ sound as* **x**.

- *The letter* **q** *is always followed by* **u**.

- **X** *rarely comes at the beginning of a word. When it does, it is pronounced /z/.*

EXAMPLES

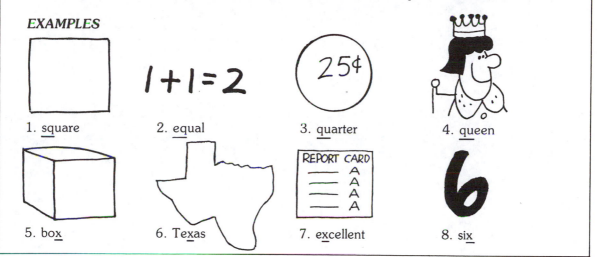

1. s<u>qu</u>are   2. e<u>qu</u>al   3. <u>qu</u>arter   4. <u>qu</u>een

5. bo<u>x</u>   6. Te<u>x</u>as   7. e<u>x</u>cellent   8. si<u>x</u>

WRITE   *Fill in the spaces with* **qu** *or* **x**.

1. The instructor e_**x**_plained the si____ e____amples to the ____estions on the ____estionnaire.

2. The students did the e____ercises on the e____amination ____ickly and ____ietly.

3. The mechanic had e____cellent ____alifications to fi____ the e____pensive e____ipment from Te____as and New Me____ico.

4. The law re____ires that you pay a ta____ of e____actly a ____arter for the ____art of oil in this bo____.

THE IMMIGRANTS

COMPETENCIES	• Describing Past Events
GRAMMAR	• Expressions of Time
	• Irregular Verbs
VOCABULARY	• Prepositions and Conjunctions: *before, during, after, for, until, in*
PRONUNCIATION	• The Letter *w* at the End of Words

LISTEN

Larry Evans is interviewing Lan Tran for the high school newspaper.

Larry: I'm Larry Evans. I'm a high school student at this school during the day. I'm writing an article for our school newspaper. The article is about ESL students who come to the adult school in the evening. Can I ask you a few questions?

Lan: OK. We can talk for a few minutes. My class doesn't start until 7.

Larry: Where are you from, and when did you come to this country?

Lan: I'm from Vietnam, and I came to this country with my husband and children last year. It will be our one-year anniversary three weeks from now.

Larry: Did you know any English before you arrived in Los Angeles?

Lan: A little. We studied English in the Philippines before we came here.

Larry: How long did you stay there?

Lan: We lived in a refugee camp for a few months until we got our visas to enter the United States.

Larry: Where did you live after you arrived?

Lan: We stayed with my uncle until we found an apartment and jobs.

Larry: Do you have any other relatives here?

Lan: No, but my brother will arrive here in two weeks. I can't wait until he's here. My uncle helped us, and now we have the chance to help another new immigrant, my brother.

UNDERSTAND   *Circle True, False, or We don't know.*

1. Larry and Lan study at the same school.   True   False   We don't know.
2. The article will be in the newspaper in two weeks.   True   False   We don't know.
3. Lan arrived in this country less than a year ago.   True   False   We don't know.
4. Lan has a relative here.   True   False   We don't know.

GRAMMAR   Expressions of Time: *before, during, after*

- *We use **before** and **after** as both prepositions and conjunctions. We use **during** only as a preposition.*

- ***Before** means **sooner than**, **in front of**, or **in the past**. **During** means **through the course of** or **in the time period**. **After** means **at a later time than** or **following**.*

EXAMPLES

I'm a high school student	**during**	the day.
We studied English	**before**	we came here.
Where did you stay	**after**	you arrived here?

READ   *Make logical complete sentences with the words in the box.*

	lived in Vietnam	during	she arrived here.
Lan	lived with relatives	before	the daytime.
Larry	studied English	after	the evening.
	studies		

PAIR PRACTICE   *Talk with another student. Use **before**, **during**, or **after** with the phrases below. Answer in your own words.*

Student 1:   What do you usually do ....?
Student 2:   I usually ....

1. breakfast
2. lunch
3. dinner
4. work
5. a test
6. a movie

7. your English lesson
8. the weekend
9. your vacation
10. a job appointment
11. a party
12. your break

WHAT DO YOU USUALLY DO DURING BREAKFAST?

I USUALLY DRINK MY COFFEE AND READ THE NEWSPAPER DURING BREAKFAST.

PAIR PRACTICE   *Use **during** with the phrases below. Answer in your own words.*

Student 1:   What do you like to do during ....?
Student 2:   I like to .... during ....

1. the weekend
2. the evening
3. the morning
4. the afternoon
5. your free time
6. the daytime

7. the night
8. the spring
9. the summer
10. the fall
11. the winter
12. ....

WHAT DO YOU LIKE TO DO DURING THE WEEKEND?

I LIKE TO REST DURING THE WEEKEND.

READ

The interview continues.

WHAT DID YOU DO DURING YOUR STAY IN THE REFUGEE CAMP?

WE WENT TO ENGLISH CLASSES FOR FOUR HOURS DURING THE DAY AND WE STUDIED DURING THE EVENING.

GRAMMAR   Expressions of Time: *during, for*

- *For* means **lasting a period of time**, and answers the question **How long?** Words that follow **for** express a specific time and often include numbers. For example: *for an hour, for two days, for three weeks.*

- *During* answers the question **When?** We usually use nonspecific time words after **during**. For example: *during the daytime, during the lesson.*

EXAMPLES

How long	did you stay?	We stayed there	**for**	5 months.
When	did you study?	We went to classes	**during**	the daytime.
		We studied	**during**	the evening.

PAIR PRACTICE   *Use the words and phrases below. Answer with **for** and your own words.*

Student 1:   How long do you ....?
Student 2:   I .... for ....

1. study
2. work
3. sleep
4. rest
5. watch T.V.
6. plan to live here
7. read
8. ....

HOW LONG DO YOU STUDY?

I STUDY FOR AN HOUR EVERY DAY.

PAIR PRACTICE   *Use the phrases below. Answer with **during** and your own words.*

Student 1:   When do you ....?
Student 2:   I .... during ....

1. eat breakfast
2. have lunch
3. have dinner
4. go on vacation
5. sleep
6. work
7. go to class
8. visit friends or relatives

WHEN DO YOU EAT BREAKFAST?

I EAT BREAKFAST DURING THE MORNING.

READ

It's the end of the interview.

GRAMMAR   Expressions of Time: *in, until*

- *In* means **within a certain period of time**, **at a later time**, or **in the future**.

- *Until* means **before a specific time** or **up to the time of**. We can also write **until** as **till** or **'til**.

EXAMPLES

The article will be in the paper	**in**	a week.
Lan's brother will arrive here	**in**	two weeks.
Lan can't wait	**until**	her brother comes.
Larry has	**until**	Monday to write it.
Lan's class doesn't start	**until**	7 p.m.

PAIR PRACTICE   *Use the phrases below. Answer with **until** and your own words.*

Student 1:   When will ....?
Student 2:   Not until ....

1. this course end
2. the end of the week be
3. the next test be
4. the end of the lesson be

5. the end of the year be
6. you get a raise
7. your birthday be
8. you take a break

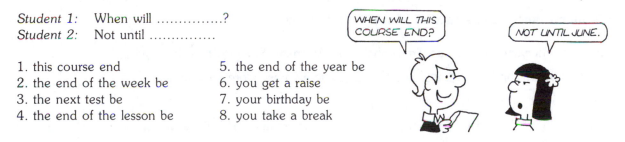

PAIR PRACTICE   *Use the phrases below. Answer with **in** and your own words.*

Student 1:   When will you ....?
Student 2:   I'll .... in ....

1. take a vacation
2. leave this room
3. take a break
4. graduate from this school

5. finish this exercise
6. have a birthday
7. finish this book
8. speak English well

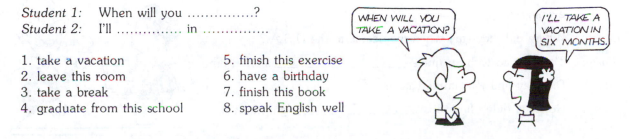

WRITE   *Match the questions with their answers. Write the letters of the answers on the lines after the questions.*

It's the following day. Larry's talking to the newspaper editor between classes.

1. How long was your interview? _c_

2. Did you speak to the ESL students after class last night? ____

3. When can I hear about the interview? ____

4. OK. When's your lunch? ____

5. Did you visit Mr. Barns' ESL class? ____

6. Did you write the article? ____

a. During lunch, OK?

b. No, I didn't finish it. It won't be ready until Monday.

c. A few minutes long.

d. No, we talked before class.

e. In an hour, after my next class.

f. Yes, I listened to his lesson for an hour after the break.

WRITE   *Fill in the spaces with **for** or **during**.*

It's lunch time. Larry's talking about the interview.

Larry: I interviewed Mrs. Lan Tran. She's from Vietnam. She said that she lived in the Philippines ___*for*___ five months before coming here.

Editor: What did they do there?

Larry: They didn't do very much _____ their stay there. They went to English classes _____ a few hours every day and they studied and practiced their English with other immigrants _____ the evening.

Editor: Where did they stay when they came to the U.S.A.?

Larry: They stayed with an uncle _____ a short time.

Editor: Did they find jobs immediately?

Larry: No, they didn't find jobs _____ eight months.

WRITE   *Fill in the spaces below with the words in the box.*

for	during	before	in	until	after

Here is Larry's newspaper article.

NEW IMMIGRANTS

Lan Tran is 44 years old, a mother, a wife, and a student at our school. How can this be, you ask? Well, she and other adult students from all over the world attend classes here. Not _____ the daytime, but _____ the evening. They are hard-working men and women who want to learn English so that they can live a normal life and get a better job in the future. Lan Tran is an excellent example of an immigrant who is trying to begin a new life in a new country.

Lan Tran, her husband, and their two children are refugees from Vietnam. _____ they came to this country they stayed in the Philippines _____ five months. _____ their stay there, they studied English because they wanted to speak the language _____ they arrived in their new home. Lan and her husband went to classes _____ the day and practiced their new language with other refugees and friends _____ their free time. They stayed in the refugee camp _____ they got their visas to enter the U.S.A.

At first, it wasn't easy. They had to live with relatives _____ a short time _____ they found their own apartment and jobs. Lan entered an ESL adult-school program immediately. Her class met every day _____ three hours _____ the morning. She studied _____ eight months _____ she found a job. _____ she began to work, she went to English classes _____ the evening. At work she used and practiced what she learned in class. Now she speaks English very well.

In the beginning their relatives helped them begin their new life, and _____ a few days, Lan's family will have the chance to help another new immigrant to this country, her brother.

DISCUSSION   *From your experience, what advice can you give new immigrants?*

READ

The adult school students are talking during the break.

GRAMMAR   Review of Irregular Verbs

- We form the past tense in English by adding **-ed** to most verbs. Some verbs have irregular forms in the past tense.
- We use the base form of the verb (infinitive without **to**) in the question and negative forms.
- We use the irregular form of the verbs in the affirmative only.
- We use **did** to signal the question and **didn't** to signal the negative.

Base Form	**Irregular Form**
go	went

EXAMPLES

QUESTION: **Did** you **go** to the movies? (base form)

NEGATIVE: No, I **didn't** **go** there. (base form)

AFFIRMATIVE: I **went** to the theater. (irregular form)

COMMON IRREGULAR VERBS

Base	*Irregular*	*Base*	*Irregular*
begin	began	make	made
buy	bought	meet	met
come	came	read	read (pronounced like
do	did	say	said the color *red*)
drink	drank	see	saw
eat	ate	send	sent
feel	felt	sit	sat
forget	forgot	sleep	slept
get	got	speak	spoke
give	gave	stand	stood
go	went	take	took
have	had	tell	told
have to	had to	think	thought
know	knew	understand	understood
leave	left	write	wrote

WRITE *Fill in the spaces with the correct form of the irregular verbs.*

It's breaktime.

1.
What did you see at the movies?

I _saw_ a good western.

2.
Did the kids give your daughter money?

No, they _____ _____ her money. They _____ her many toys.

3.
Did your son go to the birthday party?

Yes, he _____ to the party.

4.
When did the party begin?

It _____ at 10 o'clock.

5.
Why _____ Wanda _____?

She left because she didn't feel very well.

6.
What _____ he _____?

He said that the test will be next Friday.

7.
Did Mario come to class last week?

No, he _____ _____ to class because he had to work overtime.

8.
Did you have a good time in Las Vegas?

I lost a lot of money, but I _____ a good time.

READ

Peter Boulos is telling Rita Landry about his weekend trip to Las Vegas.

Peter: I spent a lot of money on a very short trip. Last Friday after work, I went to the airport, paid for a ticket, and flew to Las Vegas. I played cards and I won five thousand dollars in one evening.

Rita: Oh, really! What did you do with the money?

Peter: I lost it all the next day. I had only fifty dollars and it wasn't enough to buy an airplane ticket back home.

Rita: So what did you do?

Peter: I rode the bus.

UNDERSTAND   *Circle **True, False,** or **We don't know.***

1. Peter took $5,000 to Las Vegas.	True	False	We don't know.
2. Peter flew to and from Las Vegas.	True	False	We don't know.
3. He was in Las Vegas on Saturday.	True	False	We don't know.
4. An airplane ticket cost $75.	True	False	We don't know.

GRAMMAR   **More Irregular Verbs**

Base	*Irregular*	*Base*	*Irregular*
spend	spent	lose	lost
pay	paid	cost	cost
fly	flew	ride	rode
win	won		

WRITE   *Fill in the spaces with words from the boxes above each exercise.*

Rita is asking Peter about his trip.

1.

did	didn't	pay	paid

Rita: _Did_ you _pay_ a lot of money for the airplane ticket to Las Vegas?

Peter: No, I _____ _____ very much. I _____ only eighty dollars.

Rita: Why _____ you _____ for a return ticket when you _____ for the first ticket?

Peter: That's a very good question.

WRITE

2. | did   didn't   fly   flew |

Rita: Why _____ you _____ to Las Vegas?

Peter: I _____ there because I wanted to win some money.

Rita: _____ you _____ from Los Angeles International Airport?

Peter: No, I _____. I _____ from Long Beach Airport.

3. | did   didn't   ride   rode |

Rita: How long _____ you _____ on the bus?

Peter: We _____ on the bus for eight hours.

Rita: _____ you _____ in an air-conditioned bus?

Peter: No, we _____. We _____ in a bus with a broken air conditioner. It
was terrible!

EASY COME,
EASY GO.

4. | did   didn't   win   won |

Rita: You said that you _____ $5,000.

Peter: That's right. I _____ it all in one day.

Rita: How _____ you _____ it?

Peter: I _____ it at cards.

Rita: _____ other people _____ more than you?

Peter: No, they _____ _____ more money.

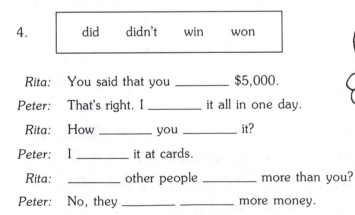

READ

Two students from the wood shop class are talking during the break.

Jack: I heard that you drove to the mountains last weekend.
John: That's right. My wife and kids went, too. We spent three days there.
Jack: How did you like it?
John: It was fun except for a few small problems. One of the kids fell down, tore his clothes, and hurt his leg. The other one cut her leg a little. My wife threw a piece of wood on the fire and burnt her hand. She wore a bandage for a few days. Luckily, we brought a first-aid kit. Everybody's OK now. We didn't have any serious problems.
Jack: Why did you take your kids?
John: My dad taught me all about camping and the outdoors as I grew up. Now my wife and I want to teach our kids about the outdoors before they grow up.

UNDERSTAND   *Circle **True**, **False**, or **We don't know**.*

1. John likes the outdoors.	True	False	We don't know.
2. John's wife likes the outdoors, too.	True	False	We don't know.
3. John grew up in the mountains.	True	False	We don't know.
4. The kids didn't tear their clothes.	True	False	We don't know.

GRAMMAR   **More Irregular Verbs**

Base	Irregular	Base	Irregular
hear	heard	fall	fell
spend	spent	throw	threw
cut	cut	hurt	hurt
bring	brought	teach	taught
tear	tore	grow	grew
wear	wore	burn	burnt

PAIR PRACTICE   *Practice using irregular verbs. Use the phrases below. Answer the questions in complete sentences.*

Student 1:   Did you ....?
Student 2:   Yes, I .... or No, I didn't ....

1. hear about Mr. Fuller
2. spend a lot of money
3. grow up in this city
4. wear that shirt/blouse before
5. tear your clothes
6. bring your dictionary to school
7. cut your finger
8. hurt your hand

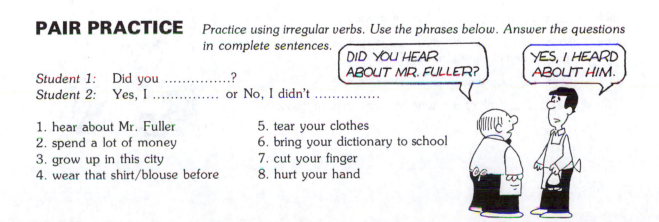

WRITE   *Fill in the spaces below with words from the boxes above each exercise.*

1.

did	didn't	grow	grew

Jack: Where _____ you _____ up?

John: I _____ up on a farm.

Jack: _____ you _____ up on a farm near here?

John: No, I _____. I _____ up in Kansas.

Jack: _____ you _____ wheat on the farm?

John: No, we _____ _____ wheat. We _____ corn.

2.

did	didn't	burn	burnt

Jack: How _____ your wife _____ her hand?

John: She _____ it when she threw some wood on the fire.

Jack: _____ she _____ both hands?

John: No, she _____. She _____ only her right hand.
Thank goodness it wasn't serious.

3.

did	didn't	spend	spent

Jack: How much time _____ you _____ in the mountains?

John: We _____ a three-day weekend.

Jack: _____ you _____ a lot of money?

John: No, we _____. We _____ very little money because we
brought and cooked our own food.

Jack: How _____ you _____ your time?

John: We _____ all of our time on small medical problems.

WRITE   *Interview a student in your class. Then write a short article. Follow the directions below.*

1. *Think about some interview questions that you want to ask. Write them on the lines below. Use some of the question words in the box.*

what	when	what kind	how long	why
where	how	how much	how many	who

INTERVIEW QUESTIONS

_____

_____

_____

_____

_____

2. *Interview a student. Ask your questions.*

3. *Write the answers to your questions on another piece of paper.*

4. *Use the information from your interview to write an article about the student. (Write a rough draft on another piece of paper first.)*

THE ESL NEWS / FEATURE ARTICLE

_____

_____

_____

_____

_____

_____

_____

_____

_____

_____

CHALLENGE   *Read your article to all the students in class.*

PRONUNCIATION   The Letter *w* at the End of Words

- *The letter **w** often occurs in the final position in many words.*
- *We use it in combination with the vowels **a**, **e**, and **o**.*
- *We pronounce **ew** as /u/ or /yu/, **aw** as /ɔ/, and **ow** as /o/ or /au/.*
- *The final **w** occurs in some irregular verbs such as:*

gr<u>ow</u>	→	gr<u>ew</u>	kn<u>ow</u>	→	kn<u>ew</u>
thr<u>ow</u>	→	thr<u>ew</u>	bl<u>ow</u>	→	bl<u>ew</u>
see	→	s<u>aw</u>	fly	→	fl<u>ew</u>
dr<u>aw</u>	→	dr<u>ew</u>			

EXAMPLES

1. l<u>aw</u>n   2. d<u>ow</u>nt<u>ow</u>n   3. a f<u>ew</u> pill<u>ow</u>s

WRITE   *Fill in the sentences with **ow**, **ew**, or **aw**. Then read the sentences with the correct pronunciation.*

1. My neph*ew* wants to borr____ my n____ yell____ car. I kn____ that he will drive it d____nt____n sl____ly.

2. The farmer didn't gr____ wheat on his farm. He gr____ corn and he also ____ned a f____ br____n c____s.

3. H____ do you kn____ that the l____yer fl____ by airplane to revi____ the l____?

7

AT THE BANK

COMPETENCIES	• Opening a Bank Account
	• Cashing a Check
	• Making Deposits
	• Using an Automatic Money Machine
	• Understanding Deductions from a Paycheck
	• Doing Simple Math Problems
GRAMMAR	• Modals
VOCABULARY	• Bank-Related Words
	• Words Found on Check Stubs
SPELLING	• Silent Letters

LISTEN

Mario and Maria Corral are at home. Maria is paying the bills.

Maria: We really ought to open a checking account.
Mario: Why?
Maria: We could pay all of our bills by check. It would be convenient.
Mario: I guess we should get a checking account. Shall we go on Friday after work?
Maria: Yes, we should go before 6 p.m. when the banks close.

Mario and Maria are at the bank.

Teller: May I help you?
Maria: Yes, we'd like to open a checking account.
Teller: I'm sorry, but I can't help you. You should talk to the clerk over there.
Maria: Thank you. We will.

Mario and Maria are talking to a clerk in the new accounts department.

Clerk: Hello, could I help you?
Mario: Yes, we would like to open an account.
Clerk: Would you like to open a checking or savings account?
Mario: A joint checking account, but we might open a savings account, too.
Clerk: Very well. Please sit down.

UNDERSTAND   *Circle **True**, **False**, or **We don't know**.*

1. Maria and Mario are buying a money order at the bank.   True   False   We don't know.
2. Maria and Mario pay their bills by check.   True   False   We don't know.
3. The teller can't help Maria and Mario.   True   False   We don't know.
4. They will open a joint savings account.   True   False   We don't know.
5. Checking and savings accounts are the same.   True   False   We don't know.

GRAMMAR   Modals

- The following are the most common modals:

can	may	shall	will	must
could	might	should	would	ought to

- We do not often use modals to express statements of fact. We use them to express actions or events that exist only in the mind: possibility, probability, potentiality, necessity, or wishes.

- Modals do not change form, so we cannot add -s to the third person singular.

- We use a modal with the simple form of the verb (an infinitive without to). The only exception is **ought to**.

EXAMPLES

We	**ought to**	**open**	a checking account.
We	**could**	**pay**	our bills by check.
It	**would**	**be**	more convenient.
We	**should**	**get**	an account.
You	**must**	**talk**	to the clerk over there.
We	**will**	**talk**	to the clerk over there.
We	**might**	**open**	a savings account, too.

- We use contractions with most of the modals.

can't	won't	mustn't
couldn't	wouldn't	shouldn't

- We do not use contractions with the following modals:

may not	might not	ought not to	shall not

- We use two forms of the negative for **can: can't** and **cannot**.

- We place modals in front of the subject to form questions.

EXAMPLES

Shall	we	go on Friday?
May	I	help you?

READ   Make logical complete sentences with the words in the box.

I	can		the clerk.
He	can't	open	Maria and Mario.
She	cannot	get	an account.
It	must	talk to	the bills.
We	will	pay	you.
You	won't	help	them.
They			so many money orders.

READ

The clerk is explaining the differences between checking accounts.

Mario: How much money must we have to open a checking account?
Clerk: You'll need $400.00 for an interest-paying checking account or $100.00 for
a regular account.
Maria: Can you explain the difference?
Clerk: Sure, look at these two signs.

REGULAR CHECKING ACCOUNT
$100.00 minimum balance
no interest
$2.00 monthly service charge
$10.00 overdraft fee

INTEREST-PAYING CHECKING ACCOUNT
$400.00 minimum balance
5 1/4% interest
no service charge
$10.00 overdraft fee

UNDERSTAND   *Circle **True**, **False**, or **We don't know**.*

1. Maria and Mario have five hundred dollars.	True	False	We don't know.
2. A regular checking account pays interest.	True	False	We don't know.
3. People must pay a twenty-four dollar service charge yearly for an interest-paying account.	True	False	We don't know.

GRAMMAR   **Review of *can, must, will,* and *would***

- *Can expresses ability and **must** expresses necessity.*

- *We use **will** to signal the future time.*

- *We use **would** with the verb **like** as a polite form of **want**.*

- *We also use **would** to express a possible present condition (see Chapter 10). The contraction for **would** is **'d**.*

PAIR PRACTICE   *Talk with another student. Practice using **can**. Use the phrases below.*

Student 1:   Can they ...?
Student 2:   Yes, they can. / No, they can't.

1. open a regular account with $50.00
2. open a regular account with $200.00
3. open an interest-paying checking account with $500.00
4. open an interest-paying checking account with $200.00
5. get interest with a regular account
6. get ten-percent interest with an interest-paying checking account
7. write a check for more than the balance

PAIR PRACTICE   *Practice using **would like** or **'d like**. Use the phrases below.*

Student 1:   What would they like?
Student 2:   They would like/They'd like ....

1. to open an account
2. to have a joint account
3. to understand the difference between accounts
4. to get interest

5. to deposit some money in an account
6. to write checks
7. to pay their bills by check

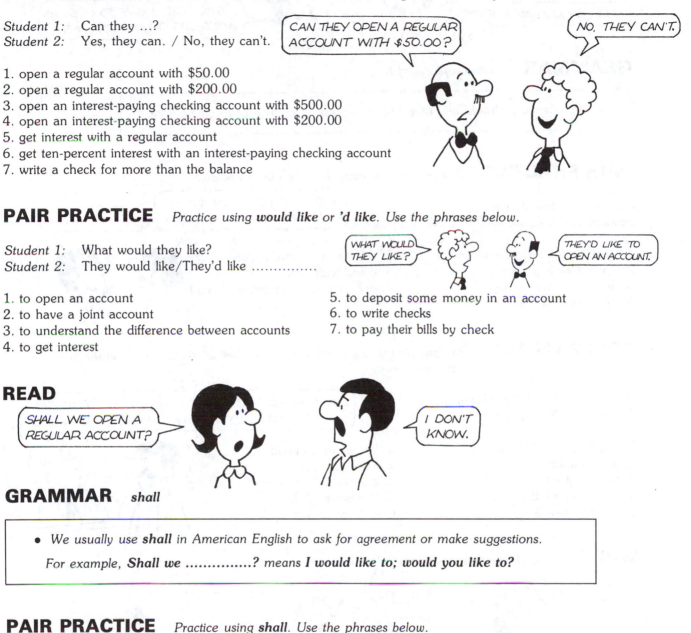

READ

GRAMMAR   *shall*

- *We usually use **shall** in American English to ask for agreement or make suggestions.*

  *For example, **Shall we ....?** means **I would like to; would you like to?***

PAIR PRACTICE   *Practice using **shall**. Use the phrases below.*

Student 1:   Shall we ....?
Student 2:   OK. / Let's not.

1. open an interest-paying checking account
2. open a regular checking account
3. open a savings account, too
4. deposit all our money

5. think about it first
6. go to another bank
7. come back later
8. go home

READ

GRAMMAR   *should* and *ought to*

• We often use **should** and **ought to** to express an opinion or to give advice.

PAIR PRACTICE   *Practice using* **should***. Use the phrases below.*

Student 1:   Should we ....?
Student 2:   Yes, we should. / No, we shouldn't.

1. open an interest-paying account
2. open a savings account
3. deposit all our money
4. think about it first

5. ask for more information
6. come back later
7. open a regular checking account

PAIR PRACTICE   *Ask* **should** *questions with the phrases below. Answer with* **ought to** *and your own words.*

Student 1:   What should you do ....?
Student 2:   You ought to ....

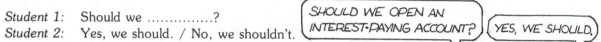

1. to pay your bills by check
2. to find a job
3. to keep a job
4. to make friends
5. to keep friends

6. if you see an accident
7. if you are sick
8. if you can't go to work
9. to learn English
10. to learn English well

WRITE   *What should these people do? Write your opinion below the pictures. Use* **should** *or* **ought to***.*

1. *He should see a doctor.*

2. _____

3. _____

4. _____

5. _____

6. _____

READ

Maria and Mario want to open a savings account, too.

Clerk: Here's your checkbook for your new interest-paying checking account.
Mario: Thank you. Could you open a savings account for us, too?
Clerk: Yes, I could.
Maria: When we first arrived in this country, we couldn't open a savings account because we didn't have enough money. Now, both of us are working, so we can save a little money every month. Could you tell us about a regular savings account?
Clerk: You need $100.00 to open an account. Our regular savings account pays 5 1/4% interest.

UNDERSTAND   *Circle* **True**, **False**, *or* **We don't know**.

1. They want to open a savings account, too.	True	False	We don't know.
2. They can save one hundred dollars a month.	True	False	We don't know.
3. The savings and the interest-paying checking account pay the same amount of interest.	True	False	We don't know.

GRAMMAR   *could*

- *We use* **could** *to ask a polite question in the present tense.*

EXAMPLES

Could	you help us?
Could	you please tell us about the regular savings account?

- **Could** *is also the past tense of* **can**.

EXAMPLE

We   **couldn't**   open a savings account when we arrived here.

PAIR PRACTICE   *Practice using* **could**. *Use the phrases below.*

Student 1: Could you ....?
Student 2: Yes, I could. / No, I couldn't.

1. help us
2. tell us about a saving account
3. explain that again
4. repeat that

5. show me a bankbook
6. tell me the time
7. ....

PAIR PRACTICE   *Practice using **could** in the past tense. Use the phrases below.*

Student 1:   Could you .... when you came to this country?
Student 2:   Yes, I could. / No, I couldn't.

1. speak English
2. open a savings account
3. open a checking account
4. save money
5. earn a lot of money

6. spend a lot of money
7. drive a car
8. buy a car
9. buy a house
10. ....

WRITE   *Help these people ask questions. Use **could**.*

1. This man needs help.

2. This woman wants to change $20.00.

3. This man wants the teller to repeat.

4. This person wants to know the time.

5. This lady wants directions to the post office.

6. This person wants to speak to the manager.

READ

The clerk explains how to use the automatic money machine.

Clerk: Here's your savings account bankbook. Do you want to use our automatic money machine?

Mario: What's that?

Clerk: When you put this card in the machine, some questions will appear on the screen. Answer them and you may withdraw or deposit money, or transfer money from one account to another. You can use the machine when the bank is closed. It's in operation twenty-four hours.

Mario: May we see how it works?

Clerk: Sure. Come on, I'll show you.

UNDERSTAND   *Circle **True**, **False**, or **We don't know**.*

1. People need to have a card to use the automatic money machine.	True	False	We don't know.
2. People may get money from the machine on the weekends.	True	False	We don't know.
3. "Withdraw" means "deposit."	True	False	We don't know.
4. "Transfer" means "change around."	True	False	We don't know.

GRAMMAR   *may*

- We use **may** to ask or give permission.

EXAMPLES

You	**May**	I help you?
	may	use the machine on the weekends.
	May	we see it?

PAIR PRACTICE   *Practice using **may** and **can**. Use the phrases below. Find the answers on the sign.*

KINDS OF SERVICES	AUTOMATIC MONEY MACHINE
1. Deposit money and checks in all accounts (no coins).	24-hour Service
2. Withdraw money from all accounts ($200.00 limit a day).	Machines in 50 States
3. Transfer money between accounts.	WELCOME
4. Information on balance.	INSERT CARD AND PUSH CODE NUMBER 1 2 3 / 4 5 6 / 7 8 9 / 0

Student 1: May/Can I ....?

Student 2: Yes, you may/can. / No, you may not/cannot.

1. deposit money
2. withdraw money
3. withdraw $500.00 in one day
4. use the machine on Sunday
5. deposit coins
6. use the machine in New York

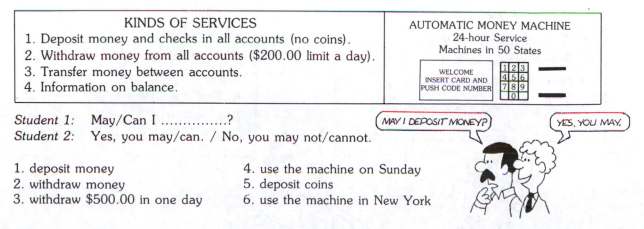

MAY I DEPOSIT MONEY?   YES, YOU MAY.

WRITE   *Help these people ask questions. Use **may**.*

May I ask
you a question?

1. This woman wants to ask a question.

2. This man wants to help the woman.

3. This man wants to use the machine.

4. This girl wants to have a puppy.

5. This man wants to speak to a teller.

6. This person wants to have a deposit envelope.

WRITE   *Match the sentences with their responses. Write the letters of the answers on the lines after the questions.*

1. Could you give me some information?
   c

2. I'd like to know how to use this machine. _____

3. Must I use this card? _____

4. What should I do to withdraw twenty dollars? _____

5. May I deposit this change? _____

6. I'd like to thank you for your help. _____

a. Yes, you must put it in the machine.

b. You should answer the questions that the machine will ask you.

c. Sure, I could.

d. I'd be happy to show you how to use it.

e. You're welcome.

f. No, you can't. You may deposit only paper money or checks.

READ

The people are waiting in line and talking.

GRAMMAR   *might*

- *We use **might** to express doubt. It means **maybe, not sure,** or **undecided**.*
- *We also use **may** in the same way, but **might** expresses more doubt.*

EXAMPLES

| We | **may** | open an account. | (not sure) |
| We | **may** **might** | open an account. | (less sure) |

WRITE   *Answer the questions in your own words with **may** or **might**.*

1. Will you come to the party tonight? — I don't know. *I might go.*

2. What are you going to eat for dinner? — I don't know. _____

3. It's a beautiful day today! What will you do? — I don't know. _____

4. Where will you go on vacation this year? — I don't know. _____

READ

It's the following week. Maria's cashing a check.

Teller: May I help you?
Maria: Yes, I'd like to cash this check.
Teller: Could I please see some I.D.?
Maria: Here's my driver's license. I'd like two twenties and a ten.
Teller: Here you are.
Maria: Thanks a lot. I'll see you next Friday.

Here's an example of a personal check.

UNDERSTAND   *Circle **True**, **False**, or **We don't know**.*

1. The check is for $693.34.	True	False	We don't know.
2. "I.D." means "identification."	True	False	We don't know.
3. Maria doesn't have any identification.	True	False	We don't know.

WRITE   *Underline all the modals in the dialog above.*

WRITE   *Help Maria write checks for her electric bill and telephone bill.*

Mario Corral
Maria Corral
369 Ship Street
Santa Monica, CA 90405
787-6935

102

_____ 19____   16-4
                          1234

Pay to the order of _____ $_____

_____ Dollars

The Neighborhood Bank
56 Main Street
Santa Monica, CA 90405
Memo: _____
1234 - 102 - 02470 - 10201

CALIFORNIA TELEPHONE COMPANY

28.46

PLEASE DEDUCT ANY PART OF THIS BILL WHICH HAS BEEN PAID

CORRAL, MARIO AND MARIA
369 SHIP STREET
SANTA MONICA, CA 90405

785   787-6935

Mario Corral
Maria Corral
369 Ship Street
Santa Monica, CA 90405
787-6935

101

_____ 19____   16-4
                          1234

Pay to the order of _____

_____ $_____

_____ Dollars

The Neighborhood Bank
56 Main Street
Santa Monica, CA 90405
Memo: _____
1234 - 101 - 02470 - 10201

CE CALIFORNIA EDISON COMPANY

**CR06

PLEASE
PAY THIS
AMOUNT
NOW   DUE

CORRAL, MARIO AND MARIA
369 SHIP STREET
SANTA MONICA, CA 90405

68 35 005 2290 07 000643 000002823   20000 $36.92

READ

Mario's depositing some money.

UNDERSTAND   *Circle **True**, **False**, or **We don't know**.*

1. Mario is depositing three checks.	True	False	We don't know.
2. He's depositing two coins.	True	False	We don't know.
3. He's depositing $475.02 in currency.	True	False	We don't know.
4. He wrote the bank numbers on the deposit slip.	True	False	We don't know.
5. He has $1,000 in his account.	True	False	We don't know.

WRITE   *Fill in the spaces below with the words in the box.*

may	would like	could	can't	can	should

The man at the next window wants to cash a check, too.

Teller: <u>May</u> I help you?

Customer: Yes, I _____ to cash this check.

Teller: Do you have an account at this bank?

Customer: No, I don't.

Teller: I'm sorry, but we _____ cash this check.

Customer: Why not?

Teller: We _____ cash checks only if you have an account with us or if it's a

check from this bank.

Customer: What _____ I do?

Teller: You _____ go to the bank whose name is on the check.

Customer: I don't have a bank account at any bank. _____ I open an account here?

Teller: Yes, you _____. Please see the clerk over there next to the door.

Customer: Thank you.

WRITE   *Fill in the short answers.*

Mario and Stephen meet in front of the bank.

1. Do you have an account at this bank, too?

2. I didn't see you at school yesterday. Were you there?

3. Will you be at school on Monday?

4. Is this your lunch hour?

5. Would you like to have lunch with me?

6. Can't you eat?

7. Why not?

1. Yes, _____

2. No, _____

3. Yes, _____

4. No, _____

5. No, _____

6. No, _____

7. I just left the dentist.

READ

Stephen is waiting in line to cash his pay check. He's looking at his check stub.

CHECK STUB	
NAME: STEPHEN BRATKO **SOC. SEC.** 573-66-2728	
HOURS WORKED: Regular: 80 **Overtime:** 0	
PAY PERIOD: 2/1/84 **TO** 2/15/84	
GROSS PAY:	$805.95
DEDUCTIONS:	
Federal Withholding	-108.79
State Withholding	- 19.36
F.I.C.A.	- 49.40
Pension Plan	- 14.65
Medical Insurance	- 12.31
Life Insurance	- 8.10
TOTAL DEDUCTIONS:	-212.61
NET PAY:	$593.34

Here's Stephen's pay check. The amount of his check is larger this month because he received a seven-percent raise. The check for this two-week pay period is $593.34. His gross pay is $805.95. He worked regular 40-hour weeks without any overtime.

There are some deductions from his check. The federal government withheld $108.79 for income tax. The state government withheld $19.36. The company deducts $49.40 for Social Security (or F.I.C.A. *). His other deductions were voluntary ones: $14.65 for the company pension plan, $12.31 for medical insurance, and $8.10 for life insurance. His total deductions were $212.61. His take-home pay or net pay is $593.34.

UNDERSTAND   *Circle **True, False,** or **We don't know.***

1. This check is for a one-week period.	True	False	We don't know.
2. Stephen worked 40 hours overtime.	True	False	We don't know.
3. "Gross pay" means "total pay before deductions."	True	False	We don't know.
4. Stephen works full time.	True	False	We don't know.
5. "Take-home pay" is "net pay."	True	False	We don't know.
6. Stephen never works overtime.	True	False	We don't know.

* F.I.C.A. = Federal Insurance Contribution Act

PAIR PRACTICE

Fold the page on the dotted line. Look at your side only.

Student 1

Listen to your partner's questions and find the answers in the bankbook below.

THE NEIGHBORHOOD BANK
SAVINGS ACCOUNT

NAME: Stephen & Wanda Bratko

ACCOUNT NUMBER: 69430-634

DATE:	WITHDRAWALS	DEPOSIT	BALANCE
5/17		500.00	500.00
6/10	100.00		400.00
7/15	50.00		350.00
8/1		200.00	550.00
10/15		25.00	575.00
2/18		75.00	650.00

Now ask your partner these questions.

1. What kind of form do you see?
2. How many checks did Stephen write in January?
3. How much did he deposit in January?
4. When did he write a check to the telephone company?
5. What kind of bill did he pay on January 20?
6. What's his balance now?
7. How much was the check to Dr. Rivers?

Student 2

Ask your partner these questions.

1. What kind of bankbook do you see?
2. Whose savings account is it?
3. Did Stephen deposit $100.00?
4. How much did he withdraw in June?
5. What was his balance in August?
6. What's his balance now?
7. How much did he withdraw on July 15?
8. What was his balance on February 18?

Now listen to your partner's questions and find the answers in the checkbook balance record.

CHECKBOOK BALANCE RECORD

CHECK NO.	DATE	ISSUED TO	DEPOSIT	CHECK	BALANCE
					243.01
643	1/6	A and B Market		43.69	199.32
644	1/7	Calif. Electric		34.29	165.03
645	1/8	Dr. Rivers		50.00	115.03
	1/15		643.17		758.20
646	1/15	Telephone Co.		19.96	138.24
647	1/16	Car Insurance		200.00	538.24
	1/18		40.00		578.24
648	1/20	Central Market		39.41	538.83

FOLD HERE

FOLD HERE

READ   *Basic Math*

- *In the United States we read math problems as follows:*

ADDITION:	$1 + 1 = 2$	One plus one equals two. *or* One and one is two.
SUBTRACTION:	$5 - 2 = 3$	Five minus two equals three.
MULTIPLICATION:	$5 \times 5 = 25$	Five times five equals twenty-five.
DIVISION:	$10 \div 2 = 5$	Ten divided by two equals five.

READ   *Read the problems orally, and then give the answer.*

$9 + 6 =$	$40 + 4 =$	$100 - 5 =$
$43 - 7 =$	$30 - 6 =$	$600 - 50 =$
$12 \times 8 =$	$99 + 1 =$	$20 \times 6 =$
$150 - 10 =$	$10 \times 4 =$	$44 - 4 =$

WRITE   *Write the answers to the math problems.*

1. The balance for your checking account is $274.91. You write three checks. The first check is for $43.90, the second check is for $10.00, and the third check is for $19.99. How much is your balance after you write the checks?

    $ _____

2. The balance for your savings account is $1,050.00. You deposit sixty-five dollars in cash in July and a seventy-dollar check in August. How much is your balance at the end of August?

    $ _____

3. You have $575.00 in a savings account. The bank pays you 5 1/4% interest. How much interest will you get after one year?

    $ _____

4. Your checking account balance is $200.00 for January, $250.00 for February, $300.00 for March, and $225.00 for April. What is your average monthly balance for the first four months of the year?

    $ _____

CHALLENGE   *Discuss how you did the problems above with the other students in your class.*

SPELLING   Review of Silent Letters

Most of the words in the crossword puzzle contain a silent letter.

ACROSS

1. I don't drive to school; I _____ there.
4. A noise that you make on a door.
6. The first day of the weekend.
8. A part of the body at the middle of your leg.
10. Spoon, fork, _____.
11. The past tense of *can.*
12. An important holiday.
15. The past tense of the verb *throw.*
17. The ball came _____ the window and broke it.
19. He likes to _____ poems.
21. Tomatoes, potatoes, and peas are _____.
24. A woman is beautiful; a man is _____.
25. I _____ food at the market.

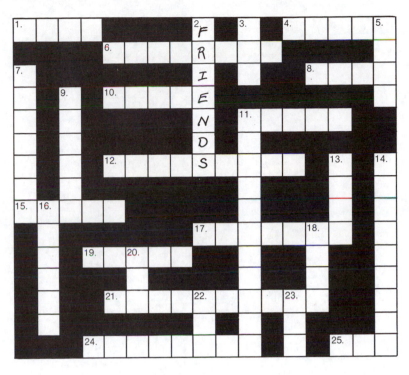

DOWN

2. People whom you know very well.
3. Past tense of *see.*
5. Past tense of *know.*
7. Past tense of *think.*
9. Can you _____ my question?
11. My armchair is very _____.
13. _____ school.
14. A day in the middle of the week.
16. My _____ is 5 feet 8 inches.
18. She _____ to school by bus.
20. Something to cool your drink.
22. One, _____, three…
23. When do you _____ dinner?

THE BUDGET

- Review Chapter
- Midterm Test

WRITE   *Fill in the spaces below with the correct past tense form of the verb under the line.*

Stephen Bratko arrives home from the bank.

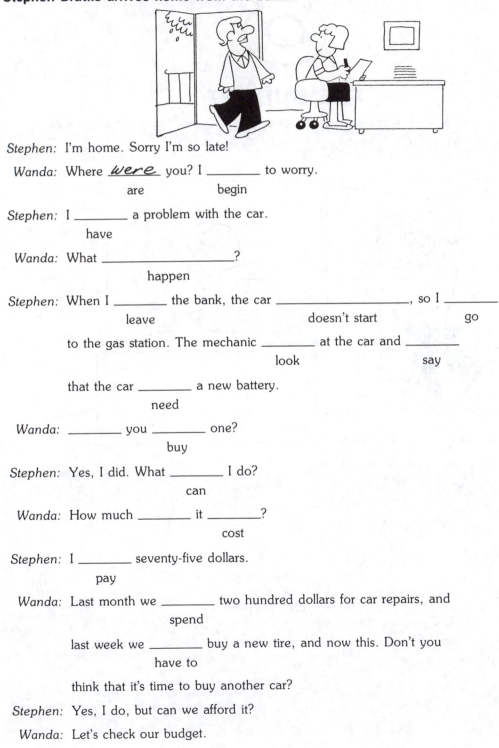

Stephen: I'm home. Sorry I'm so late!

Wanda: Where _**were**_ you? I _____ to worry.
                               are   begin

Stephen: I _____ a problem with the car.
                              have

Wanda: What _____?
                              happen

Stephen: When I _____ the bank, the car _____, so I _____
                              leave   doesn't start   go

to the gas station. The mechanic _____ at the car and _____
                                              look   say

that the car _____ a new battery.
                         need

Wanda: _____ you _____ one?
                              buy

Stephen: Yes, I did. What _____ I do?
                                        can

Wanda: How much _____ it _____?
                                       cost

Stephen: I _____ seventy-five dollars.
                         pay

Wanda: Last month we _____ two hundred dollars for car repairs, and
                                      spend

last week we _____ buy a new tire, and now this. Don't you
                         have to

think that it's time to buy another car?

Stephen: Yes, I do, but can we afford it?

Wanda: Let's check our budget.

READ

Stephen and Wanda's monthly budget.

BUDGET

FOOD

Market	$ *150.00*	
Eating out	$ *50.00*	
Total		$ *200.00*

INSURANCE PAYMENTS

Health	$ *—*	
Car	$ *30.00*	
Life	$ *10.00*	
Total		$ *40.00*

HOUSING

Rent	$ *400.00*	
Home repairs	$ *—*	
Furniture	$ *20.00*	
Utilities	$ *60.00*	
Telephone	$ *15.00*	
Other	$ *—*	
Total		$ *495.00*

CLOTHES

New	$ *20.00*	
Cleaning	$ *5.00*	
Repair	$ *—*	
Total		$ *25.00*

TRANSPORTATION

Gas	$ *50.00*	
Car repairs	$ *10.00*	
Bus fare	$ *10.00*	
Total		$ *70.00*

MISCELLANEOUS

Hair cuts	$ *20.00*	
Entertainment	$ *25.00*	
Trips	$ *—*	
Presents	$ *10.00*	
Other	$ *—*	
Total		$ *55.00*

MEDICAL EXPENSES

Doctor	$ *25.00*	
Medicine	$ *10.00*	
Total		$ *35.00*

SAVINGS	$ *100.00*
TOTAL EXPENSES	$ *1,020.00*
TOTAL INCOME	$ *1,280.00*
DIFFERENCE	$ *260.00*

PAIR PRACTICE   *Talk with another student. Use the budget above.*

Student 1: How much do they spend for ....?
Student 2: They spend $ .... for ....

DISCUSSION   *Do you think that the Bratkos can afford to pay two hundred dollars a month for a new car? Why or why not?*

WRITE   *Calculate your monthly budget.*

BUDGET

FOOD

Market	$ _____
Eating out	$ _____
Total	$ _____

HOUSING

Rent	$ _____
Home repairs	$ _____
Furniture	$ _____
Utilities	$ _____
Telephone	$ _____
Other	$ _____
Total	$ _____

TRANSPORTATION

Gas	$ _____
Car repairs	$ _____
Bus fare	$ _____
Total	$ _____

MEDICAL EXPENSES

Doctor	$ _____
Medicine	$ _____
Total	$ _____

INSURANCE PAYMENTS

Health	$ _____
Car	$ _____
Life	$ _____
Total	$ _____

CLOTHES

New	$ _____
Cleaning	$ _____
Repair	$ _____
Total	$ _____

MISCELLANEOUS

Hair cuts	$ _____
Entertainment	$ _____
Trips	$ _____
Presents	$ _____
Other	$ _____
Total	$ _____

SAVINGS	$ _____
TOTAL EXPENSES	$ _____
TOTAL INCOME	$ _____
DIFFERENCE	$ _____

PAIR PRACTICE   *Talk about your budget with another student.*

Student 1: Do we pay the same for ....?
Student 2: Yes, we do.
        or
      No, we don't. I pay more/less than you.

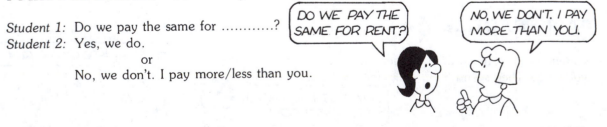

DO WE PAY THE SAME FOR RENT?

NO, WE DON'T. I PAY MORE THAN YOU.

CHALLENGE   *Exchange budgets with another student. Cut his or her budget by 10%. Then explain to the student where and why you cut the budget.*

DISCUSSION   *Talk about ways to cut down on expenses.*

READ

The following day Stephen and Wanda look at some new cars.

PAIR PRACTICE   *Find the answers in the picture above.*

Student 1: What kind of cars do you have?
Student 2: We have all kinds of cars. We have
.... ones, ... ones, and .... ones.

PAIR PRACTICE   *Ask questions with the words below. Use the picture above for answers.*

Student 1: Do you have any .... cars?
Student 2: Yes, we have some/one.
                or
             No, we don't have any.

1. American
2. small
3. inexpensive
4. used
5. sports

6. big
7. new
8. black
9. white
10. gray

PAIR PRACTICE   *Ask questions with the words below. Use the picture above for answers.*

Student 1: Do you have any ....?
Student 2: Yes, we have two.
             One is .... and the other is ....

1. American cars
2. Japanese cars
3. German cars

4. sedans
5. convertibles
6. sports cars

READ

Wanda and Stephen like three of the cars.

PAIR PRACTICE   *Ask questions with the words below. Use the picture above for answers.*

Student 1: Which car is the ....est?
                              or
                 Which car is the most ....?
Student 2: The .... is ....

1. small
2. big
3. expensive
4. long
5. short

6. cheap
7. popular
8. practical
9. economical on gas
10. ....

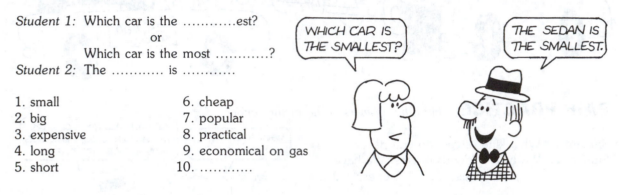

READ

Stephen and Wanda can't decide which of these two cars to buy.

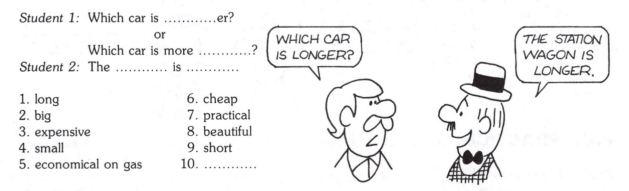

PAIR PRACTICE   *Ask questions with the words below. Use the picture above for answers.*

Student 1: Which car is ....er?
                              or
                 Which car is more ....?
Student 2: The .... is ....

1. long
2. big
3. expensive
4. small
5. economical on gas

6. cheap
7. practical
8. beautiful
9. short
10. ....

DISCUSSION   *Which car should Wanda and Stephen buy? Give your reasons.*

CHALLENGE   *How many different kinds of cars can you name?*

---

* miles per gallon

READ

Stephen and Wanda have only $1,000, so they must get a loan for the rest.

CALIFORNIA TRUST

Date: _February 20, 1985_   Loan Amount: $_5,000.00_

To Be Paid in _36_ Monthly Installments   Beginning: _April 1_ 19_85_

Kind of Loan: Boat   (Car)   Home   Other _____

APPLICANT

Name: _Stephen and Wanda Bratko_   Date of Birth: _7/14/48_ _4/23/51_

Address: _1160 Fairfax St. #3_   City: _Los Angeles_ Zip Code: _90046_

Number of Years at This Address: _1 yr._   Telephone: _765-4012_

Previous Address: _39 5th St._   Number of Years: _6 mo._

Number of Dependents: _none_ Are You Married or Unmarried? _married_

INCOME INFORMATION

Stephen: _M.O. Nee Accountants_
Employed by: Wanda: _Abby Market_   Position: _Accountant_ _Cashier_

How Long Employed: _1_ years _6_ months   Telephone: _378-0412_

Monthly Income: $_both $1,280.00_ Other Income: $_none_

EXPENSES

Living Situation: Own Home   (Rent)   Live with Relatives

Monthly Mortgage or Rent: $_400.00_   Do You Own a Car? Make and Year: _Plym 68_

Other Debts: Loans or Credit Cards

To Whom Paid	Address	Account Number	Balance	Monthly Payment
Ed Brown Furniture	_64 Main St._	_0463490_	_$250.00_	_$20.00_

BANK ACCOUNTS

Name of Bank: _Neighborhood Bank_ Address: _56 Main St., Santa Monica_

Type of Accounts: _Savings and Checking_

Signature: _Stephen Bratko_ _Wanda Bratko_   Today's Date: _2/20/85_

DISCUSSION   *Ask and answer questions about the application above.*

WRITE   *You fill out a loan application for a car, too.*

CALIFORNIA TRUST

Date: _____   Loan Amount: $_____

To Be Paid in ____ Monthly Installments   Beginning: _____ 19____

Kind of Loan: Boat   Car   Home   Other _____

APPLICANT

Name: _____   Date of Birth: _____

Address: _____   City: _____   Zip Code: _____

Number of Years at This Address: _____   Telephone: _____

Previous Address: _____   Number of Years: _____

Number of Dependents: _____   Are You Married or Unmarried? _____

INCOME INFORMATION

Employed by: _____   Position: _____

How Long Employed: _____ years _____ months   Telephone: _____

Monthly Income: $_____   Other Income: $_____

EXPENSES

Living Situation: Own Home   Rent   Live with Relatives

Monthly Mortgage or Rent: $_____   Do You Own a Car? Make and Year: _____

Other Debts: Loans or Credit Cards

To Whom Paid   Address   Account Number   Balance   Monthly Payment

_____

_____

_____

BANK ACCOUNTS

Name of Bank: _____   Address: _____

Type of Accounts: _____

Signature: _____   Today's Date: _____

WRITE   *Fill in the spaces with questions. The answers will help you figure out the questions.*

Wanda and Stephen are talking to the car salesman about the loan and their old car.

1.

May I ask you a question?

Yes, you may.

2.

_____

You must pay the state tax, too.

3.

_____

We should get a three-year loan.

4.

_____

We'd like a three-year loan.

5.

_____

We can give you $500 for your old car.

6.

_____

No, I'm sorry, but we couldn't give more than $500 for your car.

7.

_____

Your first payment will be in two months.

8.

_____

You may pick up the car on Monday if we get an OK from the bank tomorrow.

READ

On Monday, Stephen and Wanda picked up their new car.

THE BANK APPROVED YOUR LOAN. HERE ARE THE KEYS FOR YOUR NEW CAR. GOOD LUCK.

THANK YOU.

WRITE *Fill in the crossword puzzle.*

DOWN

1. ____ you please help me?
2. Susan is ____ American.
3. Joseph does ____ speak well.
4. We come ____ school every day.
5. The pencil is ____ the box.
7. ____ I help you?
9. She felt cold, so she ____ the window.
10. George will come, but Lisa ____ come.
11. ____ did you get up?
12. We ____ go to school last Friday.
14. How ____ do you go to the movies?
15. We are doing this crossword puzzle ____.
17. Will you visit Bob and Jill? Yes, I'll visit ____.
19. ____ Olga speak English?
22. I have a doctor's appointment, so I ____ come to school tomorrow.
23. What ____ is it?
25. Is ____ your pen?
28. How do ____ do?
30. How much ____ does it cost?
31. ____ do you live?
33. ____ do you feel today?
34. If you want to learn English, you ____ study.
35. One, ____, three, four . . .
39. ____ is my brother.
40. The short form of "Hello."

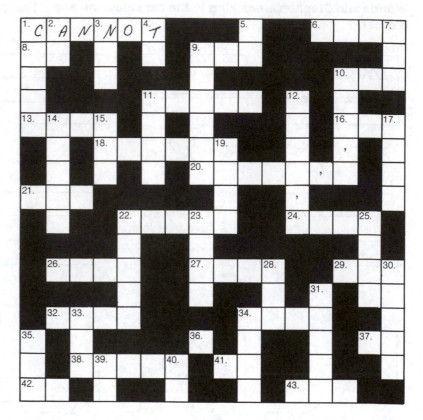

ACROSS

1. I can swim, but he ____.
6. With ____ do you come to school?
8. The book is ____ the table.
9. He ____ swim very well.
10. ____ do you want to learn English?
11. ____ book is this?
13. Upstairs/____stairs
16. You may ____ smoke in class!
18. She ____ the windows.
20. He ____ know how to dance well.
21. Girls/women; boys/____
22. He ____ to learn English.
24. She said ____ she didn't feel well.
26. ____ did you come to the U.S.A.?
27. How ____ people are there in class?
29. Did you see Jim? Yes, I saw ____.
32. ____ did you say?
34. How ____ does it cost?
36. Please give me ____ piece of paper.
37. Where will you ____ this time tomorrow?
38. ____ is your favorite color?
41. We are lost! Could you please help ____?
42. The United States ____ America.
43. Do you know Mary? Yes, I know ____.

GROUP ACTIVITY

Talk with the people in your class. Write the names of those who have the following qualities.

1. _____
   is the youngest person in the class.

2. _____
   has the longest hair.

3. _____
   has an older brother.

4. _____
   lives nearest to school.

5. _____
   is the tallest person in the class.

6. _____
   has a younger sister.

7. _____
   gets up the earliest every morning.

8. _____
   is the best student in the class.

9. _____
   has the most work experience.

10. _____
    has the biggest family.

11. _____
    has the most brothers and sisters.

12. _____
    takes the longest coffee break.

MIDTERM TEST   *Circle the correct answer.*

1. *James:* I need a stamp.
   Betty: There's _____ in the drawer.
   a. some   c. it
   (b.) one   d. any

2. *James:* Did you see my pen?
   Betty: I saw _____ on the table.
   a. some   c. it
   b. its   d. any

3. *James:* Do you want me to pay the bills?
   Betty: Yes, please pay _____.
   a. it   c. one
   b. its   d. them

4. *James:* Are there any letters on the desk?
   Betty: No, there aren't _____.
   a. any   c. one
   b. some   d. them

5. *James:* Will you give your mother money for her birthday?
   Betty: No, I'll buy _____ a present.
   a. her   c. you
   b. him   d. them

6. Can I send this letter _____ first class mail?
   a. in   c. buy
   b. on   d. by

7. I have two packages. One is big and _____ is small.
   a. one another   c. the other
   b. other   d. others

8. I got three birthday cards today. One's from my mother, _____ is from my brother, and _____ is from my sister.
   a. another   c. the others
   b. other   d. others

9. Help me carry these two packages. You carry _____ and I'll carry the other.
   a. another   c. the other
   b. one   d. ones

10. *Waitress:* What would you like?
    Customer: _____ some coffee, please.
    a. I like   c. I'm like
    b. I'd want   d. I'd like

11. Do you like chocolate ice cream?
    Yes, _____.
    a. I would   c. I do
    b. I'd like   d. I am

12. Wake up! I hear _____ downstairs.
    a. anything   c. nothing
    b. something   d. anybody

13. Go to sleep. I didn't hear _____.
    a. anything   c. nothing
    b. something   d. somebody

14. Does _____ live in that old house?
    a. nothing   c. anybody
    b. nobody   d. no one

15. I want a job _____ pays high wages.
    a. what   c. who
    b. that   d. whom

16. Do you know the name of the person _____ sits behind you?
    a. what   c. who
    b. which   d. whom

17. Who do you go to school _____?
    a. to   c. in
    b. with   d. by

18. What address should I send the letter _____?
    a. to   c. in
    b. with   d. by

19. She _____ that the company needed to hire another salesperson.
    a. say   c. tell
    b. said   d. told

20. What did you _____ them?
    a. say   c. tell
    b. said   d. told

21. Bob can work _____ than Gale.
    a. more fast   c. faster
    b. fastest   d. more faster

22. Gale has _____ experience than Bob.
    a. most   c. more
    b. bigger   d. the most

23. Gale can work _____ than Bob.
    a. good   c. best
    b. more good   d. better

24. The Super X-100 is the _____ dangerous car in America today.
    a. least   c. fewest
    b. less   d. better

25. It's the _____ economical car of all.
    a. most   c. less
    b. more   d. must

26. What's the _____ car in the world?
    a. better   c. best
    b. worse   d. most bad

27. What's the _____ country in the world?
    a. bigest   c. biger
    b. biggest   d. bigger

28. People work _____ they can pay for food and rent.
    a. for   c. in order to
    b. to   d. so that

29. People work _____ support their families.
    a. for   c. so that
    b. because   d. to

30. Lan can't wait _____ her brother arrives.
    a. until   c. during
    b. for   d. in

31. Lan studies English _____ three hours every day.
    a. for   c. in
    b. during   d. until

32. How much did the airplane ticket _____?
    a. cost   c. pay
    b. costs   d. paid

33. Where did you _____?
    a. grow up   c. growed up
    b. grew up   d. grewed up

34. I didn't _____ in the city.
    a. grow up   c. growed up
    b. grew up   d. grewed up

35. _____ you like to open an account?
    a. Do   c. Would
    b. May   d. Could

36. _____ you please explain the difference between accounts?
    a. Ought to   c. May
    b. Should   d. Could

37. _____ see how this machine works?
    a. I should to c. Maybe can
    b. Can   d. May I

38. I'd like to _____ this check.
    a. change   c. withdraw
    b. cash   d. account

39. I'd like to open a _____ account.
    a. deposit   c. savings
    b. withdrawal   d. balance

40. Do you _____ an account at this bank?
    a. have   c. has
    b. had   d. can have

9

A FIRE

LISTEN

Roberto Monte and a fellow employee were talking when their boss arrived.

Roberto: What a day!

   Boss: Are you all right?

Roberto: Yes, but there was a fire here a few hours ago.

   Boss: I heard about it on the radio while I was driving here. Did anybody get hurt?

Roberto: Some people got a few small cuts and bruises, but there were no serious injuries. They were fighting the fire when the fire fighters arrived.

   Boss: How did it happen?

Roberto: Mr. Sam Blazes accidentally set fire to some chemicals in the warehouse while he was smoking.

   Boss: What did you and the other employees in our department do?

Roberto: We were helping to evacuate the nearby buildings while the fire fighters were putting out the fire.

   Boss: Was there much damage?

Roberto: There was only a little damage. The fire fighters put out the fire quickly.

UNDERSTAND *Circle True, False, or We don't know.*

1. Roberto was working when the fire started.	True	False	We don't know.
2. The boss was working when the fire started.	True	False	We don't know.
3. Nobody was hurt.	True	False	We don't know.
4. The fire was an accident.	True	False	We don't know.
5. Some employees were trying to put out the fire before the fire fighters arrived.	True	False	We don't know.

GRAMMAR   The Past Continuous Tense

- *Use the past continuous to describe an action that interrupts another action in the past.*
- *Use the simple past tense after words like **before**, **when**, and **after**, and the past continuous after **while**.*

EXAMPLES

They **were fighting** the fire **when** the fire fighters **arrived**.
Mr. Sam Blazes accidentally set the fire **while he was smoking**.
I heard about it on the radio **while I was driving** here.

- *We also use the past continuous to describe two past actions that were happening at the same time.*

EXAMPLE

We **were evacuating** the nearby buildings while the fire fighters **were putting** out the fire.

READ   *Make logical complete sentences with the words in the boxes.*

| Roberto The people The fire fighters Sam Blazes Some employees We He | was were | fighting the fire watching the fire evacuating people working smoking helping coming | when while | the fire began. the fire fighters were working. the employees were working. the fire fighters were coming. an employee set the fire. |

| What | was were | Roberto the fire fighters some employees Sam Blazes you | doing | when while | the fire fighters were working? the fire started? employees were helping? his boss arrived? the fire fighters were coming? |

PAIR PRACTICE   *Talk with another student. Use the phrases below.*

Student 1: What were you doing when ....?
Student 2: I was ....

1. the fire started/working in the office
2. the fire began/going to the lunch room
3. the fire fighters arrived/evacuating the building
4. the fire fighters came/leaving the building
5. you heard about the fire/sitting at my desk
6. Roberto told you about the fire/having a meeting

WHAT WERE YOU DOING WHEN THE FIRE STARTED?

I WAS WORKING IN THE OFFICE.

PAIR PRACTICE   *Practice the past continuous tense. Use the pictures and phrases below.*

The fire started at 2:35 p.m.

Student 1: What was/were .... doing when the fire began?
Student 2: .... was/were ....

1. Linda/make photocopies

2. Bill/work in the warehouse

3. the managers/have a meeting

4. Albert/work on the assembly line

5. Dr. Dennis/work in the laboratory

6. Tom and Jim/discuss a new project

7. Mr. Leo Getty/speak on the phone

8. security guard/walk around

9. Jill/take a break

PAIR PRACTICE   *Use the pictures and phrases above.*

Student 1: Was/Were .... when the fire began?
Student 2: Yes, ... was/were.
             or
      No, ... wasn't/weren't.

READ

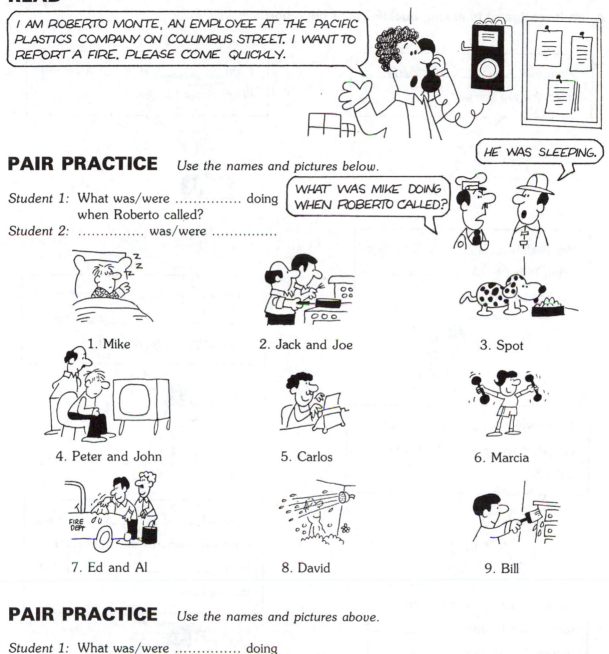

I AM ROBERTO MONTE, AN EMPLOYEE AT THE PACIFIC PLASTICS COMPANY ON COLUMBUS STREET. I WANT TO REPORT A FIRE. PLEASE COME QUICKLY.

HE WAS SLEEPING.

PAIR PRACTICE   *Use the names and pictures below.*

Student 1: What was/were .... doing when Roberto called?

WHAT WAS MIKE DOING WHEN ROBERTO CALLED?

Student 2: .... was/were ....

1. Mike

2. Jack and Joe

3. Spot

4. Peter and John

5. Carlos

6. Marcia

7. Ed and Al

8. David

9. Bill

PAIR PRACTICE   *Use the names and pictures above.*

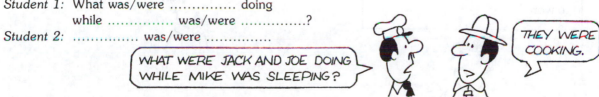

Student 1: What was/were .... doing while .... was/were ....?

Student 2: .... was/were ....

WHAT WERE JACK AND JOE DOING WHILE MIKE WAS SLEEPING?

THEY WERE COOKING.

WRITE   *Write sentences describing the pictures. Use the past continuous.*

WRITE   *Fill in the blanks with the correct form of the past continuous tense.*
A fire investigator is asking questions for his report.

1. What (do) *were* you *doing* when the fire started?

2. I (sit)_____ at my desk when I heard about the fire.

3. We (walk)_____ to the office when Roberto told us to evacuate the nearby buildings.

4. When I heard the alarm, I (move) _____ some boxes in the shipping department.

5. We (have)_____ an important budget meeting when the fire fighters arrived.

6. I (come) _____ from the warehouse when I saw Sam Blazes. He (try) _____ to put out the fire alone.

7. I learned about the fire on the radio while I (drive) _____ to work.

WRITE   *Fill in the blanks with the simple past or past continuous form of the word under the line.*

FIRE REPORT

The fire __*began*__ about 2:35 p.m. at the Pacific Plastics Company in a storeroom
        begin

at the back of the warehouse. Mr. Sam Blazes _____ that he _____ when he
                                       say   smoke

accidentally _____ the fire.
         start

    Mr. Roberto Monte, an employee at the company, _____ the fire and _____
                                       see   call

the fire department immediately. Then he _____ the fire to the company security guard.
                  report

When the fire fighters _____ at 2:55 p.m., some employees _____ to put out
           arrive   try

the fire, and others _____ the nearby buildings. The fire fighters _____ the fire
        evacuate   put out

quickly and _____ at 4:15 p.m. There _____ no serious injuries and damage
        leave   be

_____ light.
  be

    After the fire, while the fire investigators _____ the warehouse and storerooms, they
               inspect

noticed that there _____ no fire extinguishers or safety signs. The fire investigators
        be

_____ the company president that the company _____ ten days to install fire ex-
 tell   have

tinguishers and put up safety signs.

Fire Investigator

Juan Francisco

READ

Roberto Monte is speaking to his boss.

    Boss: How is Sam Blazes?

Roberto: He'll be OK. He was lucky that he didn't kill himself. He tried to put out the fire by himself. When he realized that he couldn't, he asked some employees to help him. You know, they almost put it out by themselves before the fire fighters arrived.

    Boss: What about the other people?

Roberto: The paramedics treated a few people. A woman cut herself on some broken glass, and a man burned himself on some hot metal. Two fire fighters injured themselves slightly while they were breaking down a door.

    Boss: Did you and the other employees injure yourselves while you were trying to evacuate the building?

Roberto: No, we didn't hurt ourselves at all.

    Boss: Thank heavens!

Roberto: Oops! (Roberto trips.)

    Boss: Are you all right? Did you hurt yourself?

Roberto: No, I didn't hurt myself. I'm fine. I just slipped.

UNDERSTAND   *Circle **True**, **False**, or **We don't know**.*

1. Mr. Sam Blazes is in the hospital.	True	False	We don't know.
2. Mr. Sam Blazes put out the fire alone.	True	False	We don't know.
3. Some employees put out the fire.	True	False	We don't know.
4. A woman injured herself.	True	False	We don't know.
5. Roberto slipped and hurt himself.	True	False	We don't know.
6. "Slightly" means "badly."	True	False	We don't know.

WRITE   *Underline all the words in the sentences above that end in **-self**.*

GRAMMAR   Reflexive Pronouns

- Forms of the reflexive pronouns:

Singular	Plural
myself	ourselves
yourself	yourselves
himself	
herself	themselves
itself	

- Use reflexive pronouns to refer to the subject of the sentence.

EXAMPLES		Subject		Reflexive Pronoun
		Sam Blazes	didn't kill	**himself.**
		A woman	cut	**herself.**
		A man	burned	**himself.**
		Two fire fighters	injured	**themselves.**
	Did	you	injure	**yourselves?**
		We	didn't hurt	**ourselves.**
	Did	you	hurt	**yourself?**
		I	didn't hurt	**myself.**

- We also use the reflexive pronoun with **by** to mean **alone**.

EXAMPLES

He tried to put out the fire	**by himself.**
They almost put out the fire	**by themselves.**

READ   Make logical complete sentences with the words in the box.

I	hurt	themselves.
A man	didn't hurt	yourselves.
A woman	cut	ourselves.
Two fire fighters	injured	herself.
Some people	didn't injure	himself.
We	burned	yourself.
You	didn't burn	myself.

READ   Make logical questions with the words in the box. Then answer the questions.

Do	your best friend	like to be		yourself?
	your friends	live		himself?
	your brother/father	work		herself?
Does	your sister/mother	do homework	by	ourselves?
	you	go to the movies		yourselves?
Can	you and I	like to work		themselves?

PAIR PRACTICE   *Practice reflexive pronouns. Use the words and pictures below.*

Student 1: What happened to ....?
Student 2: ....

WHAT HAPPENED TO THIS WOMAN?

NOTHING, SHE DIDN'T HURT HERSELF.

1. this woman

2. this man

3. these fire fighters

4. Mr. Sam Blazes

5. Roberto

6. these people

7. this boy

8. this woman

9. the boss

PAIR PRACTICE   *Use the words below. Answer in your own words.*

Student 1: When was the last time you .... yourself?
Student 2: ....

1. hurt
2. cut
3. burned
4. injured

5. bruised
6. enjoyed
7. amused

WHEN WAS THE LAST TIME YOU HURT YOURSELF?

I HURT MYSELF LAST WEEK AT A BASEBALL GAME.

CHALLENGE   *How do people injure themselves at home or work? Make a list below.*

1. _____
2. _____
3. _____
4. _____
5. _____
6. _____

7. _____
8. _____
9. _____
10. _____
11. _____
12. _____

DISCUSSION   *How can people prevent the injuries above?*

PAIR PRACTICE   *Use the pictures and phrases below.*

Student 1: Can .... by ....?
Student 2: Yes, he/she/they can.
           or
        No, he/she/they can't.

CAN THE WOMAN LIFT THE BOX BY HERSELF?

YES, SHE CAN.

1. lift

2. put out the fire

3. do this job

4. operate the machine

5. protect the company

6. fix

7. calculate

8. run the company

9. repair the damage

PAIR PRACTICE   *Use the pictures and words below.*

Student 1: How can .... protect .... against ....?
Student 2: He/She/They ....

HOW CAN THIS MAN PROTECT HIMSELF AGAINST FIRES?

HE SHOULDN'T SMOKE NEAR THE BOXES.

1. fires

2. industrial accidents

3. car accidents

4. poisoning

5. earthquakes

6. drowning

7. electrocution

8. robberies

DISCUSSION   *Talk about the ways to prevent the misfortunes above.*

CHALLENGE   *Look at the First Aid section in the front of your telephone book.*

WRITE *Fill in the blanks with the correct reflexive pronouns.*

At the fire station.

1.
Do you need any help?

No, thank you. I can do it by *myself*.

2.
Did you hurt _____?

No, I'm OK. I didn't hurt _____.

3.
Where's Willy?

He's over there. He's sitting by _____.

4.
Do you and your wife live by _____?

No, we don't live by _____.
My mother-in-law lives with us.

5.
Can Marcia move that equipment by _____?

Sure she can. She did it
by _____ last time, too.

6.
How are Carlos and Frank?
Did they injure _____ badly?

They'll be OK in a few days.
They only hurt _____ slightly.

READ

Mr. Baxter, the company president, has some safety signs for the company.

WRITE   *Where should Mr. Baxter put the signs? Write the words on the signs in the pictures below.*

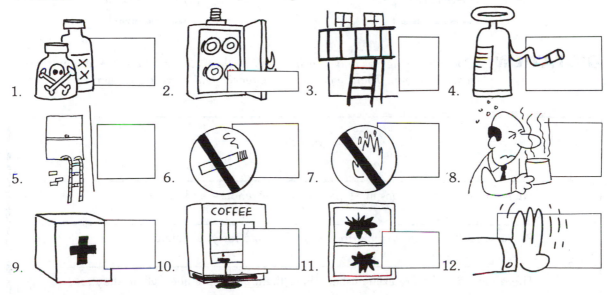

1.

2.

3.

4.

5.

6.

7.

8.

9.

10.

11.

12.

CHALLENGE   *How many other safety signs can you name?*

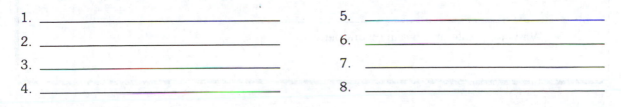

1. _____   5. _____

2. _____   6. _____

3. _____   7. _____

4. _____   8. _____

WRITE   *Match the signs with their meanings. Write the letter of the answer in the blank in front of the sign.*

Roberto asks, "What do these new signs mean?"

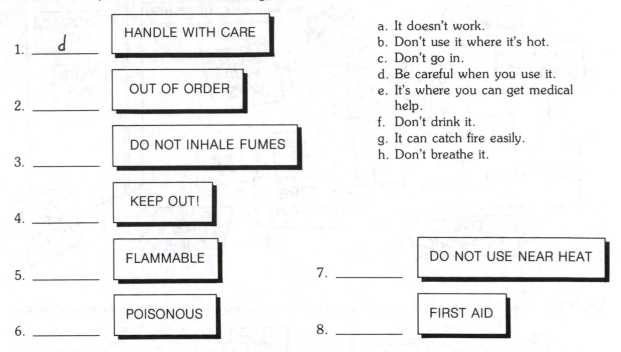

1. ___d___   HANDLE WITH CARE

2. _____   OUT OF ORDER

3. _____   DO NOT INHALE FUMES

4. _____   KEEP OUT!

5. _____   FLAMMABLE

6. _____   POISONOUS

7. _____   DO NOT USE NEAR HEAT

8. _____   FIRST AID

a. It doesn't work.
b. Don't use it where it's hot.
c. Don't go in.
d. Be careful when you use it.
e. It's where you can get medical help.
f. Don't drink it.
g. It can catch fire easily.
h. Don't breathe it.

DICTATION   *Cover the sentences under each line. Write the dictation on the line as your teacher reads it to you. Then uncover the sentences and correct your writing.*

MEMO

1. _____
There are new safety signs in all parts of the warehouse and offices.

2. _____
Please read them and do what they say. They are for your safety.

3. _____
There are also new fire extinguishers. Find them and remember where they are.

4. _____
If you see any other dangerous situations, please let me know.

5. _____
We want a safe and healthy work place.

PAIR PRACTICE

Fold the page on the dotted line. Look at your side only. Compare your pictures after you both fill in all the empty signs.

Student 1

Fill in the blank signs below with the signs your partner describes to you.

Now describe to your partner the locations of the signs in your picture. Read what's on the signs.

Student 2

Describe to your partner the locations of the signs in your picture. Read what's on the signs.

Now fill in the blank signs below with the signs your partner describes to you.

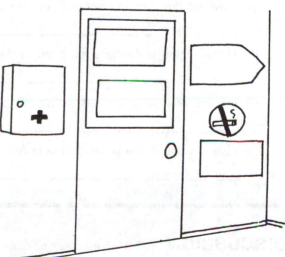

WRITE   *Answer the questionnaire.*

QUESTIONNAIRE
HOW WELL DO YOU KNOW YOURSELF?

1. Do you like to live by yourself or with others? _____

_____

2. Do you work better by yourself or with others? _____

_____

3. Do you think people sometimes need to be by themselves? When? Why? _____

_____

4. When do you like to be by yourself? _____

_____

5. Do you often injure yourself? If so, how and how often? _____

_____

6. How can you avoid injuring yourself? _____

_____

7. Did you ever handle an emergency by yourself? If so, what kind? _____

_____

8. How do you handle yourself in an emergency? _____

_____

9. How do you prepare yourself for difficulties? _____

_____

10. How do you feel when you listen to yourself on a tape recorder? Why? _____

_____

11. Do you ever sing to yourself? When? _____

_____

12. How do you enjoy yourself in your free time? _____

_____

DISCUSSION   *Talk about other possible answers to the questions above.*

WORD BUILDING   The Prefix *mis-*

- *We use **mis-** as a negative prefix with verbs to mean **error**, **wrong**, **bad**, or **opposite**.*

EXAMPLES

1. He miscalculated the amount of the budget.

2. She misplaced her briefcase.

3. He misunderstood the directions.

WRITE   *Rewrite the sentences below using the prefix **mis-**.*

1. Mr. Sam Blazes handled the emergency badly.

   Mr. Sam Blazes mishandled the emergency.

2. The employee didn't read the sign right.

   _____

3. The security guard didn't inform the fire fighters correctly.

   _____

4. The manager used his power in a wrong way.

   _____

5. The manager handled the situation badly.

   _____

10
RESOURCES

COMPETENCIES	• Finding Job Resources
	• Reading Newspaper Job Ads
	• Reading Abbreviations Used in Want Ads
	• Using Telephone Book Yellow Pages
GRAMMAR	• Present Unreal
	• Present Unreal with *could*
	• Present Unreal with *were*
VOCABULARY	• Job Titles
	• Job Ad Abbreviations
WORD BUILDING	• The Suffixes *-ful* and *-less*

LISTEN

David Fernandez and Paul Green are talking on their way to the library.

David: I need a job badly. If you needed a job, what would you do, Paul?

Paul: If I needed a job, I'd tell all of my friends and relatives. They're often the best contacts. I would also go to the local state employment office. It's a free government service for all unemployed people.

David: What about private employment agencies?

Paul: Most of those agencies help highly qualified people and professionals find jobs. If I went to a private agency, I'd be very careful. Some agencies require you to pay a percentage of your first wages to them as a fee, others require the employer to pay the fee. There are a lot of ads for employment agencies in the newspaper and telephone book.

David: What else would you do?

Paul: If I knew of an industrial or commercial area, I would drive or walk around it. You can sometimes see signs for job openings on the walls or windows of some companies.

David: Would you write to companies?

Paul: Yes, I would. And I would also write to unions and professional societies. There are books in the library that have the names, addresses, and descriptions of many of these organizations. The library also has many other job resources such as the Dictionary of Occupational Titles that describe jobs in detail.

UNDERSTAND   *Circle True. False, or We don't know.*

1. Paul Green needs a job.	True	False	We don't know.
2. People pay fees at the state employment office.	True	False	We don't know.
3. David is a highly qualified professional.	True	False	We don't know.
4. All agencies require employers to pay fees.	True	False	We don't know.
5. If David did what Paul Green told him to do, he would find a job.	True	False	We don't know.

GRAMMAR   The Present Unreal

- *We form the present unreal by using the past tense in the dependent clause (after **if**) and the conditional (**would**) in the main clause.*

- *The contracted form of would is **'d**.*

EXAMPLES	*Dependent Clause*	*Independent Clause*
	If you **needed** a job,	what **would** you **do**?
	If I **needed** a job,	**I'd tell** all of my friends.
	If I **went** to a private agency,	**I'd** be careful.
	If I **knew** of an industrial area,	I **would drive** around it.

READ   *Make logical complete sentences with the words in the box.*

If I	needed wanted went knew had	a job, about a job opening, an interview, to an interview,	I	would 'd wouldn't	be happy. have to look for a job. go to the employment office. tell all of my friends. make an appointment.

READ   *Make logical questions with the words in the box. Then answer them.*

What Where Who	would you	call contact do go	if you	needed to find a telephone number? wanted to find an address? wanted some information about unions? needed a job?

PAIR PRACTICE   *Talk with another student. Practice the present unreal. Use the phrases below.*

Student 1: What would you do if you ....?
Student 2: If I ...., I'd ....

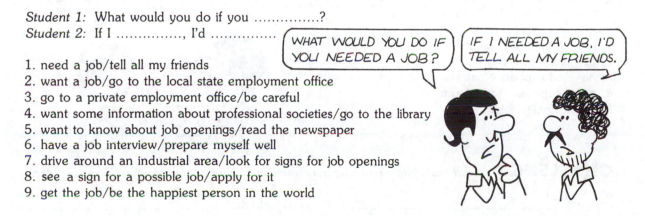

1. need a job/tell all my friends
2. want a job/go to the local state employment office
3. go to a private employment office/be careful
4. want some information about professional societies/go to the library
5. want to know about job openings/read the newspaper
6. have a job interview/prepare myself well
7. drive around an industrial area/look for signs for job openings
8. see a sign for a possible job/apply for it
9. get the job/be the happiest person in the world

PAIR PRACTICE   *Talk with another student. Use the phrases and pictures below.*

Student 1: .... doesn't/don't ....
Student 2: Yes, I know, but if ...., ... would ....

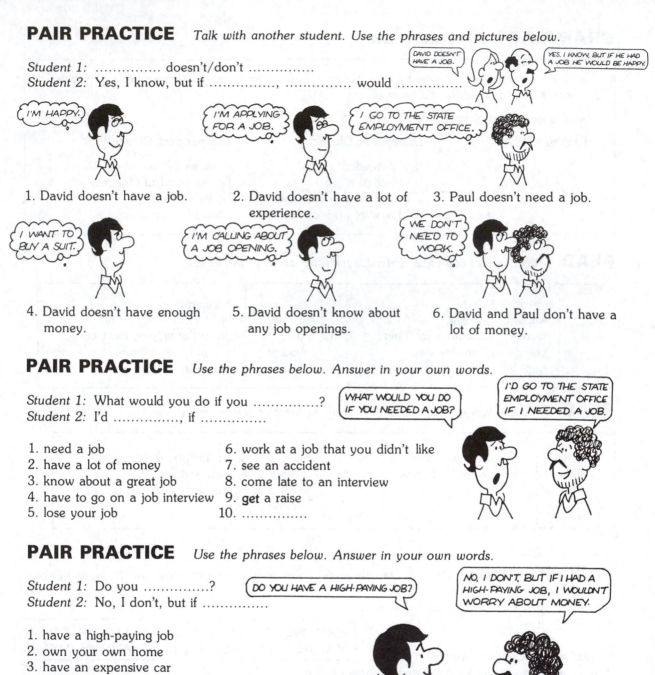

1. David doesn't have a job.

2. David doesn't have a lot of experience.

3. Paul doesn't need a job.

4. David doesn't have enough money.

5. David doesn't know about any job openings.

6. David and Paul don't have a lot of money.

PAIR PRACTICE   *Use the phrases below. Answer in your own words.*

Student 1: What would you do if you ....?
Student 2: I'd ...., if ....

1. need a job
2. have a lot of money
3. know about a great job
4. have to go on a job interview
5. lose your job
6. work at a job that you didn't like
7. see an accident
8. come late to an interview
9. **get** a raise
10. ....

PAIR PRACTICE   *Use the phrases below. Answer in your own words.*

Student 1: Do you ....?
Student 2: No, I don't, but if ....

1. have a high-paying job
2. own your own home
3. have an expensive car
4. go to expensive restaurants
5. speak English well
6. ....

CHALLENGE   *Find the address and telephone number of your nearest state employment office.*

Address: _____   Telephone: _____

READ

David and Paul are still talking.

Paul: What about the newspaper? Do you read the want ads?

David: Not very often.

Paul: If you read the classified ads more often, you could learn a lot.

David: What could I learn?

Paul: You could learn some useful job vocabulary that you might need in an interview. If you read them over a long period of time, you could learn what the average wages and minimum qualifications are for your occupation.

David: When's the best day to buy the paper?

Paul: I would buy the Sunday newspaper. It has more ads than the daily papers.

David: I didn't find many jobs in my occupation in the last newspaper I bought.

Paul: I would look under different job titles that are related to your work. For example, if you had experience as a bookkeeper, you could look under other job titles such as accountant, office worker, or clerk.

David: What about a carpenter or painter?

Paul: If you wanted to find job titles that are related to "painter," you could look under construction worker or handyperson.

UNDERSTAND   *Circle True, False, or We don't know.*

1. David reads the paper twice a week.	True	False	We don't know.
2. A person could learn some useful vocabulary if he or she read newspaper ads.	True	False	We don't know.
3. "Want ads" means "classified ads."	True	False	We don't know.
4. Paul Green is a bookkeeper.	True	False	We don't know.
5. Daily papers usually have fewer ads than the Sunday paper.	True	False	We don't know.

GRAMMAR   Present Unreal with *could*

- *We use **could** to mean **would be able to**.*

- *It expresses possibility dependent on an unreal condition.*

EXAMPLES

If you read the classified ads, you **could** learn a lot.

If you wanted to find job titles that are related to "painter," you **could** look under construction worker or handyperson.

READ   *Make logical complete sentences with the words in the box.*

If David	wanted to learn some useful vocabulary, found a job ad in the paper, read the newspaper more often, asked his friends about job openings,	he could	find a job. learn a lot. look in the paper. call about it.

PAIR PRACTICE   *Practice the present unreal with **could**. Use the phrases below.*

Student 1: What could I learn from ....?
Student 2: You could learn a lot from ....
   if you ....

1. people/talk to them
2. want ads/study the vocabulary in them
3. a newspaper/buy and read it often
4. a library/use it

5. classified ads/read the paper
6. a job counselor/see one
7. ....

PAIR PRACTICE   *Use the phrases below. Answer in your own words.*

Student 1: If I needed ....,
   where could I find it?
Student 2: You could find ....

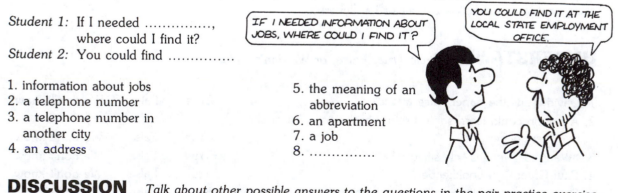

1. information about jobs
2. a telephone number
3. a telephone number in another city
4. an address

5. the meaning of an abbreviation
6. an apartment
7. a job
8. ....

DISCUSSION   *Talk about other possible answers to the questions in the pair practice exercise above.*

READ

David's at the library. He is looking at some job titles in the Dictionary of Occupational Titles.

Accountant	Contractor	Manufacturing Engineer
Accountant Clerk	Controller	Marketing Director
Administrative Assistant	Cook	Mechanic
Administrator	Cosmetologist	Medical Technician
Advertising Secretary	Counselor	Mold Maker
Air Conditioner Installer	Credit Manager	Motorcycle Mechanic
Air Conditioning Service Mechanic	Custodian	Nurse
Aircraft Engineers and Designers	Data Processor	Nurse's Aid
Aircraft Mechanic	Delivery Person	Office Clerk
Airlines Reservation Clerk	Dental Hygienist	Order Desk Clerk
Alarm Technicians and Installers	Dental Assistant	Parking Attendant
Alterations	Dentist	Pattern Maker
Appraiser	Designer	Pharmacist
Architect	Drafter	Photo Lab Finisher
Artist	Dry Cleaning Worker	Photographer
Art Director	Educator	Physical Therapist
Assembler	Electrical Worker	Pipe Fitter
Attorney	Electrician	Plastic Injection Molder
Auditor	Electronic Assembler	Plater (Electropolisher)
Auto Service Mechanic	Electronic Technician	Plumber
Auto Body Worker	Engineer	Pressman
Baker	Estimator	Printer
Bank Teller	File Clerk	Purchasing Clerk
Barber	Food Service Manager	Receptionist
Bartender	General Office Aid	Restaurant Worker
Beautician	Glass Worker	Retail Assistant
Billing Clerk	Glazier (mirrors)	Sales Order Clerk
Binder (books)	Guard	Salesperson
Biochemist	Handyperson	Secretary
Bookkeeper	Hospital Worker	Seamstress
Bus Driver	Hotel Worker	Security Guard
Busboy	Housekeeper	Service Station Worker
Buyer	Illustrator	Sewing Machine Worker/Operator
Cameraman	Import Clerk	Sheet Metal Worker
Carpet Layer	Instructor	Shipping Clerk
Cashier	Insurance Sales	Social Worker
Chemist	Inventory Clerk	Steel Worker
Chiropractor	Investigator	Tailor
Civil Engineer	Janitor	Taxi Driver
Clerk	Jeweler	Teacher
Computer Operator	Keypunch Operator	Tool and Die Maker
Computer Programmer	Medical Technician	Tool Designer
Construction Worker	Laboratory Technician	Typist
	Liquor Clerk	Waiter or Waitress
	Machinist	Warehouse Worker/Clerk
	Maintenance Mechanic	Welder

CHALLENGE   *Answer some questions about jobs and job titles.*

1. Circle your job title.
2. Underline job titles that are related to your occupation.
3. Check the job titles of the people in your class.

READ

David's looking at some ads in the newspaper.

AUTO BODY
repair & painting
needs own equip 203-0851

AUTOMOTIVE PAINTER
5 yrs min exp.
xlnt pay plan
Call Phil Delphy 666-7676

CONSTRUCTION
Maint. pers. w/exp.
needed for single-family housing.
Very steady work. Apply in per.
at 29418 Walnut St. L.A.

CONSTRUCTION
Painter, long-term job
Must have truck
and travel around city
Xlnt bene. 874-0126

HANDYPERSON
repair, paint, cleaning,
maint, odd job for hosp.
Contact Mrs. Snow 852-8274

PAINTER
f/t work, no exp. req.
see last Sunday's ad
for more details

AUTO BODY
repair and painting
needs own equipment, 203-0851

AUTOMOTIVE PAINTER
five years minimum experience
excellent pay plan
Call Phil Delphy at 666-7676

CONSTRUCTION
Maintenance person with experience
needed for single-family housing.
Very steady work. Apply in person
at 29418 Walnut St., Los Angeles

CONSTRUCTION
Painter, long-term job
Must have truck
and travel around city
excellent benefits, 874-0126

HANDYPERSON
repair, paint, cleaning,
maintenance, odd jobs for hospital
Contact Mrs. Snow 852-8274

PAINTER
full-time work, no experience required
see last Sunday's advertisement
for more details

PAIR PRACTICE   *Use the phrases below. Look at the ads above.*

Student 1: Can David apply for the .... ad?
Student 2: No, he can't. He could apply for
          the .... ad if he ....

1. first/have his own equipment
2. second/have five years experience
3. third/know how to do maintenance work
4. fourth/have his own truck
5. fifth/do repair and maintenance work, too
6. sixth/have last Sunday's newspaper

CAN DAVID APPLY
FOR THE FIRST AD?

NO, HE CAN'T. HE COULD APPLY
FOR THE FIRST AD IF HE HAD
HIS OWN EQUIPMENT.

READ

ACCOUNTING CLERK, typing, bkkpg,* gen. office. Knowledge of credits & bus. mach. Growing comp. Good benefits. Tel. 123-4567	**ELECTRONIC TECH.** Auto Radio & Stereo equip. Must have 3 yrs. expr. Full time, 5 days week, top pay, co. benefit. Apply in person 10-4 p.m. Mon.-Fri. Joe's Electronics, 654 Maple St.	**MEDICAL ASSISTANT/LVN** Full time. Large med. group seeks exp. back office persons to assist physician. Excl. benefits. Call 999-1233 ext. 34 for appointment or apply in person 9 a. to 4 p. week days. VALLEY MED. GROUP 1234 Rhode Island St.
AIR CONDITIONING & HEAT Service technician, exp. only, good fringe benefits. Co. pays group health, dental, life ins., uniforms furnished. Steady work. Tel. 987-5432	**JANITOR—HANDYPERSON** clean, wax floors, polish furniture, exp. req. Must be able to lift heavy furn. Perm. Tel. 321-7654	**PAINT Lab.** Super—paint & coating dvlpmt. Sal. commensurate w/ability. Complete employee bene. Send resume Box M-999, L.A. 91405
AUTO MECHANIC, must have foreign car exper. Top benefits, profit sharing, top pay, paid holidays. 4 day wk., free ins. Ask for Ted or Tim. 123-9876	**KEYPUNCH/KEY ENTRY** Key Entry Oper. IBM 3742 experience required, min. 1 year. Salary open. Fringe benefits. Please call 987-1234 Personnel for appointment.	**PLASTICS**, 2nd shift (m/f) for plastic injection molding plant. Must have mechanical knowledge of injection molding machines. Good co. benefits, sal. open. Call. 634-0087
BOOKKEEPER, exp. in payroll, cost acctg., accts. payable/recv. & other general acct. functions. Salary commensurate w/exp. Good co. benefits. Tel. 300-1010	**LAB TECH** Work part time, evenings Mon.-Fri. 6 pm to 9 pm. Must have exp. in all lab procedures & must be licensed. Contact Rob Tanka. 345-6789	**PLUMBERS**—exp. in res. plumbing & heating repair—great job oppt. with xlnt. wages. We need honest, dependable people to grow with the company. Top pay, vacation, profit share & more. Clark Plumbing 678 N. ''C'' Street. S.F.
CASHIER, with retail exp. Paid holidays, vacation. Bilingual helpful. Local references. Hamilton Outlet Stores. Interview Mon. thru Fri. 10 a.m. to 4 p.m. 45 S. 10th St. L.A.	**MACHINISTS** to operate boring mills, lathes, grinders, etc. in job shop type environment. Nat'l co. offering xlnt. bnft. pkg. & overtime. Call ACME Service Corp. 789-1234 for an interview. E.O.E.	**SALESPEOPLE WANTED** Items made by the blind. Comm. work, daily pay, transp. furn. Full-pt. time, xlnt. earnings. Retired/handicap. OK. (213) 987-6543
DENTAL TECHNICIAN needed in all phases of denture, crown, and bridge work for our modern well-eqpt. lab. We also need a metal finisher. Both full or part time. If you qualify, please call 678-9101	**MAINTENANCE PERSON** Large corp. seeking a person capable of gen. repairs to work with plumb, carpet, welding & electrical. Full time, good wages, excellent benefits. For appoint. call 321-1234	**TOOL & DIE MAKER**—Must be proficient w/draw dies & compound dies, piercing, blanking. Apply Paul's Radiator Co. 543 S. 4th St.
ELECTRICIAN, comm'l/indust'l maintenance & installation. No new const. Uniform & health ins. furnished. Pref. mature person. Good pay and working conditions. 911-2233		

PAIR PRACTICE   *Use the ads above.*

CAN YOU APPLY FOR THE AD FOR AN AUTO MECHANIC?

NO, I CAN'T. I COULD APPLY IF I KNEW SOMETHING ABOUT THAT OCCUPATION.

Student 1: Can you apply for the ad for an ....?
Student 2: No, I can't. I could apply for it if ....

---

* See the list of abbreviations at the end of this chapter.

WRITE *Match the abbreviations with their meanings. Place the letter of the meaning on the line in front of the abbreviation.*

Paul, what do these abbreviations mean?

1. __c__ &
2. _____ f/t
3. _____ pd.
4. _____ ins.
5. _____ xlnt.
6. _____ gd.
7. _____ yr.
8. _____ exp.
9. _____ req.
10. _____ w/

a. experience
b. year
c. and
d. required
e. with
f. insurance
g. good
h. full time
i. excellent
j. paid

WRITE *Write the abbreviations for the following words.*

1. salary __sal.__
2. hour _____
3. location _____
4. month _____

5. part time _____
6. business _____
7. engineer _____
8. evening _____

9. advertisement _____
10. male/female _____
11. department _____
12. company _____

CHALLENGE *Write an ad for a job you would like to have. Use abbreviations.*

_____

_____

_____

_____

CHALLENGE *Exchange ads with another student. Read your partner's ad and make sure that you understand all the abbreviations.*

READ

Paul and David are still talking.

Paul: Don't forget to use the telephone book. That's a good resource, too.

David: It is? How?

Paul: If I were you, I'd look at the ads in the yellow pages of the phone book. If there were some ads that interested me, I would visit the company and ask to fill out an application. Who knows? Maybe you'd be lucky and get a job. If there weren't any job openings, maybe they could tell you where there are some. After all, what's the worst thing that they could do to you?

David: I don't know. What?

Paul: They could say that they don't have any job openings.

David: Maybe it's worth a try.

Paul: I'd do it if I were you. You have nothing to lose.

UNDERSTAND   *Circle **True**, **False**, or **We don't know**.*

1. Paul Green believes that the phone book is a good resource for jobs.   True   False   We don't know.
2. If Paul were David, he would call some of the companies that advertise in the phone book.   True   False   We don't know.
3. David filled out applications for some of the companies that advertise in the phone book.   True   False   We don't know.
4. Some of the companies that advertise in the phone book have job openings.   True   False   We don't know.
5. "It's worth a try" means "I should do it because I have nothing to lose."   True   False   We don't know.

GRAMMAR   **Present Unreal with *were***

- *The dependent clause of the present unreal uses the past tense of all verbs except **to be**. We use **were** in all persons in such clauses.*

EXAMPLES

Dependent Clause

If I **were** you,	I'd look in the telephone book.
If there **were** some ads that interested me,	I'd visit the company.
If there **weren't** any jobs at that company,	maybe they could tell you where there are some.
If I **were** you,	I'd do it.

READ   *Make logical complete sentences with the words in the box.*

If	I Paul David he there	were	a boss, Paul, David, smart, jobs,	he'd visit some companies. I'd look in the phone book. maybe he could get one. he would hire him. he'd fill out some applications.

PAIR PRACTICE   *Practice the present unreal with **were**. Use the phrases below.*

Student 1: What would you do if you were ....?
Student 2: If I were ...., I would ....

1. me/read the ads in the phone book
2. unemployed/look for a job
3. the boss of a company/give David a job
4. at a company/ask to fill out an application
5. at an interview/answer all the questions as best I can
6. .... / ....

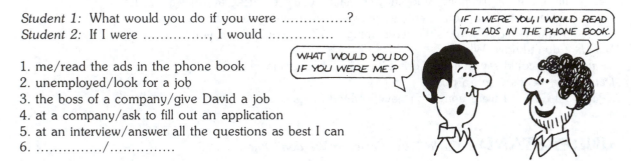

READ

David's looking at the index in the back of the yellow pages.

THIS INDEX IS YOUR GUIDE TO THE YELLOW PAGES.

A	page		page	B	page
Accountants	1	Art Galleries	57	Banks	229
Adult Education		Attorneys	65	Barbers	235
Center	1168	Automobile		Bathroom	
Advertising		Body Repair		Equipment	240
Agencies	8	and Paint	108	Bookkeeping	
Air Conditioning	107	Automobile		Service	270
Appliances	868	Insurance	652	Books	
Architects	56	Automobile		Sales	1147
		Sales	763		

PAIR PRACTICE   *Ask about the occupations below. Use the index above.*

Student 1: Where would you look
   if you were a/an ....?
Student 2: If I were a/an ....,
   I'd look under ....

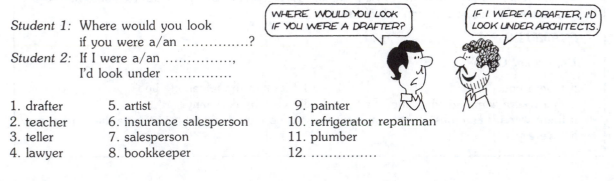

1. drafter
2. teacher
3. teller
4. lawyer
5. artist
6. insurance salesperson
7. salesperson
8. bookkeeper
9. painter
10. refrigerator repairman
11. plumber
12. ....

READ

AIR

DELUXE AIR CONDITIONING & HEATING
REPAIR - SERVICE - INSTALLATION
RESIDENTIAL - COMMERCIAL
Maintenance Contracts
6411 Cleon............................764-6318

AUTOMOTIVE

THE AUTOMOBILE SHOPPE
COMPLETE AUTOMOTIVE
SERVICE/PARTS
FOREIGN - DOMESTIC
31126 Burbank Bl...............761-6272

BUILDING

VALLEY CONSTRUCTION MATERIALS
ROCK - SAND - CEMENT
BRICK - BLOCK - STONE
LATH - PLASTER - REBAR
18149 W. Agoura Rd..........889-2124

CLEANERS

BATES CLEANERS
PICK-UP & DELIVERY
LEATHER & SUEDE - BLANKETS
ALTERATIONS
7717 W Burbank Bl............842-8176

CONSTRUCTION

**HOME REMODELING
ROOM ADDITIONS
KITCHENS - BATHS**

DESIGN & PLANNING SERVICE
FINANCING AVAILABLE
FREE ESTIMATES

COTT CONSTRUCTION......957-2688

DENTISTS

Baker Thos. M DDS
    Member American Dental
    Association
    57354 Van Nuys Bl..........783-7780
Bell Jas D DDS
    Endodontics – Member American
    Dental Association
    11020 Sherman Wy..........992-4415

Brill Ann G
    Member American Dental
    Association
    2833 Victory Bl................881-0431

EMPLOYMENT

Ready Personnel Services Inc.
    22544 Ventura Bl.............985-7805

SPECIAL EMPLOYMENT AGENCY
SINCE 1962
OFFICE - FACTORY - INDUSTRIAL
OFFICE SALES - MEDICAL &
DENTAL - FINANCE
ENGINEERING - PROFESSIONALS
AUTOMOTIVE - TECHNICAL
TRAINEES TO SPECIALISTS
PERSONALIZED ATTENTION TO
EMPLOYERS & EMPLOYEES
8151 Owensmouth Av........348-2172

GLASS

GUY'S GLASS CO
DOOR & WINDOW PARTS
SALES & REPAIRS
ALUMINUM SLIDING DOORS
4223 Oxnard........................785-6152

INSURANCE

DALTON WILLIAM J
AUTO - LIFE - FIRE &
HOMEOWNERS
HEALTH & DISABILITY
SAFETY INSURANCE
COMPANIES
8302 W Sunset Bl...............876-5130

OFFICE SUPPLIES

MILLER'S OFFICE EQUIPMENT
ELECTRONIC CALCULATORS &
TYPEWRITERS
NEW & USED - SALES - SERVICE -
RENTALS
17071 Ventura Bl................342-7228

PHARMACY

DEPENDABLE PHARMACY
DELIVERY SERVICE
12246 Hamlin.....................997-2727

PLUMBING

Lee Plumbing & Heating
    9218 Victory Bl................996-3642
LOTT, RUSSELL A & SONS
24-HOUR
EMERGENCY SERVICE
6834 Crebs Av....................342-3475
MARK PLUMBING CO
21010 W Magnolia Bl......845-5289
MEDALLION PLUMBING
8124 Ethel Av...................764-7631
MIGUEL'S ROOTER SERVICE
FLAT PRICE QUOTED ON THE
PHONE
SE HABLA ESPANOL
8827 Morella Av.................765-9691

SCHOOLS

MOTHER GOOSE SCHOOL
Pre-School - Kindergarten
After School Care
8214 Baird Av.....................342-9962

TELEVISION

RELIABLE T.V.
SALES & SERVICE
MOST MAKES & MODELS
COLOR - BLACK & WHITE - STEREO
HOME CALLS
14913 Ventura Bl...............784-8852

TIRES

NORTHERN TIRE CO
TIRES - BRAKES - ALIGNMENT
TIRE TRUING & BALANCING
902 S Victory Bl.................842-3512

TOOLS

ACME WHOLESALE TOOL & SUPPLY
AIR - POWER - HAND TOOLS
HOME & INDUSTRIAL

Automotive Tools
Complete Line of Supplies

OPEN TO THE PUBLIC

26109 Roscoe Bl................996-1700

PAIR PRACTICE   *Ask about the items below. Use the ads in the yellow pages.*

Student 1: Who would you call if you
          had a problem with your ....?
Student 2: I'd call .... at ....

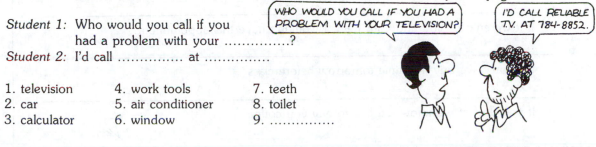

WHO WOULD YOU CALL IF YOU HAD A PROBLEM WITH YOUR TELEVISION?

I'D CALL RELIABLE T.V. AT 784-8852.

1. television
2. car
3. calculator
4. work tools
5. air conditioner
6. window
7. teeth
8. toilet
9. ....

PAIR PRACTICE

Ask about the items below. Use the ads in the yellow pages on the previous page.

Student 1: Who would you contact
     if you wanted to buy ....?
Student 2: I'd contact ....

1. some medicine
2. car insurance
3. car tires
4. a television
5. a typewriter
6. an electric saw
7. tools
8. a heater
9. ....

PAIR PRACTICE

Ask about the items below. Use the ads in the yellow pages on the previous page.

Student 1: Who would you telephone
     if you needed information about ....?
Student 2: I'd telephone ....

1. building a house
2. a kindergarten
3. renting a typewriter
4. building materials
5. a job
6. your teeth
7. car brakes
8. insurance
9. ....

DICTATION

Cover the sentences under each line. Write the dictation on the line as your teacher reads it to you. Then uncover the sentences and correct your writing.

Paul received a note a few days later.

1. _____
   I went to the library and looked for last Sunday's newspaper.

2. _____
   I found an interesting ad for a painter.

3. _____
   I went to the company and applied for the job.

4. _____
   They gave me an appointment for next Tuesday at 11:30.

5. _____
   If it weren't for you and your help, I wouldn't have this appointment.

6. _____
   Do you have any free time tomorrow before class?

7. _____
   If you do, let me know. I'd like to buy you coffee.

David

PAIR PRACTICE

Fold this page on the dotted line. Look at your side only.

Student 1	Student 2

Student 1

Listen to your partner's questions and find the answers in the ads below.

PAINTER

xlnt. wages
med. & den. ins.
5 yrs. exp.
f/t work
call 871-0936
for appoint

CARPENTER

gd. sal. & bene.
pd. ins., 3 yrs
loc exp. & ref.
req. apply in
per. Mr. Warner
239 Commercial St.
L.A. CA 90028

Now ask your partner these questions.

1. What kind of advertisements do you see?

2. How many ads are there for painters?

3. What kind of abbreviations are there in the ads?

4. Do all the companies do the same kind of work?

5. Do the companies have licenses?

6. Which company would you call if you needed a painter to paint your home? Why?

Student 2

Ask your partner these questions.

1. What kind of ads do you see?

2. Do both ads require the same amount of experience?

3. Are the jobs full time or part time?

4. How can you find out more information about the jobs?

5. What kind of benefits are there?

6. What abbreviations are there in the ads?

7. How much is the salary for both jobs?

Listen to your partner's questions and find the answers in the telephone ads below.

P   878   Painting

AAA Painting and Decorating
    28321 Melrose Ave. L.A.   **883-3635**
Class Act Painting   **873-0345**
    Industrial, Residential, Commercial
    Quality Work
    State Contractor's License # 273478
    1296 Main St. L.A.
Great Outdoors Painting Co. **976-2813**
    Exterior/Interior
    Carpentry/Tree Cutting
     Excellent Rates
    8750 6th St. L.A.
Home Painting Co.   **203-0346**
    Home & Apt. Specialist
    Over 20 Years Experience
    4381 Atoll Ave. L.A.

FOLD HERE

FOLD HERE

WORD BUILDING   The Suffixes *-ful* and *-less*

- The suffix *-ful* means **full of** or **characterized by**.

EXAMPLES

1. beautiful   2. playful   3. helpful

- The suffix *-less* means **without**.

EXAMPLES

1. penniless   2. helpless   3. careless

WRITE   *Add -ful or -less to the word in parentheses.*

1. David is very (hope) *hopeful* about a job.

2. Paul Green is a very (help) _____ person.

3. David was (thank) _____ that Paul could help him.

4. David doesn't have a job, but he isn't (penny) _____ or (home) _____.

5. If David went on a job interview, he wouldn't be (care) _____; he'd try to be (care) _____.

6. David must try to be (skill) _____, (thought) _____, and (truth) _____ when he answers the interview questions.

7. Looking for a job sometimes seems (end) _____, (hope) _____, (use) _____, and (worth) _____.

CHALLENGE   *How many sentences can you make with the following words?*

1. playful   4. powerful   7. restless   10. colorful   13. thankless
2. useful   5. powerless   8. hateful   11. colorless   14. lifeless
3. peaceful   6. restful   9. forceful   12. tasteless   15. ageless

ABBREVIATIONS

A

Acct.	accountant
acctg.	accounting
Acct.P.	
Accts Pay	
A/Pay	accounts payable
A/P	
Accts Rec	
Accts R	
A/Rec	accounts receivable
A/R	
ad	advertisement
Air Con., A/C	air conditioning
AM	morning
appoint.	appointment
ASAP	as soon as possible
asst.	assistant
atty.	attorney
avail.	available

B

B.A.	Bachelor of Arts
bef.	before
ben.	
bene.	benefits
bnft.	
bkgrnd.	background
bkkpg.	bookkeeping
blk.	block
brks.	brakes
Bros.	brothers
B.S.	Bachelor of Science
BSME	Bachelor of Science in Mechanical Engineering
bus.	business

C

C.E.	civil engineer
Ch.E.	chemical engineer
clk.	clerk
clng.	cleaning
co., comp.	company
comm'l.	commercial
conds.	conditions
const.	construction
contr.	control

corp.	corporation
CPA	Certified Public Accountant
cpl.	couple
ctr.	center
cust.	customer

D

DC	direct current
del.	deliver or delivery
dent.	dentist
dept.	department
des.	designer
des.	desirable
Dir.	director
dist.	district
div.	division
dlrshp.	dealership
DMV	Department of Motor Vehicles
dntn.	downtown
dr. lic.	driver's license
dvlpmt.	development

E

E.	east
E.E.	electrical engineer
EDP	electronic data processing
EKG	electrocardiogram
elect.	electrical
engr.	engineer
EOE	equal opportunity employer
equip.	equipment
etc.	et cetera
excl., exlnt.	excellent
exec.	executive
exp.	
exp'd.	
exper.	experience, experienced
exper'd.	
exper.	expert
ext.	extension
eve.	evening

F

f/b	full benefits
F.C., F/C	full charge
fin.	financial
flex.	flexible
Fri.	Friday
frt.	front
F.T.	full time
full-pt.	full or part time
furn.	furnished, furniture

G

gen.	general
gd.	good
gov't.	government
grad.	graduate

H

hi. qual.	high quality
hosp.	hospital
hr., hrs.	hour, hours
HVAC	heating, ventilation, and air conditioning
hvy.	heavy

I

ICU	intensive care unit
immed.	immediate
Inc.	incorporated
incl.	included, including
indust'l.	industrial
info.	information
int'l.	international
ins.	insurance

K

k	thousand

L

lab.	laboratory
lic.	license
loc.	location
lt.	light
ltd.	limited
LVN	licensed vocational nurse

M

M	thousand
M.A.	Master of Arts

mach.	machine
maint.	maintenance
max.	maximum
MBA	Master of Business Administration
M/Care	Medicare
mdse.	merchandise
M.E.	mechanical engineer
mech.	mechanic or mechanical
med.	medical
M-F	Monday thru Friday
m/f	male or female
mfg.	manufacturing
mgmt.	management
mgr.	manager
min.	minimum
min.	minute
misc.	miscellaneous
mkr.	maker
mo.	month
Mon.	Monday
M.S.	Master of Science
MVR	motor vehicle record

N

N.	north
NA	nursing assistant
N/A	not applicable
nat'l.	national
nites	nights
no exp. nec.	no experience necessary
nr.	near

O

ofc.	office
ofr.	offer
op., oper.	operator
open'g.	opening
oppt., oppty.	opportunity
OR	operating room
organ.	organization
O/T	overtime
OJT	on the job training

P

PC	
PC board	printed circuit board
PCB	
pd. vac.	paid vacation

per., perm.	permanent
per diem	per day
Ph.D.	Doctor of Philosophy
pkg.	package
P&L	posting and ledger
plsnt.	pleasant
PM	afternoon, evening
P.O. Box	post office box
postn.	position
prep.	preparation
pri., pvt.	private
prog.	progress
prog.	programmer
proj.	project
pref., pref'd.	preferred
pt.	part
p/t, P.T.	part time

Q

| QC | quality control |
| qual. | qualified |

R

rcpt.	receipt
recv., rec.	receivable
R/D	research and development
ref.	reference
RN	registered nurse
rep.	represent
req., req'd.	required
res.	residential

S

S.	south
sal.	salary
sec.	secretary
ser.	service
S.H.	short hand
spk.	speak
Spn.	Spanish
sr.	senior
st.	street
stmts.	statements
supt.	superintendent
supv.	supervisor
surg.	surgical or surgery
sys.	system

T

T.B.	trial balance
tech.	technical or technology
tel.	telephone
temp.	temporary
trans., transm.	transmission
transp.	transportation
trans. furn.	transportation furnished
trn.	trainee

U

| util. | utility |

V

| vac. | vacation |
| vlly. | valley |

W

W.	west
w/	with
wk.	week
wkend., wknds.	weekend, weekends
WPM, wpm	words per minute
wrhs.	warehouse

X

| xlnt. | excellent |

Y

| yr., yrs. | year, years |

SYMBOLS

@	at, each
#	number
$	dollar
%	percent
¢	cent
&	and
–	minus
+	plus
=	equals
/	or
5'	5 feet
8''	8 inches

11

HAVE YOU MADE A DECISION ABOUT THE JOB?

COMPETENCIES	• Going on an Interview
	• Answering Job-Related Questions
	• Filling Out an Application
	• Rating an Interview
	• Understanding Gestures
GRAMMAR	• The Present Perfect
	• Regular and Irregular Forms of the Past Participle
VOCABULARY	• *for* and *since*
	• Expressions of Time Used with the Present Perfect
	• Job Application Terms
	• Irregular Past Participles
WORD BUILDING	• The Suffix *-able*

LISTEN

David Fernandez has arrived for his job interview a few minutes early. He's talking to Sue Dennis, the receptionist. He also meets Jeff Harris, another applicant.

Sue: May I help you?

David: My name is David Fernandez. I have an appointment with the personnel manager at 11:30.

Sue: Mr. Gabriel has interviewed applicants all morning and he's running a little late. This gentleman, Jeff Harris, is ahead of you, and he's next. I've changed his appointment several times already. He has waited for a long time. I've rescheduled your appointment for after lunch, at 1:30. I hope it isn't too inconvenient for you, Mr. Fernandez.

David: Not at all.

Sue: Have you filled out an application?

David: No, I haven't.

Sue: Here's an application form. Please fill it out and bring it to the interview. You have more than an hour before your interview. If you wanted, you could have lunch in the cafeteria.

David: Where's the cafeteria?

Sue: It's in the basement.

Jeff: May I join you?

David: Please do.

Jeff: My name's Jeff Harris.

David: I'm David Fernandez. Pleased to meet you.

Jeff: Pleased to meet you, too. It seems that we've both applied for the same job.

David: I guess so.

UNDERSTAND   *Circle **True, False,** or **We don't know**.*

1. It's 11:30.	True	False	We don't know.
2. Mr. Gabriel is the personnel manager.	True	False	We don't know.
3. Jeff Harris has filled out an application.	True	False	We don't know.
4. The cafeteria is downstairs.	True	False	We don't know.
5. Sue Dennis has rescheduled David's appointment for before lunch.	True	False	We don't know.

GRAMMAR   The Present Perfect

- *We form the present perfect by combining the present tense of* **have** *and the past participle.*

EXAMPLES   *Past Participle*

David Fernandez	**has**	**arrived**	for his job interview.
Mr. Gabriel	**has**	**interviewed**	applicants all morning.
He	**'s**	**waited**	a long time.
I	**'ve**	**changed**	his appointment several times.
I	**'ve**	**rescheduled**	your appointment.
We	**'ve**	**applied**	for the same job.

- *The simple past tense and the past participle of* **regular** *verbs are the same, and end in* **-ed**.

Simple Form	Past Tense	Past Participle
apply	applied	applied
arrive	arrived	arrived
change	changed	changed
interview	interviewed	interviewed
reschedule	rescheduled	rescheduled
wait	waited	waited

- *We use the contractions* **'ve** *for* **have** *and* **'s** *for* **has**.

- *We place* **have** *or* **has** *before the past participle to form questions and add* **n't** *to* **have** *and* **has** *to form the negative.*

EXAMPLES

Have you **filled** out an application? (Question)
I **haven't filled** out an application. (Negative)

- *The present perfect expresses an indefinite time in the past and the simple past tense implies a specific time. The present perfect also indicates that we still feel its effects.*

EXAMPLES

I've **rescheduled** your appointment. (indefinite time)
I **rescheduled** Mr. Harris's appointment **an hour ago**. (specific time)
Mr. Gabriel **has interviewed** many people. (and will interview more)
Mr. Gabriel **interviewed** five people **yesterday**. (specific time)

- *The present perfect can also indicate a repeated time in the past.*

EXAMPLE

I've **changed** his appointment **several times**. (and may do so again)

READ   *Make logical complete sentences with the words in the box.*

David	have	interviewed	David's appointment.
Sue	've	arrived	applicants all morning.
Mr. Gabriel	has	rescheduled	a long time.
Jeff	's	waited	the same job.
I		applied for	Jeff's appointment several times.
They		changed	for the interview a little early.

READ   *Make logical questions with the words in the box. Then answer them.*

Have	you	waited a long time?
	David	rescheduled the appointments?
	Jeff	interviewed Jeff or David?
Has	Sue	applied for the same job?
	Mr. Gabriel	changed any appointments?
	they	arrived early?

Yes,	I	have.
	he	haven't.
No,	she	has.
	they	hasn't.

PAIR PRACTICE   *Talk with another student. Practice the present perfect tense. Use the phrases below.*

Student 1: Have you ....?
Student 2: Yes, I have. / No, I haven't.

1. wait a long time/yes
2. receive a new appointment/yes
3. fill out an application/yes
4. complete the whole application/yes
5. answer all the questions/no
6. apply for other jobs/yes
7. live here long/no
8. work as a painter a long time/yes
9. talk to the boss/no
10. ask about the job/no

PAIR PRACTICE   *Use the phrases below.*

Student 1: Has ....?
Student 2: Yes, he/she has.
          or
          No, he/she hasn't.

1. the receptionist reschedule your appointment/yes
2. Mr. Gabriel interview you/no
3. the receptionist call you about the job/no
4. the other man wait long/no
5. the receptionist ask you about your qualifications/no
6. the receptionist look at your application/yes
7. the receptionist check your application/yes
8. the personnel manager finish the interviews/no
9. the manager talk to you/no
10. the manager ask to see another applicant before lunch/no

PAIR PRACTICE   *Use the phrases below.*

Student 1: How many times have/has ....?
Student 2: ....

1. Jeff/apply for a job here

2. the receptionist/reschedule Jeff's appointment

3. the receptionist/check Jeff's application

4. Jeff/talk to Mr. Gabriel

5. Jeff/call to make an appointment

6. Jeff/look for a job

7. the secretary/ask Jeff about his qualifications

8. Jeff/fill out an application

9. Jeff/answer some questions on the application incorrectly

WRITE   *Answer with **Yes, I did/have.** or **No, I didn't/haven't**.*

1. Did you apply for the job yesterday?   No, _____

2. Have you waited for a long time?   Yes, _____

3. Have you talked to the other applicants?   No, _____

4. Did you hear anything about the job?   No, _____

5. Did you learn about this job from the newspaper?   Yes, _____

6. Have you applied for many other jobs?   No, _____

WRITE   *Put the words in the correct order.*

1. a long time/city/Have/in/lived/this/you/for/?

   Have you lived in this city for a long time?

2. many/arrived/Have/interview/the/for/people/?

   _____

3. Have/most of/you/the morning/waited/for/?

   _____

4. many/applicants/the manager/How/interviewed/has/?

   _____

5. the receptionist/How/rescheduled/many/appointments/has/?

   _____

6. the appointments/Why/rescheduled/has/the receptionist/?

   _____

No, for only three weeks.

No, not many.

Yes, I have.

I don't know.

Most of them.

Because the manager is running late.

DICTATION   *Cover the sentences under each line. Write the dictation on the line as your teacher reads it to you. Then uncover the sentences and correct your writing.*

TO: Mr. Gabriel   **MEMO**

1. _____

   David Fernandez has arrived for his interview.

2. _____

   I have rescheduled his appointment for 1:30.

3. _____

   I have also changed Mr. Harris's appointment to 1 o'clock.

4. _____

   I told the two applicants to come back after lunch.

5. _____

   I have finished my work, and I'm going to lunch.

6. _____

   Do you want me to bring you something from the cafeteria?

7. _____

   Let me know before noon.

READ

David and Jeff are in the cafeteria.

Clerk: May I help you?

Jeff: I think I'll have a salad in pita bread.

David: In pita bread? What's pita bread?

Jeff: Haven't you ever eaten pita?

David: No, I haven't.

Jeff: It's great. It's flat bread with a pocket. How long have you been here?

David: About a year and a half.

Jeff: You've been here that long and you haven't tried a pita?

David: No, I've never had one.

Clerk: And you, sir? What are you going to have?

David: I guess I'll have a salad in pita bread, too.

UNDERSTAND   *Circle* ***True, False,*** *or* ***We don't know.***

1. Jeff has eaten pita bread many times.	True	False	We don't know.
2. David has never had pita bread before.	True	False	We don't know.
3. David has been here for less than a year.	True	False	We don't know.
4. David and Jeff have ordered the same thing.	True	False	We don't know.
5. Salad in pita bread is popular in your city.	True	False	We don't know.

GRAMMAR   The Present Perfect with Irregular Verbs

- *More than two hundred past tense and past participle forms of English verbs are irregular.*

EXAMPLES

Irregular Form

David	has never	**eaten**	pita bread.
David	has never	**had**	a salad in pita bread.
David	has	**been**	here about a year and a half.

- *Here's a list of some of the most common ones. See the end of this chapter for a more complete list.*

Simple Form	Simple Past	Past Participle
am, is, are	was, were	been
bring	brought	brought
buy	bought	bought
come	came	come
do	did	done
drink	drank	drunk
eat	ate	eaten
get	got	got, gotten
go	went	gone
have/has	had	had
hear	heard	heard
know	knew	known
make	made	made
meet	met	met
see	saw	seen
send	sent	sent
take	took	taken
think	thought	thought
write	wrote	written

READ   *Make logical complete sentences with the words in the box.*

I	have	seen	to the office.
You	've	gone	him a long time.
He	haven't	been	a resume to the interview.
She	has	met	to the cafeteria.
It	's	brought	an interview.
We	hasn't	gotten	lunch.
They		known	the personnel manager.
		come	in this city a year and a nalf.
		had	the job.

PAIR PRACTICE   *Use the words and pictures below.*

Student 1: Have you ever eaten/had ....?
Student 2: Yes, I have. / No, I haven't.

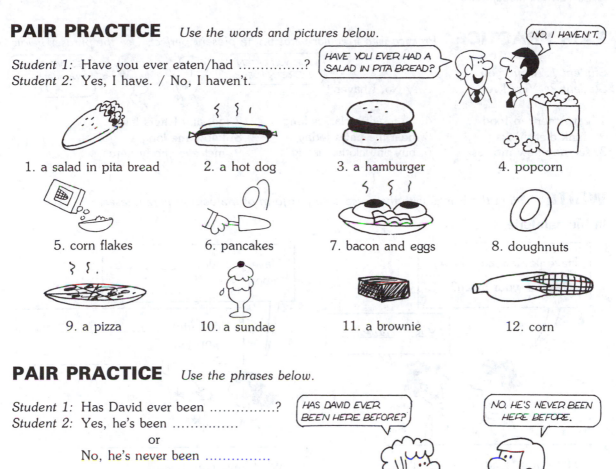

1. a salad in pita bread
2. a hot dog
3. a hamburger
4. popcorn

5. corn flakes
6. pancakes
7. bacon and eggs
8. doughnuts

9. a pizza
10. a sundae
11. a brownie
12. corn

PAIR PRACTICE   *Use the phrases below.*

Student 1: Has David ever been ....?
Student 2: Yes, he's been ....

or

No, he's never been ....

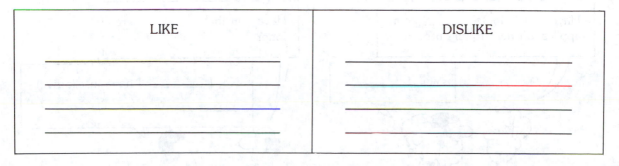

1. here before/no
2. to this company before/no
3. to the restaurant across the street/yes
4. on a job interview/yes
5. to the local adult school/yes
6. to the state employment office/no
7. to a private employment agency/no

CHALLENGE   *What kinds of American food have you had? What do you like or dislike? Why?*

LIKE	DISLIKE

PAIR PRACTICE   *Practice with irregular verbs in the present perfect. Use the phrases below.*

Student 1: Have you ....?
Student 2: Yes, I've .... / No, I haven't ....

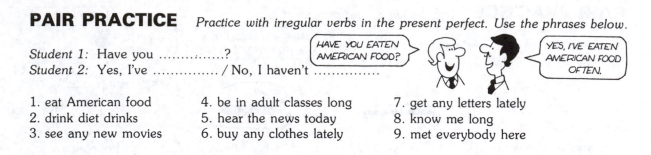

HAVE YOU EATEN AMERICAN FOOD?

YES, I'VE EATEN AMERICAN FOOD OFTEN.

1. eat American food
2. drink diet drinks
3. see any new movies

4. be in adult classes long
5. hear the news today
6. buy any clothes lately

7. get any letters lately
8. know me long
9. met everybody here

WRITE   *Fill in the blanks with the present perfect form of the verb in parentheses.*

In the cafeteria.

1.
Have you already (have) *had* your lunch?

Yes, I *have*.

2.
Have you (do) _____ the report?

No, I (do) _____ _____ the report yet.

3.
Have you (send) _____ the package to New York?

No, I _____. I'll send it out after lunch.

4.
What have you (hear) _____ about the job opening?

Nothing. I (hear) _____ _____ anything.

5.
Have you (bring) _____ your application here to fill out?

Yes, I _____.

6.
Have you (be) _____ here long?

No, I _____. I have just (arrive) _____.

READ

David has finished lunch. He's now in the interview with the personnel manager.

Mr. Gabriel: Hello, I'm Morris Gabriel.
    David: I'm David Fernandez.
Mr. Gabriel: Pleased to meet you. Please come and take a seat.
    David: Thank you. Here's my application.
Mr. Gabriel: I see from your application that you're from Puerto Rico.
    David: That's right.
Mr. Gabriel: How long have you been in this city?
    David: For a year and a half.
Mr. Gabriel: And how long have you worked as a painter?
    David: Since 1981.
Mr. Gabriel: Have you had any carpentry experience?
    David: Some. I've taken carpentry courses at the adult school for a year.

A half an hour has gone by. The interview is ending.

Mr. Gabriel: I haven't made a decision about the job. I'll decide next week. We'll contact you then.
    David: Can I call you?
Mr. Gabriel: OK. Call me next Tuesday morning. Thank you for coming.
    David: Thank you for your time.

UNDERSTAND   *Circle **True**, **False**, or **We don't know**.*

1. David has worked as a painter for five years.	True	False	We don't know.
2. David has lived here since 1981.	True	False	We don't know.
3. "Take a seat" means "Please sit down."	True	False	We don't know.
4. "Make a decision" means "decide."	True	False	We don't know.
5. Mr. Gabriel will make a decision about the job during the weekend.	True	False	We don't know.

GRAMMAR   The Present Perfect with *for* and *since*

- *Use the present perfect to express an action that began in the past, continues to the present, and will possibly continue into the future.*

EXAMPLES

David **has lived** here **for** a year and a half. (He still lives here.)
He**'s worked** as a painter **since** 1981. (He continues to work as a painter.)
He**'s taken** carpentry courses **for** a year. (He's still taking a course.)

- *The preposition **for** precedes a quantity of time and **since** precedes the starting point.*

EXAMPLES

How long has Jeff lived here?

Since January. (start)   For six months. (duration)

January   February   March   April   May   June

READ   *Make logical complete sentences with the words in the box.*

David	have	had	here		6 months.
Jeff	've	been	at the adult school	for	1981.
We	haven't	lived	a course		September.
They	has	worked	a carpentry course	since	2 months.
She	's	taken	a job		a long time.
I	hasn't				last year.

READ   *Make logical questions with the words in the box. Then answer them.*

How long		you	had a job?
	have	your family	worked?
		your friend	lived in this city?
	has	your parents	taken this class?
		your neighbor	known your neighbors?

PAIR PRACTICE   *Use the phrases below.*

Student 1: Have you .... long?
Student 2: Yes, I have. / No, I haven't.

HAVE YOU LIVED HERE LONG?   *NO, I HAVEN'T.*

1. live here
2. work
3. go to school
4. know the people here
5. wait here
6. take adult classes
7. have a job
8. ....

PAIR PRACTICE   *Practice with **for** and **since**. Use the phrases below.*

Student 1: How long has David ....?
Student 2: He's .... for/since ....

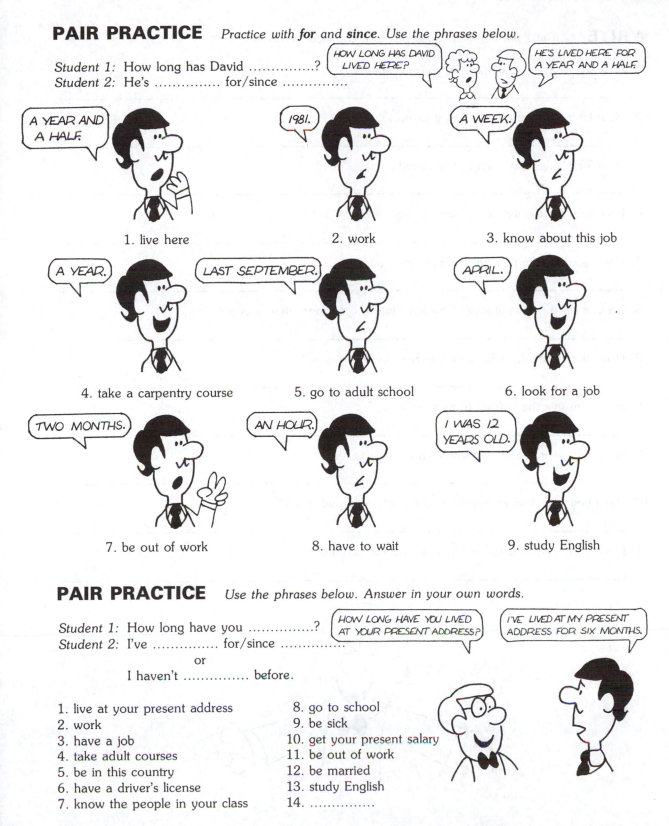

HOW LONG HAS DAVID LIVED HERE?

HE'S LIVED HERE FOR A YEAR AND A HALF.

A YEAR AND A HALF.

1. live here

1981.

2. work

A WEEK.

3. know about this job

A YEAR.

4. take a carpentry course

LAST SEPTEMBER.

5. go to adult school

APRIL.

6. look for a job

TWO MONTHS.

7. be out of work

AN HOUR.

8. have to wait

I WAS 12 YEARS OLD.

9. study English

PAIR PRACTICE   *Use the phrases below. Answer in your own words.*

Student 1: How long have you ....?
Student 2: I've .... for/since ....
                    or
             I haven't .... before.

HOW LONG HAVE YOU LIVED AT YOUR PRESENT ADDRESS?

I'VE LIVED AT MY PRESENT ADDRESS FOR SIX MONTHS.

1. live at your present address
2. work
3. have a job
4. take adult courses
5. be in this country
6. have a driver's license
7. know the people in your class

8. go to school
9. be sick
10. get your present salary
11. be out of work
12. be married
13. study English
14. ....

WRITE   *Answer the interview questions with complete sentences.*

1. How long have you worked in your occupation?

_____

2. How long have you worked at your present job?

_____

3. How long have you been in this country?

_____

4. How long have you lived at your present address?

_____

5. Have you lived in this city for more than a year?

_____

6. Do you have any references who have known you more than a year?

_____

7. How many different jobs have you had in your lifetime?

_____

8. Have you ever been fired from a job?

_____

9. Have you ever received unemployment insurance?

_____

10. Have you ever had an accident on the job? If so, what kind?

_____

11. Have you ever used American tools and measurements?

_____

READ

Morris Gabriel and Alida Cohen, his supervisor, are talking about David.

Morris: I've interviewed a lot of applicants, and I think I've finally made a decision. I think we should hire Mr. David Fernandez.

Alida: Tell me something about him.

Morris: Mr. Fernandez is from Puerto Rico. He started to work in 1978 as a stockperson in a store. In 1981 he began to work as a painter. He left Puerto Rico in 1983. He lived in New York for a few months, and then moved here about a year and a half ago. He worked for a painting contractor until two months ago. He started to look for a job when the company laid him off, and he's still looking. He has experience as a painter, but not much as a carpenter. He said that he took a wood shop class last year and is taking another one now. He saw our ad in the newspaper last week and called. I interviewed him a few minutes ago, and I think he's the best applicant for the job.

WRITE

Find the answers to the questions in the dialog above. Use the present perfect or the simple past tense.

1. How long has David worked?

   He has worked since 1978.

2. When did he start his first job?

3. How long has he worked as a painter?

4. How long did he live in New York?

5. How long has he lived in Los Angeles?

6. How many wood shop courses has he taken?

7. When did he see the ad in the paper?

8. How long has he known about the job?

READ

Mr. Gabriel makes a call the following Monday.

THIS IS MORRIS GABRIEL. I INTERVIEWED YOU LAST WEEK ABOUT A JOB. WHEN CAN YOU BEGIN?

GOOD. COME IN TOMORROW AT EIGHT O'CLOCK.

I CAN BEGIN IMMEDIATELY!

READ

EMPLOYMENT APPLICATION
Please Print

Personal Data

Name: _Fernandez,   David   Juan_   Date: _4/6/84_
           Last   First   Middle   Month/Day/Year

Address: _13   Theater St.   #1   L.A.   CA   90038_
         Number   Street   Apartment   City   State   Zip Code

Telephone: _(213) 421-9605_   Social Security Number: _032-66-2526_

Have you worked for this company before? _No_   When? _N/A_

Any relatives or friends employed by this company? Name: _None_

What position are you applying for? _painter_   Wages expected? _open_

Date ready to start: _immediately_ Have you ever been convicted of a crime? _No_

If yes, please explain: _N/A_

Do you have any disabilities that might interfere with your ability to do the job that you are

applying for? _No_   If yes, please explain: _N/A_

References

Name	Address	Phone	Occupation
1. Mr. Castell	6439 River St. L.A. 90038	964-2301	manager
2. Mrs. Faber	120 Southwood St. L.A. 90046	943-0061	supervisor

Education

	Name of School	Address	Dates From To	Did you graduate?	Course or Degree
Elementary	Columbus School	San Juan, Puerto Rico	1967/75	Yes	
High School	Martin High School	San Juan, Puerto Rico	1976/80	Yes	Diploma
Vocational, Business, or Trade	Fairfax Community Adult School	7850 Melrose West Hollywood	1983/84	No	wood work
College	No				

Previous Employment   (Most recent employer first)

Name and Address of Company	Kind of Business	Supervisor	Salary
Max's Printing Co. 63 Main St. Santa Monica	Printing	Mr. Roberts	$7.00/hr.
Ace Painting Co. San Juan, Puerto Rico	Painting	Mr. Lopez	$5.00/hr.
Pepe's Shoe Store, Puerto Rico	Stockperson	Mrs. Sanchez	$3.00/hr.

Date: _April 6, 1984_ Signature: _David Fernandez_

WRITE   *You fill out an application, too.*

EMPLOYMENT APPLICATION
Please Print
Personal Data

Name: _____ Date: _____
Last   First   Middle   Month/Day/Year

Address: _____
Number   Street   Apartment City   State   Zip Code

Telephone: _____ Social Security Number: _____

Have you worked for this company before? _____ When? _____

Any relatives or friends employed by this company? Name: _____

What position are you applying for? _____ Wages expected? _____

Date ready to start: _____ Have you ever been convicted of a crime? _____

If yes, please explain: _____

Do you have any disabilities that might interfere with your ability to do the job that you are

applying for? _____ If yes, please explain: _____

References   Name   Address   Phone   Occupation

1. _____

2. _____

Education   Name of   Address   Dates   Did you   Course or
School   From To graduate?   Degree

Elementary _____

High School _____

Vocational,
Business, or Trade _____

College _____

Previous Employment   (Most recent employer first)

Name and Address of Company   Kind of Business   Supervisor   Salary

_____

_____

_____

Date: _____ Signature: _____

PAIR PRACTICE   *Applicants have to answer many questions during an interview. Many questions will be specifically about the job. However, there are some general questions that you can practice before an interview. Practice asking and answering the following questions with another student. Be brief and clear. The parentheses after the questions contain either possible answers or helpful hints.*

QUESTIONS TO APPLICANTS

1. What's your name?
2. What's your occupation or profession? (Give job title.)
3. What did you do at your last job? (Describe your last job in detail.)
4. What did you study in high school, college, or vocational school?
5. What shift can/can't you work? (day, swing, graveyard shifts)
6. What are some of your strong/weak points? (Be positive.)

7. Where are you from?
8. Where do/did you live/work?
9. Where are you presently employed? (I'm employed at ..../I'm unemployed.)

10. When can you begin/start work? (anytime, immediately)
11. When can you come in for another interview? (at your convenience)
12. When did you finish your education/school? (Give date.)

13. How's your health? (fine, good, very good, excellent)
14. How will you get to work? (by car, bus, foot)
15. How do you work under pressure?
16. How's your English? (improving quickly, better every day)

17. What kind of tools can you use? (Name as many as you can. Be specific.)
18. What kind of machines can you operate? (Name as many as you can.)
19. What kind of skills do you have?
20. What kind of experience/background do you have?
21. What kind of job are you looking for?

22. How much experience do you have? (I have .... years experience.)
23. How much money did you earn at your last job?
24. How much do you expect to earn at this job? (It's open; negotiable.)

25. How many dependents do you have?
26. How many different kinds of jobs have you had?

27. How long have you worked in your field/occupation/profession?
28. How long have you lived here?
29. How long can you work a day/week?

QUESTIONS TO EMPLOYERS

30. What are the qualifications for the position?
31. What kind of training is there?
32. Is the job temporary or permanent/full time or part time?
33. What would my duties be?
34. What are the beginning wages?
35. What kind of benefits are there?

CHALLENGE   *Role-play a job interview with another student in front of the class. One student is the employer and the second student is an applicant. Use some of the questions on the previous page. The rest of the class rates the interview with the rating form below.*

INTERVIEW RATING FORM	Very Good	Good	Fair	Poor	Bad
Posture					
Manners					
Language					
Voice					
Eye Contact					
Attitude					
Personality					
Motivation					
Self-Confidence					
Clothes					
Potential					

GROUP DISCUSSION

1. Talk about how people can improve themselves in some of the categories in the rating form.

2. How important is body language in an interview? How should an applicant sit and act?

3. What kind of gestures are there for the following ideas?

yes	Quiet please.	Who me?	I forgot.
no	OK.	Stop!	This way please.
money	Good luck.	Please come here.	Here you are.
perfect	Please sit down.	I don't know.	No, thank you.

4. How many other gestures can you identify? Are these gestures acceptable in your country?

_____   _____

_____   _____

_____   _____

WORD BUILDING   The Suffix *-able*

- The suffix *-able* means **capable of**, **fit for**, or **worthy of**. We generally add it to verbs to make adjectives.

EXAMPLES

1. David is a reli<u>able</u> person.   2. David is a lik<u>able</u> person.   3. This glass is unbreak<u>able</u>.

WRITE   *Change the words in bold face to words ending in -able. Some of the words will need a negative prefix. Some of the forms are irregular.*

1. Mr. Gabriel cannot **change** the schedule; it's *unchangeable* .

2. People **like** Mr. Gabriel very much. He is a very _____ person.

3. David couldn't **forget** his interview. It was an _____ experience.

4. Jeff couldn't **drink** the coffee in the cafeteria. He said that it was terrible and _____.

5. Mr. Gabriel can **depend** on David; David's a very _____ person.

6. David **knows** a lot about his job. He's _____ about painting.

7. David had to **use** Jeff's pen to fill out his application because his own pen was _____. It was out of ink.

8. David didn't **think** of coming late to the job interview with the personnel manager. That's _____!

9. When a question does not **apply** to you, it is not _____.

WRITE   *How many other words do you know that end in -able?*

_____   _____   _____

_____   _____   _____

_____   _____   _____

CHALLENGE   *Use the words in the list above in complete sentences.*

PRINCIPAL PARTS OF COMMON IRREGULAR VERBS

Present	Past	Past Participle	Present	Past	Past Participle
awake	awoke	awakened	lose	lost	lost
bear	bore	born	make	made	made
beat	beat	beaten	mean	meant	meant
become	became	become	meet	met	met
begin	began	begun	pay	paid	paid
bet	bet	bet	quit	quit	quit
blow	blew	blown	read	read	read
bring	brought	brought	ride	rode	ridden
build	built	built	ring	rang	rung
catch	caught	caught	rise	rose	risen
choose	chose	chosen	run	ran	run
come	came	come	see	saw	seen
cost	cost	cost	sell	sold	sold
cut	cut	cut	send	sent	sent
deal	dealt	dealt	set	set	set
dig	dug	dug	shake	shook	shaken
do	did	done	shoot	shot	shot
draw	drew	drawn	show	showed	shown
drink	drank	drunk	shrink	shrank	shrunk
drive	drove	driven	shut	shut	shut
eat	ate	eaten	sing	sang	sung
fall	fell	fallen	sink	sank	sunk
feed	fed	fed	sit	sat	sat
feel	felt	felt	sleep	slept	slept
fight	fought	fought	speak	spoke	spoken
find	found	found	speed	sped	sped
fly	flew	flown	spend	spent	spent
forget	forgot	forgotten	spin	spun	spun
forgive	forgave	forgiven	spread	spread	spread
freeze	froze	frozen	stand	stood	stood
get	got	got, gotten	steal	stole	stolen
give	gave	given	stick	stuck	stuck
go	went	gone	strike	struck	struck
grow	grew	grown	swear	swore	sworn
hang	hung	hung	sweep	swept	swept
have/has	had	had	swim	swam	swum
hear	heard	heard	take	took	taken
hide	hid	hidden	teach	taught	taught
hold	held	held	tear	tore	torn
hurt	hurt	hurt	tell	told	told
keep	kept	kept	think	thought	thought
know	knew	known	throw	threw	thrown
lay	laid	laid	wake	woke	woken
lead	led	led	wear	wore	worn
leave	left	left	wet	wet	wet
lend	lent	lent	win	won	won
let	let	let	wind	wound	wound
lie*	lay	lain	wring	wrung	wrung
light	lit	lit	write	wrote	written

* *Lie* meaning *to tell an untruth* is regular.

12

WE'VE BEEN EXPECTING YOU

COMPETENCIES	• Reporting to Work
	• Filling Out a W-4 Form
	• Discussing Stress
GRAMMAR	• The Present Perfect Continuous
	• *already/yet*
	• *still/not...anymore*
VOCABULARY	• Common Job Words
	• Stressful Events
WORD BUILDING	• Past Participles as Adjectives

LISTEN

David Fernandez is reporting for work. He's talking to the receptionist.

Receptionist: May I help you?

David: Yes. My name is David Fernandez, and I'm reporting for work. This is my first day.

Receptionist: Oh yes, we've been expecting you. Please be seated. I'll tell Mr. Gear that you're here. He's been meeting with some of the other bosses about a new project. They've been talking all morning. Here are the company rules and regulations. You can read them while you're waiting.

David meets the supervisor, Mr. Albert Gear.

Mr. Gear: David?

David: Yes.

Mr. Gear: Please come in. Have you been waiting long?

David: No, I haven't. I've been sitting here and reading some papers for only a very short time.

Mr. Gear: I'm sorry that I couldn't see you sooner. I've been having a meeting all morning. We've been trying to solve a few minor problems about a new construction project. Please sit down.

David: Thank you.

UNDERSTAND   *Circle **True**, **False**, or **We don't know**.*

1. David arrived to work early.	True	False	We don't know.
2. David has been waiting a long time.	True	False	We don't know.
3. Mr. Gear has been trying to solve a problem alone.	True	False	We don't know.
4. While David has been waiting, he has been reading the company rules and regulations.	True	False	We don't know.
5. The people in the meeting have solved the minor problem.	True	False	We don't know.
6. "Please be seated" means "please sit down."	True	False	We don't know.

GRAMMAR   The Present Perfect Continuous

- *We form the present perfect continuous with the present tense form of **have** (**have** or **has**), the past participle **been**, and the present participle of the main verb (the **-ing** form of the verb).*

EXAMPLES	have/has	been	Present Participle	
We	've	been	expecting	you.
He	's	been	meeting	with some other bosses.
They	've	been	talking	all morning.
I	've	been	waiting	a short time.
I	've	been	reading	some papers.
I	've	been	having	a meeting.
We	've	been	trying	to solve a problem.

- *We use the present perfect continuous to describe an action that began in the past and has continued up to the present. It is almost interchangeable with the first use of the present perfect in the Grammar Box on page 175.*

READ   Make logical complete sentences with the words in the box.

I	have		typing	with some people	for a short time.
You	've		sitting	to solve a problem	all morning.
He		been	meeting	a letter	since 1981.
She	has		working	here	for fifteen minutes.
We	's		trying	in the waiting room	since 7 a.m.
They			waiting	for the supervisor	for a few minutes.

READ   Make logical questions with the words in the box. Then answer them.

		I		waiting	at your present job?
		he		doing	English?
	have	she		sitting	in this city?
How long		you	been	working	this exercise?
	has	we		living	to this school?
		they		coming	at your desk?
		it		speaking	here?

PAIR PRACTICE   Talk with another student. Practice the present perfect continuous. Use the phrases below.

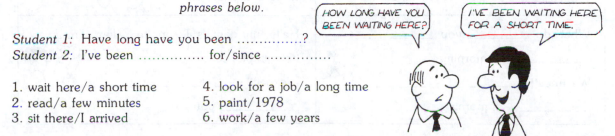

HOW LONG HAVE YOU BEEN WAITING HERE?

I'VE BEEN WAITING HERE FOR A SHORT TIME.

Student 1: Have long have you been ....?
Student 2: I've been .... for/since ....

1. wait here/a short time
2. read/a few minutes
3. sit there/I arrived

4. look for a job/a long time
5. paint/1978
6. work/a few years

PAIR PRACTICE   *Use the phrases below.*

Student 1: Has .... been ....?
Student 2: Yes, he/she has. / No, he/she hasn't.

> HAS DAVID BEEN WAITING LONG?

> NO, HE HASN'T.

1. David/wait long
2. Mr. Gear/meet with people
3. the receptionist/expect David
4. David/work here long
5. Mr. Gear/try to solve a problem

6. David/fill out forms
7. David/help Mr. Gear solve a problem
8. the receptionist/wait for David
9. Mr. Gear/have a meeting all morning
10. Mr. Gear/talk with David all morning

PAIR PRACTICE   *Use the phrases below.*

Student 1: Have you been .... long?
Student 2: Yes, I have. / No, I haven't.

> HAVE YOU BEEN SITTING HERE LONG?

> NO, I HAVEN'T.

1. sit here
2. live here
3. work
4. read the newspaper
5. write letters in English

6. study English
7. go to this school
8. do this exercise
9. look for a job
10. ....

PAIR PRACTICE   *Use the phrases below. Answer in your own words.*

Student 1: How long have you been ....?
Student 2: I've been .... / I haven't been ....

> HOW LONG HAVE YOU BEEN LIVING IN THIS AREA?

> I'VE BEEN LIVING IN THIS AREA FOR OVER A YEAR.

1. live in this area
2. work at your present job
3. drive
4. take adult classes
5. learn English

6. come to adult school
7. earn a salary
8. look for a job
9. speak English
10. ....

WRITE   *Fill in the blanks with the correct form of the verbs in parentheses.*

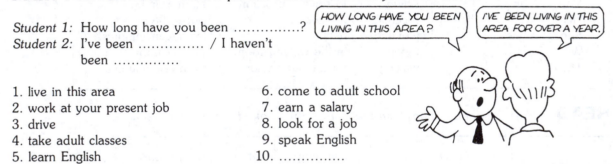

(wait) *Has* _____ Mr. Fernandez *been* _____ *waiting* _____ very long?

No, he _____ _____ _____ only for a few minutes.

Let's have another meeting tomorrow morning. We (talk) _____ _____ _____ all morning about this problem without any results.

What (do) _____ you _____ _____ all morning?

We (meet) _____ _____ _____ all morning.

Hello, my name's Jeannette Yakan. I'm a new employee.

I (expect) _____ _____ you.

READ

David is in Mr. Gear's office.

Mr. Gear: Have you filled out any forms yet?
David: No, I haven't.
Mr. Gear: What about the company rules and regulations? Have you received them yet?
David: The receptionist has already given them to me, but I haven't read all of them yet.
Mr. Gear: Has she given you a W-4 form yet?
David: No, she hasn't.
Mr. Gear: And what about the insurance forms?
David: No, I haven't received any forms yet.
Mr. Gear: Here's a W-4 form and a few other necessary forms. You can sit here and fill them out. Then read the rules and regulations. If there is anything that you don't understand or if you have any questions, please feel free to ask. Let me know when you finish. Then I'll introduce you to your section manager.

UNDERSTAND   *Circle **True, False,** or **We don't know**.*

1. David has already filled out a W-4 form.	True	False	We don't know.
2. David has already gotten the company rules and regulations.	True	False	We don't know.
3. Mr. Gear hasn't given David the insurance forms to fill out yet.	True	False	We don't know.
4. David has already met his section manager.	True	False	We don't know.
5. David has understood all of the company rules and regulations.	True	False	We don't know.

WRITE   *Underline all the verbs in the present perfect tense in the dialog above.*

GRAMMAR   *already/yet*

- *We often use the present perfect with **already** and **yet**.*

- ***Already** and **yet** mean **by a point in time** or **up to a point in time**. We use **already** in the affirmative, and it precedes the main verb. We use **yet** for questions and negatives, and it follows the main verb.*

EXAMPLES

Affirmative

The receptionist	has	**already**	given	them to me.
I	've	**already**	received	the company rules.
David	has	**already**	met	the supervisor.

Question

Have you filled out any forms	**yet?**
Have you received them	**yet?**
Has she given you the insurance forms	**yet?**

Negative

| I | **haven't** | received any forms | **yet.** |
| I | **haven't** | read all of them | **yet.** |

READ   *Make logical complete sentences with the words in the box.*

David	have	already	filled out the form	
Mr. Gear	've		seen the supervisor	
The personnel manager	haven't		met the manager	
The supervisor	has		interviewed David	
He	's		spoken to Mr. Gear	yet.
They	hasn't		read all the rules	
			finished the meeting	

READ   *Make questions with the words in the box. Then answer them.*

Have you	finished this exercise	
	started work	
	read all the papers	
	filled out an application form	yet?
Has David	been on an interview	
	seen a W-4 form	
	had a test	

PAIR PRACTICE   *Practice using **yet**. Use the phrases below.*

Student 1: Has David .... yet?
Student 2: Yes, he has. / No, he hasn't.

1. fill out all the forms/no
2. receive the rules and regulations/yes
3. read the rules and regulations/no
4. get the W-4 form/no
5. look at the insurance policy/no

6. be in the work area/no
7. see the supervisor/yes
8. speak to his new boss/no
9. begin work/no
10. fill out an application/yes

PAIR PRACTICE   *Practice using **yet** and **already**. Use the phrases below.*

Student 1: Have you .... yet?
Student 2: Yes, I've already ....

1. punch in
2. take your break
3. type my letter
4. finish the report

5. deliver the report
6. mail the letters
7. pick up the mail
8. call the supervisor

PAIR PRACTICE   *Use the phrases below.*

Student 1: Have you .... yet?
Student 2: No, I haven't .... yet.

1. have your lunch
2. see the supervisor
3. order some supplies
4. use the computer

5. learn the new computer program
6. tell the other secretary what to do
7. be next door to pick up some forms
8. make a photocopy of this letter

PAIR PRACTICE   *Use the phrases below.*

Student 1: Have you .... yet?
Student 2: Yes, I've already ....
          or
          No, I haven't .... yet.

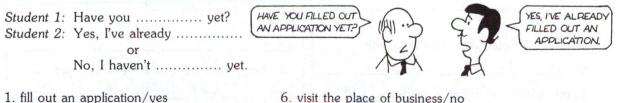

1. fill out an application/yes
2. read the rules and regulations/no
3. start work/no
4. be to the office/yes
5. meet the personnel manager/yes

6. visit the place of business/no
7. punch in/no
8. see your new boss/no
9. speak to the secretary/yes
10. give the secretary the W-4 form/yes

READ

Mr. Gear and some of the other bosses are talking about some of the company employees during the meeting.

Mr. Grant: Mr. Gear, could you please give us a report on recent raises and promotions?
Mr. Gear: Moe Jackson got a raise and a higher position last week. Now he's a supervisor. He'll get an office and a secretary in a few days. Harry Williams will get a raise next month and he'll get some new equipment and responsibilities, too. Joe Robb became a group manager last Monday, but he won't get a five percent raise until tomorrow. Larry Fox started to work here only a few months ago and won't get a raise or promotion until next year.

PAIR PRACTICE   *Ask and answer questions about the information in the dialog above.*

Student 1: Has .... yet?
Student 2: Yes, he's already ....
            or
            No, he hasn't .... yet.

HAS MOE GOTTEN A RAISE YET?

YES, HE'S ALREADY GOTTEN A RAISE.

WRITE   *Write questions or answers as needed. Find the information in the dialog above.*

1. Has Moe Jackson gotten a higher position yet?

Yes, he's already gotten a higher position.

2. _____

No, Moe hasn't moved into his new office yet.

3. Has Harry Williams received a raise yet?

_____

4. _____

Yes, Joe Robb has already received a promotion.

5. Has Joe Robb received a raise yet?

6. _____

No, Larry Fox hasn't received a raise yet.

7. Has Larry Fox gotten a promotion yet?

_____

READ

Mr. Gear is talking to one of the bosses.

Mr. Gear: Come on. Let's all take a short break.

Mr. Grant: OK. I could use a break. It's been ages since I've been at this location. How is everything here?

Mr. Gear: It's still the same.

Mr. Grant: Do you still work a lot of overtime?

Mr. Gear: Not anymore! I haven't worked overtime since my doctor told me to take it easy.

Mr. Grant: What was the matter? Were you working too hard?

Mr. Gear: Yes, I was, and I had a minor heart attack.

Mr. Grant: How are you now?

Mr. Gear: Much better!

Mr. Grant: Good. I'm glad to hear that. Let's go to the cafeteria for something to drink. Do they still make that horrible coffee?

Mr. Gear: I don't know. I don't drink coffee anymore. My doctor told me to give up coffee and smoking. He also told me to begin to exercise and watch my diet, too.

Mr. Grant: Why?

Mr. Gear: My doctor said that this job was too stressful and that I would have to manage the stress better if I wanted to live longer. What about you? Are you still working long hours?

Mr. Grant: Oh, yes, you know me. I'm still working hard, but maybe I should take it easy, too.

Mr. Gear: Yes, maybe you should!

UNDERSTAND   *Circle **True**, **False**, or **We don't know**.*

1. Mr. Gear still works overtime.	True	False	We don't know.
2. Mr. Grant still works long hours.	True	False	We don't know.
3. Mr. Grant still drinks coffee.	True	False	We don't know.
4. Mr. Grant doesn't work at this location anymore.	True	False	We don't know.
5. "It's been ages" means "It's been a long time."	True	False	We don't know.

GRAMMAR   *still/not...anymore*

- *Still describes a continuing condition in which there is no change. We use it in the affirmative and question forms. **Still** precedes the main verb, but follows the verb **to be** and modals.*

EXAMPLES

Affirmative

| It's | **still** | the same. |
| I'm | **still** | working hard. |

Question

Do you	**still**	work a lot of overtime?
Are you	**still**	working long hours?
Do they	**still**	make horrible coffee?

- *Not...anymore describes a condition that has stopped. We use it in the negative. **Anymore** follows the main verb.*

EXAMPLES

Negative

| I | **don't** | work overtime | **anymore.** |
| I | **don't** | drink coffee | **anymore.** |

READ   *Make logical complete sentences with the words in the box.*

Mr. Gear		drinks coffee.	
Mr. Grant	still	doesn't drink coffee	
He		works at the same place.	
The secretary		sells horrible coffee.	
David		doesn't work here	anymore.
The cafeteria		works hard.	

READ   *Make logical questions with the words in the box. Then answer them.*

			work overtime?
			study English?
Do	Mr. Gear		working at the same place?
Does	Mr. Grant	still	speak your language at home?
Is	you		drink coffee or tea?
Are	your friends		remember where you were 10 years ago?
			living at the same place?
			doing this exercise?

PAIR PRACTICE   *Practice using **still**. Use the phrases below.*

Student 1: Does .... still ....?
Student 2: Yes, he does. / No, he doesn't.

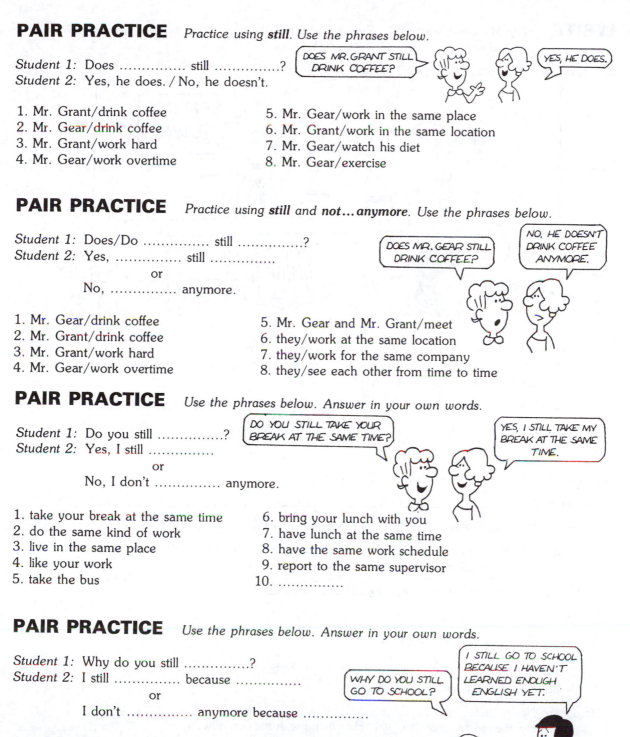

1. Mr. Grant/drink coffee
2. Mr. Gear/drink coffee
3. Mr. Grant/work hard
4. Mr. Gear/work overtime

5. Mr. Gear/work in the same place
6. Mr. Grant/work in the same location
7. Mr. Gear/watch his diet
8. Mr. Gear/exercise

PAIR PRACTICE   *Practice using **still** and **not...anymore**. Use the phrases below.*

Student 1: Does/Do .... still ....?
Student 2: Yes, ... still ....
              or
          No, ... anymore.

1. Mr. Gear/drink coffee
2. Mr. Grant/drink coffee
3. Mr. Grant/work hard
4. Mr. Gear/work overtime

5. Mr. Gear and Mr. Grant/meet
6. they/work at the same location
7. they/work for the same company
8. they/see each other from time to time

PAIR PRACTICE   *Use the phrases below. Answer in your own words.*

Student 1: Do you still ....?
Student 2: Yes, I still ....
              or
          No, I don't .... anymore.

1. take your break at the same time
2. do the same kind of work
3. live in the same place
4. like your work
5. take the bus

6. bring your lunch with you
7. have lunch at the same time
8. have the same work schedule
9. report to the same supervisor
10. ....

PAIR PRACTICE   *Use the phrases below. Answer in your own words.*

Student 1: Why do you still ....?
Student 2: I still .... because ....
              or
          I don't .... anymore because ....

1. go to school
2. work
3. live in the same place
4. exercise

5. watch your diet
6. want a better job
7. need to know more English
8. ....

WRITE   *Help Mr. Gear answer Mr. Grant's questions. Write complete sentences using* **still** *or* **not...anymore**.

Mr. Gear and Mr. Grant are still talking.

Mr. Grant: It's too bad that I work at the main office now. I really liked this location when I was here. Do you remember Shirley? She was a very charming and friendly person. Is she still here?

Mr. Gear: No, *She isn't here anymore.* _____

Mr. Grant: And what about funny old Mr. Brown. Is he still here?

Mr. Gear: Yes, _____

Mr. Grant: Do you still remember our first boss?

Mr. Gear: No, _____

Mr. Grant: You don't remember Mr. Fisher? He was so kind and easy-going.

Mr. Gear: Oh, Mr. Fisher. Yes, of course, I remember him. He hired both of us on the same day. That was about twenty years ago.

Mr. Grant: I still remember that day very clearly. Don't you?

Mr. Gear: Yes, _____

Mr. Grant: Do you know if he's still alive?

Mr. Gear: Yes, _____

Mr. Grant: Does he still live around here?

Mr. Gear: No, _____
              He moved to Ohio last year. He's living with his son now.

Mr. Grant: Our break is over. Let's go back to our meeting. Do we still have a lot to talk about at the meeting?

Mr. Gear: Yes, _____

WRITE   *Complete the answers to the questions.*

1.
> Have you been
> waiting long?

> No, _____
>
> _____

2.
> Have you begun
> the meeting yet?

> No, _____
>
> _____

3.
> Do we still have
> a lot to discuss?

> Yes, _____
>
> _____

4.
> Have we talked
> about the budget
> yet?

> Yes, _____
>
> _____

5.
> Have you hired
> any new
> employees for
> our new project?

> Yes, _____
>
> _____

6.
> Have any of the
> new employees
> begun work yet?

> No, _____
>
> _____

DICTATION   *Cover the sentences under each line. Write the dictation on the line as your teacher reads it to you. Then uncover the sentence and correct your writing.*

Dear Albert,

1. _____

   I've been thinking about what you said about stress.

2. _____

   I've already made an appointment to see my doctor for an examination.

3. _____

   I'm sure that the doctor will tell me not to work so hard anymore.

4. _____

   I'm already sixty years old and I'm still in good health.

5. _____

   I really should take it easy and take care of myself better.

6. _____

   How about lunch next Friday so that I can tell you what the doctor said?

   Bill Grant

READ

David has just filled out a W-4 form.

Form **W-4** (Rev. January 1982)	Department of the Treasury—Internal Revenue Service **Employee's Withholding Allowance Certificate**	OMB No. 1545-0010

1 Type or print your full name
David Juan Fernandez

Home address (number and street or rural route)
13 Theater Street #1

City or town, State, and ZIP code
Los Angeles, CA 90038

2 Your social security number
032-66-2526

3 Marital Status
☒ Single   ☐ Married
☐ Married, but withhold at higher Single rate
Note: If married, but legally separated, or spouse is a nonresident alien, check the Single box.

4 Total number of allowances you are claiming (from line F of the worksheet on page 2) . . . .

5 Additional amount, if any, you want deducted from each pay . . . . $ 0

6 I claim exemption from withholding because (see instructions and check boxes below that apply):
  a ☐ Last year I did not owe any Federal income tax and had a right to a full refund of **ALL** income tax withheld, **AND**
  b ☐ This year I do not expect to owe any Federal income tax and expect to have a right to a full refund of **ALL** income tax withheld. If both a and b apply, enter "EXEMPT" here . . . . . . ▶
  c If you entered "EXEMPT" on line 6b, are you a full-time student? . . . . ☐ Yes ☐ No

Under the penalties of perjury, I certify that I am entitled to the number of withholding allowances claimed on this certificate, or if claiming exemption from withholding, that I am entitled to claim the exempt status.

Employee's signature ▶ David Fernandez   Date ▶ April 9, 1984

7 Employer's name and address (including ZIP code) (FOR EMPLOYER'S USE ONLY)   **8** Office code   **9** Employer identification number

UNDERSTAND   *Circle **True** or **False**.*

1. "Spouse" means "husband or wife."   True   False
2. "Withhold" means "keep."   True   False
3. "Alien" means "non-citizen."   True   False
4. "Allowance" means the number of persons you support.   True   False

WRITE   *Fill out the W-4 form below.*

Form **W-4** (Rev. January 1982)	Department of the Treasury—Internal Revenue Service **Employee's Withholding Allowance Certificate**	OMB No. 1545-0010

1 Type or print your full name

Home address (number and street or rural route)

City or town, State, and ZIP code

2 Your social security number

3 Marital Status
☐ Single   ☐ Married
☐ Married, but withhold at higher Single rate
Note: If married, but legally separated, or spouse is a nonresident alien, check the Single box.

4 Total number of allowances you are claiming (from line F of the worksheet on page 2) . . . .

5 Additional amount, if any, you want deducted from each pay . . . . $

6 I claim exemption from withholding because (see instructions and check boxes below that apply):
  a ☐ Last year I did not owe any Federal income tax and had a right to a full refund of **ALL** income tax withheld, **AND**
  b ☐ This year I do not expect to owe any Federal income tax and expect to have a right to a full refund of **ALL** income tax withheld. If both a and b apply, enter "EXEMPT" here . . . . . . ▶
  c If you entered "EXEMPT" on line 6b, are you a full-time student? . . . . ☐ Yes ☐ No

Under the penalties of perjury, I certify that I am entitled to the number of withholding allowances claimed on this certificate, or if claiming exemption from withholding, that I am entitled to claim the exempt status.

Employee's signature ▶   Date ▶ 19

7 Employer's name and address (including ZIP code) (FOR EMPLOYER'S USE ONLY)   **8** Office code   **9** Employer identification number

PAIR PRACTICE   *Fold this page on the dotted line. Look at your side only.*

Student 1	Student 2

Student 1

Listen to your partner's questions and find the answers in the description of Mr. Gear below.

Bill Gear moved here in 1960. He's worked at the same company for over twenty years. He's planning to retire in a few years. He's married and has two married daughters in Washington. He has one grandchild.

Now ask your partner these questions about Mr. Grant.

1. How long has Mr. Grant been living in this city?

2. How long has Mr. Grant been working?

3. Does he still work for the same company?

4. Is he married?

5. Is he the vice-president of the company yet?

6. Has he retired yet?

7. What year was Mr. Grant born in?

Student 2

Ask your partner these questions about Mr. Gear.

1. Has Mr. Gear been living here long?

2. Has he been working long?

3. Is he still working?

4. Has he retired yet?

5. Is he married?

6. Do his children still live with him?

7. Does he have any grandchildren yet?

Listen to your partner's questions and find the answers in the description of Mr. Grant below.

Mr. Grant is sixty years old. He's widowed and has one son. He was born in this city and never left it. He started work when he was only 15 years old. He worked with Mr. Gear in the same company for many years. Now he has a position in another location of the same company. He would like to become vice-president of the company before he retires in a few years.

FOLD HERE

CHALLENGE   *What do you think are the most stressful situations for people? Read the list of life events. Put them in order of the most stressful (number 1) to least stressful (number 28). Compare your answers with the other students in your class.*

_____ death of a husband or wife	_____ buying a house
_____ divorce	_____ change in work responsibilities
_____ going to jail or prison	_____ son or daughter leaves home
_____ death of a family member	_____ begin or finish school
_____ personal injury or illness	_____ change in living conditions
_____ marriage	_____ change of personal habits
_____ being fired from a job	_____ trouble with the boss
_____ retirement	_____ change in work schedule or condition
_____ change in the health of a family member	_____ move to a new home or new country
_____ pregnancy	
_____ sex difficulties	_____ change schools
_____ a new family member	_____ change in social activities
_____ change in financial condition	_____ fewer family get-togethers
_____ death of a close friend	_____ change in eating habits
_____ change of occupation	

GROUP DISCUSSION

1. What is stress? Define it. Use a dictionary.

2. Is all stress bad? Why or why not?

3. What other kinds of stressful situations can you name that are not in the list above?

4. Discuss some of the symptoms of stress:

weight problem	no sleep	difficulty in breathing
high blood pressure	always tired	crying
loss of appetite	headaches	sex difficulties
desire to eat a lot	need of medicine daily	nervous energy

5. What can people do to help themselves manage stress better?

6. What kinds of stressful situations have you had in your life? How did you handle them?

7. How do you manage day-to-day stress?

WORD BUILDING   Past Participles as Adjectives

- *Past participles (regular and irregular forms) are often used as adjectives.*

EXAMPLES

1. Mr. Fisher is a <u>retired</u> person.

2. Mr. Gear is a happily <u>married</u> man.

3. The secretary tried to use a <u>broken</u> typewriter.

- *Past participles preceded by the negative prefix* **un-** *are very often used as adjectives, too.*

EXAMPLES

1. The bosses talked about some <u>unfinished</u> projects.

2. They also discussed some <u>unpaid</u> bills.

3. The secretary handed Mr. Gear an <u>unopened</u> letter.

WRITE   *Fill in the blanks with the correct past participle form of the verb in parentheses.*

1. Mr. Fisher is an eighty-year-old (retire) _____ man who now lives with his son in Ohio.

2. David Fernandez has a job; now he's an (employ) _____ person.

3. Mr. Grant took out a (write) _____ report from his briefcase and read it to everybody.

4. The report said that the company reported some (lose) _____ or (steal) _____ equipment to the police.

5. Mr. Grant wanted to buy some new equipment, but the other bosses decided to buy some (use) _____ equipment because it was cheaper.

WRITE   *Choose some of the words below to write five sentences in which the past participles are used as adjectives.*

unwanted	unchanged	unknown	unread
unanswered	unwritten	unforgotten	unseen
unheard	uncooked	unbroken	unwashed

1. _____

2. _____

3. _____

4. _____

5. _____

CHALLENGE   *Make a list of other past participles you can use as adjectives.*

HOW MUCH IS THAT IN FEET AND INCHES?

COMPETENCIES	• Understanding American Standard Measures
	• Converting Metric to American Standard Measures
	• Doing Basic Math
GRAMMAR	• *it takes*...
	• The Preposition *by*
VOCABULARY	• Adjectives Used in Measurements
	• Lines and Shapes
WORD BUILDING	• The Prefix *dis-*

LISTEN

Mr. Gear is introducing David Fernandez and another new employee, Boris Kubis, to their section manager.

Mr. Gear: This is your new section manager, Mr. Ed Brady. He'll get you started.

    Ed: First, let's get you a uniform. What size you do wear?

  David: I wear a medium.

  Boris: I don't know what size I take.

    Ed: What's your height?

  Boris: I'm 179 centimeters tall.

    Ed: How much is that in feet and inches?

  David: That's about 5 feet 11 1/2 inches.

    Ed: How much do you weigh?

  Boris: I weigh 82 kilos.

    Ed: How much is that in pounds?

  David: That's about 180 pounds.

    Ed: I think you take a large. Try this on.

UNDERSTAND   *Circle True, False, or We don't know.*

1. David knows his uniform size.	True	False	We don't know.
2. David wears a larger size than Boris.	True	False	We don't know.
3. David weighs less than 150 pounds.	True	False	We don't know.
4. Boris doesn't know his height and weight.	True	False	We don't know.
5. David knows how to convert kilos to pounds.	True	False	We don't know.

READ

WEIGHT

16 ounces (oz.) =
1 pound (lb.)

Pounds	/ Kilograms
1	0.5*
2	0.9
3	1.4
4	1.8
5	2.3
6	2.7
7	3.2
8	3.6
9	4.1
10	4.5

1 pound =
.45 kilograms (kg.)

Pounds	/ Kilograms
11	5.0
12	5.4
13	5.9
14	6.4
15	6.8
16	7.3
17	7.7
18	8.2
19	8.6
20	9.1

1 kilogram =
2.2 pounds

Pounds	/ Kilograms
25	11.34
30	13.61
40	18.14
50	22.68
60	27.22
70	31.75
80	36.29
90	40.82
100	45.36

PAIR PRACTICE
Talk with another student. Convert the kilogram weights below to approximate weights in pounds. Use the table above.

Student 1: How much does .... weigh?
Student 2: He/It weighs about .... pounds.

1. Boris
82 kg.

2. Ed
78 kg.

3. David
68 kg.

4. a ladder
5 kg.

5. Mr. Gear
77 kg.

6. a uniform
1/2 kg.

7. a paint brush
1 kg.

8. a tool box
10 kg.

---

* These numbers have been rounded off.

PAIR PRACTICE   *Convert the pounds below to approximate weights in kilograms.*

Student 1: How much does .... weigh?
Student 2: It weighs about .... kilograms.

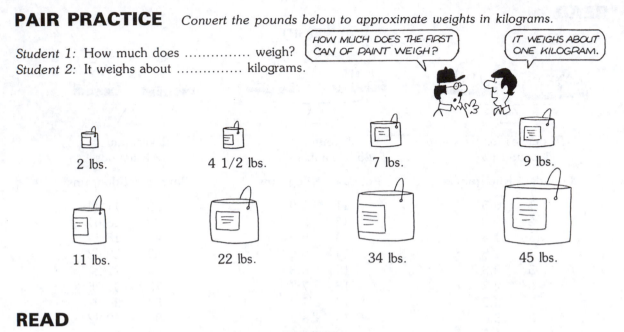

2 lbs.   4 1/2 lbs.   7 lbs.   9 lbs.

11 lbs.   22 lbs.   34 lbs.   45 lbs.

READ

HEIGHT

CONVERSION FACTORS		
When you know	Multiply by	To find
inches	2.54	centimeters
feet	30.48	centimeters
centimeters	.39	inches
meters	3.28	feet

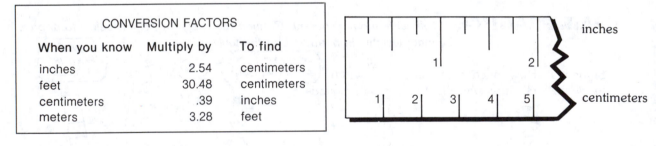

1 inch (in.) = 2.54 centimeters (cm.)   12 inches = 1 foot = 30 1/2 cm.

Note: We also use the symbols (') for feet and (") for inches.

Feet, Inches/Centimeters		Feet, Inches/Centimeters		Feet, Inches/Centimeters	
4'	120*	4' 9"	143	5' 6"	165
4' 1"	123	4' 10"	145	5' 7"	168
4' 2"	125	4' 11"	148	5' 8"	170
4' 3"	128	5'	151	5' 9"	173
4' 4"	130	5' 1"	153	5' 10"	175
4' 5"	133	5' 2"	155	5' 11"	178
4' 6"	135	5' 3"	158	6'	180
4' 7"	138	5' 4"	160	6' 1"	183
4' 8"	140	5' 5"	163	6' 2"	186

* These numbers have been rounded off.

PAIR PRACTICE

Convert the centimeters below to approximate heights in feet and inches. Use the table on the previous page.

Student 1: How tall is ....?
Student 2: He's/She's about .... feet
.... inches tall.

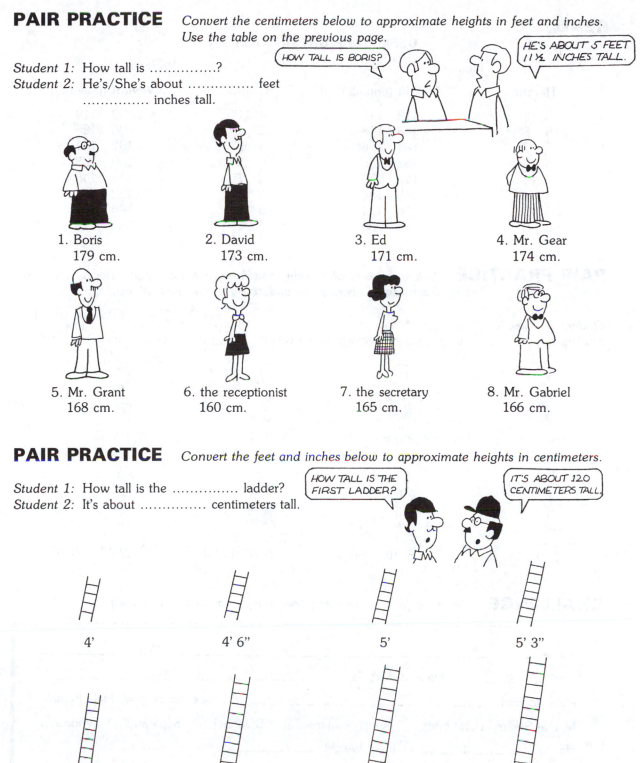

HOW TALL IS BORIS?

HE'S ABOUT 5 FEET 11½ INCHES TALL.

1. Boris
179 cm.

2. David
173 cm.

3. Ed
171 cm.

4. Mr. Gear
174 cm.

5. Mr. Grant
168 cm.

6. the receptionist
160 cm.

7. the secretary
165 cm.

8. Mr. Gabriel
166 cm.

PAIR PRACTICE

Convert the feet and inches below to approximate heights in centimeters.

Student 1: How tall is the .... ladder?
Student 2: It's about .... centimeters tall.

HOW TALL IS THE FIRST LADDER?

IT'S ABOUT 120 CENTIMETERS TALL.

4'

4' 6"

5'

5' 3"

5' 6"

5' 9"

6'

6' 3"

READ

DESIRED HEIGHT AND WEIGHT

Men		Women	
Height	**Weight (pounds)**	**Height**	**Weight (pounds)**
5' 3"	112 - 141	4' 11"	92 - 119
5' 5"	118 - 148	5' 1"	96 - 125
5' 7"	124 - 156	5' 3"	102 - 131
5' 9"	132 - 166	5' 5"	108 - 138
5' 11"	140 - 174	5' 7"	114 - 146
6' 1"	148 - 184	5' 9"	122 - 154
6' 3"	156 - 194	5' 11"	130 - 163
6' 5"	164 - 204	6' 1"	138 - 173

PAIR PRACTICE

Below are some of the other employees in the company. Decide if they are **overweight**, **average**, *or* **underweight**. *Use table above.*

Student 1: How is ....?
Student 2: .... is overweight/average/underweight.

1. Suzie
   4' 11"/110 lbs.

2. Ralph
   5' 9"/174 lbs.

3. Bert
   6' 1"/140 lbs.

4. Ellen
   5' 5"/120 lbs.

5. Jack
   5' 9"/131 lbs.

6. Ben
   5' 10"/150 lbs.

7. Sid
   5' 8"/190 lbs.

8. Linda
   5' 6"/100 lbs.

CHALLENGE

Fill in the form below with personal information about yourself.

Name: _____ Date: _____

Age: _____ Date of Birth: _____

Place of Birth: _____ Sex: (circle one) Male Female

Marital Status: (circle one)   Single   Married   Divorced   Separated   Widowed

Height: _____ ft. _____ in.   Weight: _____ lbs.

Color of Hair: _____   Color of Eyes: _____

READ

Ed is giving David and Boris their first assignment.

Ed: We have to do some painting at a new job site across town. Help me put this equipment in the truck.

David: What kind of painting job is it?

Ed: It's a huge new apartment building.

Boris: How long will it take us to finish the job?

Ed: It'll take us about a week to do the job.

David: How far is the site?

Ed: About 5 miles away.

Boris: How long does it take to get there?

Ed: Normally it takes about 15 minutes, but yesterday it took me more than half an hour.

Boris: Why did it take you so long?

Ed: I went in rush-hour traffic.

UNDERSTAND   *Circle **True**, **False**, or **We don't know**.*

1. David, Boris, and Ed are going to work at the main office of the company.   True   False   We don't know.

2. The job site is only a few minutes away.   True   False   We don't know.

3. It usually takes less time to go from one place to another in rush-hour traffic.   True   False   We don't know.

4. It will take them 15 minutes to get to the job site.   True   False   We don't know.

5. The new job site is a new office building.   True   False   We don't know.

CHALLENGE   *Name the equipment that they are putting in the truck.*

GRAMMAR *it takes...*

• We use the expression **it takes...** to express the amount of time that is necessary to complete an action. The amount of time is followed by an infinitive.

EXAMPLES		Take		Infinitive	
How long will	it	**take**	us	**to finish**	the job?
	It 'll	**take**	us about a week	**to do**	the job.
How long does	it	**take**		**to get**	there?
	It	**takes**	about 15 minutes	**to get**	there.
	It	**took**	me half an hour	**to get**	there.

READ *Make logical complete sentences with the words in the box.*

It	takes	us too long	to finish	here.
	's taking	me 10 minutes	to understand	the work.
	will take	a few minutes	to do	the directions.
	took	four years	to walk	English.
	has taken	a few weeks	to learn	the job.

READ *Make logical questions with the words in the box. Then answer them.*

How long	does		take	to go	a better job?
	will	it	taken	to walk	English well?
	has			to learn	home from here?
	did			to finish	to the market?
				to find	a chapter of this book?

PAIR PRACTICE *Use the phrases below. Answer in your own words.*

Student 1: How long does it take to ....?
Student 2: It takes ....

1. get to work or school
2. fill out an application
3. become a citizen
4. find a job
5. make good friends
6. get home from here
7. learn to speak well
8. send a letter to another country
9. receive a letter from another country
10. ....

HOW LONG DOES IT TAKE TO GET TO WORK?

IT TAKES FIFTEEN MINUTES.

READ

Ed, David, and Boris are talking on their way to the job site.

David: Where did you live before you came here?
Boris: In New York.
David: How far is that from here?
Boris: About 4,500 kilometers.
Ed: How many miles is that?
David: About 2,800 miles.

UNDERSTAND   *Circle* **True, False,** *or* **We don't know.**

1. Ed lived in New York.	True	False	We don't know.
2. New York is 3,000 kilometers from Los Angeles.	True	False	We don't know.
3. Ed doesn't know how to calculate miles from kilometers.	True	False	We don't know.

READ

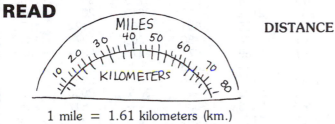

DISTANCE

1 mile = 1.61 kilometers (km.)

1 kilometer = .62 miles

Miles / Kilometers		Miles / Kilometers	
1	1.6	6	9.7
2	3.2	7	11.1
3	4.8	8	12.9
4	6.4	9	14.5
5	8.0	10	16.1

CONVERSION FACTORS		
When you know	**Multiply by**	**To find**
miles	1.61	kilometers
kilometers	.62	miles

PAIR PRACTICE   *Calculate miles from the kilometers below. Use the tables above.*

Student 1: How many miles are there in ....?
Student 2: There are about .... miles.

HOW MANY MILES ARE THERE IN 8 KILOMETERS?

THERE ARE ABOUT 5 MILES.

1. 8 kilometers   4. 15 kilometers   7. 50 kilometers
2. 9 kilometers   5. 20 kilometers   8. 75 kilometers
3. 3 kilometers   6. 25 kilometers   9. 100 kilometers

PAIR PRACTICE   *Calculate kilometers from the miles below.*

Student 1: How many kilometers are there in ....?
Student 2: There are about .... kilometers.

1. 1 mile   4. 10 miles   7. 50 miles
2. 2 miles   5. 20 miles   8. 75 miles
3. 5 miles   6. 25 miles   9. 100 miles

HOW MANY KILOMETERS ARE THERE IN ONE MILE?

THERE ARE ABOUT 1½ KILOMETERS.

READ

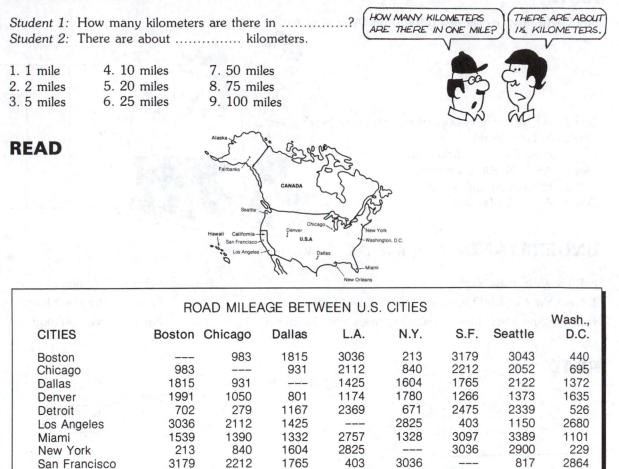

ROAD MILEAGE BETWEEN U.S. CITIES

CITIES	Boston	Chicago	Dallas	L.A.	N.Y.	S.F.	Seattle	Wash., D.C.
Boston	---	983	1815	3036	213	3179	3043	440
Chicago	983	---	931	2112	840	2212	2052	695
Dallas	1815	931	---	1425	1604	1765	2122	1372
Denver	1991	1050	801	1174	1780	1266	1373	1635
Detroit	702	279	1167	2369	671	2475	2339	526
Los Angeles	3036	2112	1425	---	2825	403	1150	2680
Miami	1539	1390	1332	2757	1328	3097	3389	1101
New York	213	840	1604	2825	---	3036	2900	229
San Francisco	3179	2212	1765	403	3036	---	817	2864
Seattle	3043	2052	2122	1150	2900	817	---	2755
Washington, D.C.	440	695	1372	2680	229	2864	2755	---

PAIR PRACTICE   *Find the road distances between the American cities above.*

THEY'RE 2,825 MILES APART.

Student 1: What's the distance between .... and ....?
Student 2: They're .... miles apart.

WHAT'S THE DISTANCE BETWEEN NEW YORK AND LOS ANGELES?

CHALLENGE   *Figure out the distances in kilometers between the cities below.*

Los Angeles to New York: _____ kilometers
Chicago to San Francisco: _____ kilometers
Boston to Miami: _____ kilometers

CHALLENGE   *In which states are the cities in the table above?*

READ

David and Boris are beginning to paint.

David: Please hand me the paint brush over there.
Boris: Which one?
David: The narrow two-inch brush.
Boris: Two inches?
David: Give me the brush that's five centimeters wide.
Boris: There are two of them. Do you want the thin or thick one?
David: Give me the thick one.
Boris: Here you are.

UNDERSTAND *Circle **True**, **False**, or **We don't know**.*

1. There are seven brushes on the floor.	True	False	We don't know.
2. The brush that David wants is thick.	True	False	We don't know.
3. There are three narrow three-inch brushes on the floor.	True	False	We don't know.
4. Boris knows how to convert centimeters to inches.	True	False	We don't know.

READ

INCHES AND CENTIMETERS

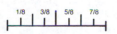

1 inch (in.) = 2.54 centimeters (cm.)   1 centimeter = 0.3937 inch

The most common divisions of an inch are in halves, quarters, eighths, and sixteenths.

Halves

Quarters

Eighths

Sixteenths

CONVERSION FACTORS		
When you know	Multiply by	To find
inches	2.54	centimeters
millimeters	0.04	inches
centimeters	0.39	inches

READ   *Read the sizes of the paint brushes and wrenches below.*

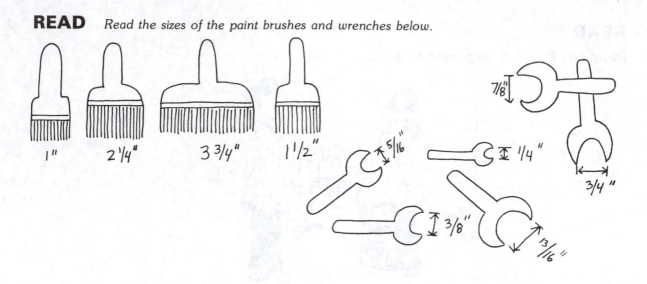

PAIR PRACTICE   *Calculate centimeters from the inches below. Use the ruler.*

Student 1: How many centimeters are there in ....?
Student 2: There are about .... centimeters.

1. 2 inches
2. 3 inches
3. 3 1/2 inches

4. 4 inches
5. 4 1/4 inches
6. 5 inches

7. 5 3/4 inches
8. 6 inches
9. 6 5/8 inches

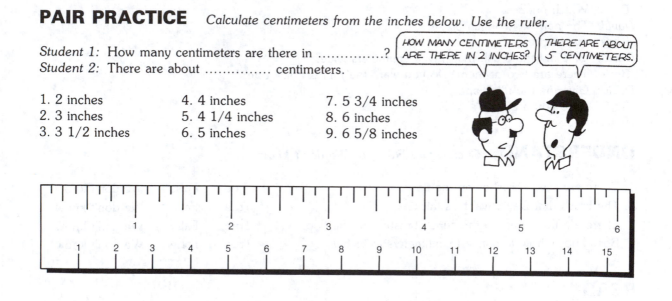

PAIR PRACTICE   *Calculate inches from the centimeters below. Use the ruler above.*

Student 1: How many inches are there in ....?
Student 2: There are about .... inches.

1. 5 centimeters
2. 3 centimeters
3. 6 centimeters

4. 8 centimeters
5. 8 1/2 centimeters
6. 10 centimeters

7. 11 centimeters
8. 12 centimeters
9. 15 centimeters

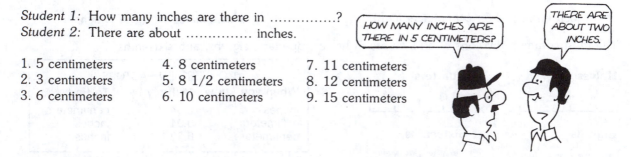

PAIR PRACTICE   *Measure the length and width of the items below in inches.*

Student 1: How long/wide/thick is the ....?
Student 2: It's .... inches long/wide/thick.

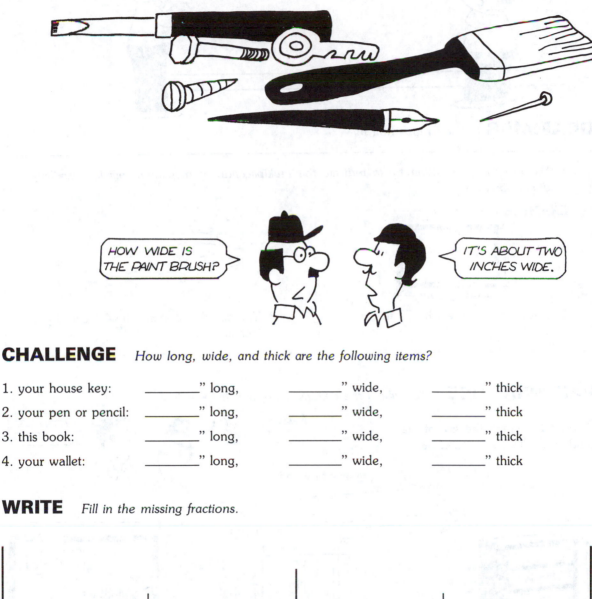

CHALLENGE   *How long, wide, and thick are the following items?*

1. your house key: _____" long,   _____" wide,   _____" thick

2. your pen or pencil: _____" long,   _____" wide,   _____" thick

3. this book: _____" long,   _____" wide,   _____" thick

4. your wallet: _____" long,   _____" wide,   _____" thick

WRITE   *Fill in the missing fractions.*

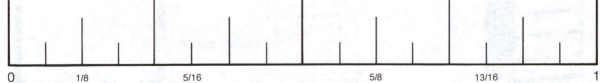

0   1/8   5/16   5/8   13/16   1

READ

GRAMMAR   The Preposition *by*

- *We use the preposition* **by** *to indicate the multiplication of measurements in describing dimensions.*

EXAMPLES

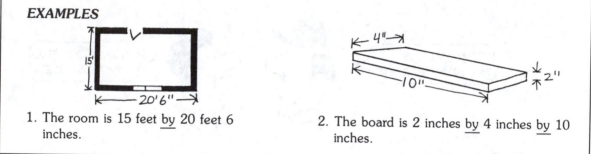

1. The room is 15 feet <u>by</u> 20 feet 6 inches.

2. The board is 2 inches <u>by</u> 4 inches <u>by</u> 10 inches.

PAIR PRACTICE   *Talk about the dimensions of the things below.*

Student 1: What's the size of the ....?
Student 2: It's .... by ....

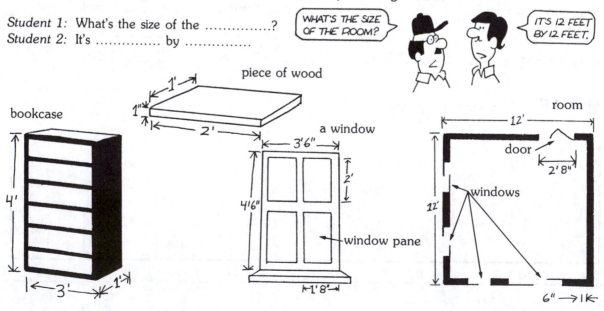

READ

It's after lunch. Ed is telling David and Boris where to hang some wallpaper.

   Ed: Here's some wallpaper.
David: There are so many different designs and patterns!
Boris: How do we know where to hang them all?
   Ed: Here's a list. It indicates where to hang each pattern.

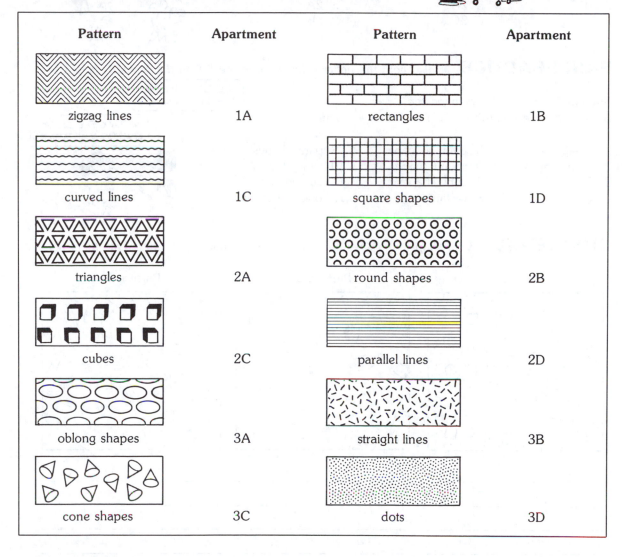

Pattern	Apartment	Pattern	Apartment
zigzag lines	1A	rectangles	1B
curved lines	1C	square shapes	1D
triangles	2A	round shapes	2B
cubes	2C	parallel lines	2D
oblong shapes	3A	straight lines	3B
cone shapes	3C	dots	3D

UNDERSTAND   *Circle **True**, **False**, or **We don't know**.*

1. There are ten different patterns.	True	False	We don't know.
2. Cubes are shapes.	True	False	We don't know.
3. A rectangle has four straight lines.	True	False	We don't know.

PAIR PRACTICE

Talk about what patterns of wallpaper go in the apartments below. Use the list on the previous page.

Student 1: What pattern do we hang in apartment ....?
Student 2: We hang the .... in apartment ....

1. 3A   4. 1A   7. 1C
2. 1B   5. 2B   8. 2A
3. 2C   6. 3C   9. 3B

PAIR PRACTICE

Talk about the patterns below. Use the list on the previous page.

Student 1: Where do we hang the ....
Student 2: We hang the .... in apartment ....

1. zigzag lines   5. triangle shapes   9. parallel lines
2. cone shapes   6. round shapes   10. straight lines
3. dots   7. cube shapes   11. curved lines
4. squares   8. rectangles   12. oblong shapes

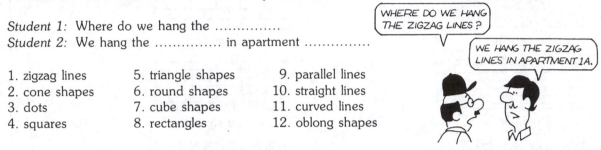

CHALLENGE

What shapes and lines are in the three wallpaper patterns? Write them below.

Pattern 1   Pattern 2   Pattern 3

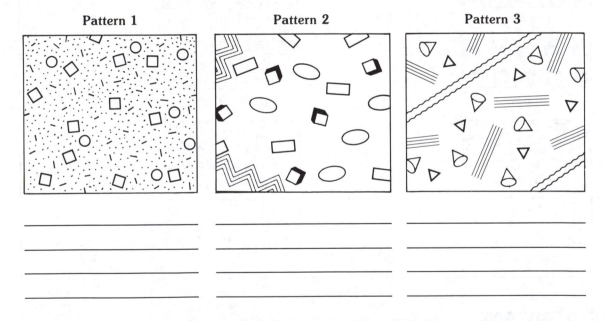

_____   _____   _____
_____   _____   _____
_____   _____   _____
_____   _____   _____

CHALLENGE

How many objects can you describe with the shapes and lines above?

EXAMPLES   1. A ruler is a long rectangle.   2. The clock has a round shape.

READ

David and Boris are calculating the square footage of a wall.

Boris: How many rolls do we need for this wall?
David: I don't know. What's the size of the wall?
Boris: It's 8 by 12. How many square feet is that?
David: It's 96 square feet.
Boris: How many square feet does a roll cover?
David: 50 square feet.

UNDERSTAND   *Circle **True**, **False**, or **We don't know**.*

1. They need two rolls of wallpaper.	True	False	We don't know.
2. The wall is eight by twelve inches.	True	False	We don't know.
3. Two rolls of wallpaper can cover one hundred square feet.	True	False	We don't know.

READ

We calculate square feet (sq. ft.) by multiplying the height by the width.

EXAMPLE

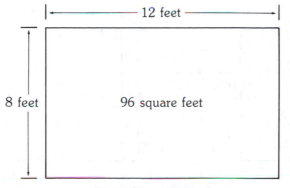

8' x 12' = 96 sq. ft.

PAIR PRACTICE   *Calculate square feet and square inches from the dimensions below.*

Student 1: How many square feet/inches is ....?
Student 2: It's ....,. square feet/inches.

1. 8' x 12'   4. 9" x 12"   7. 3 1/2" x 2"
2. 8" x 11"   5. 10 1/2" x 8'   8. 20' x 30'
3. 10' x 8'   6. 4' x 6'   9. ....

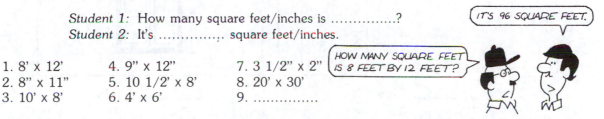

WRITE   *Calculate the square footage for the following areas.*

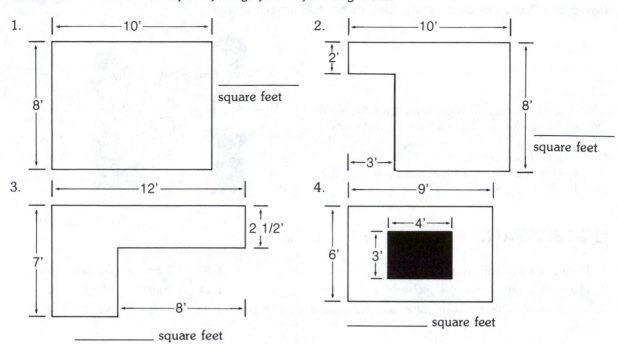

WRITE   *How many rolls of wallpaper do David and Boris need for the walls below? Each roll covers 50 square feet.*

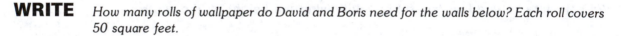

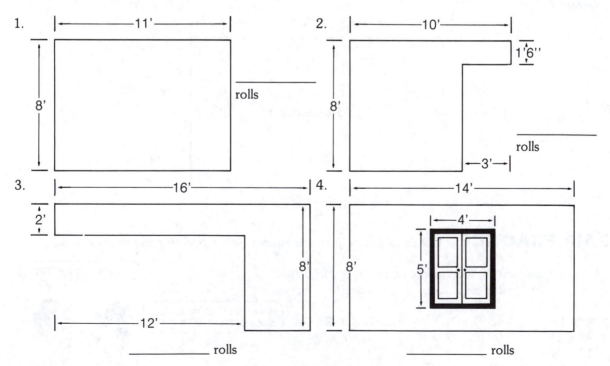

PAIR PRACTICE   *Fold the page on the dotted line. Look at your side only.*

Student 1	Student 2

Student 1

Listen to your partner's questions and find the answers in the picture below.

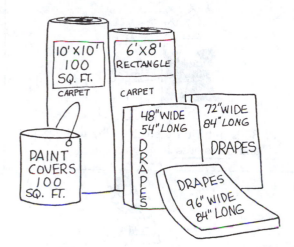

Now ask your partner these questions.

1. What do you see in the picture?
2. What are the sizes of the wrenches?
3. Will any of the wrenches fit a 7/8" bolt?
4. What size is the narrower brush?
5. How wide are the paint brushes?
6. How long are the nails?
7. Are any of the nails longer than an inch and a half?

Student 2

Ask your partner these questions.

1. What do you see in the picture?
2. What are the sizes of the carpets?
3. What are the shapes of the carpets?
4. Can the square carpet be used to cover a 9' x 12' floor?
5. What are the sizes of the drapes?
6. Will any of the drapes cover a window that is 68" wide and 80" high?
7. Will the can of paint cover a wall that is 15' x 8'?

Now listen to your partner's questions and find the answers in the picture below. Use a ruler if you have one.

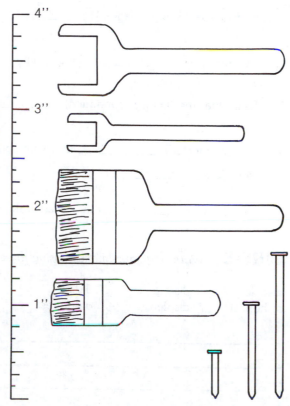

WORD BUILDING   The Prefix *dis-*

- We use **dis-** as a negative prefix with verbs and adjectives to mean **not**, **the opposite of**, or **the absence of**.

EXAMPLES

1. David disliked the wallpaper.

2. Boris put a dirty brush in the white paint and discolored it.

WRITE   Add the prefix **dis-** to the words in parentheses.

1. Ed thinks that Boris is a (organized) *disorganized* person.

2. Boris and David never (agree) _____.

3. Ed (approves) _____ of long lunches.

4. Ed said that the factory (continued) _____ this kind of wallpaper.

5. David (connected) _____ the paint sprayer, and then he
   (assembled) _____ it.

6. Ed (believed) _____ that it was broken.

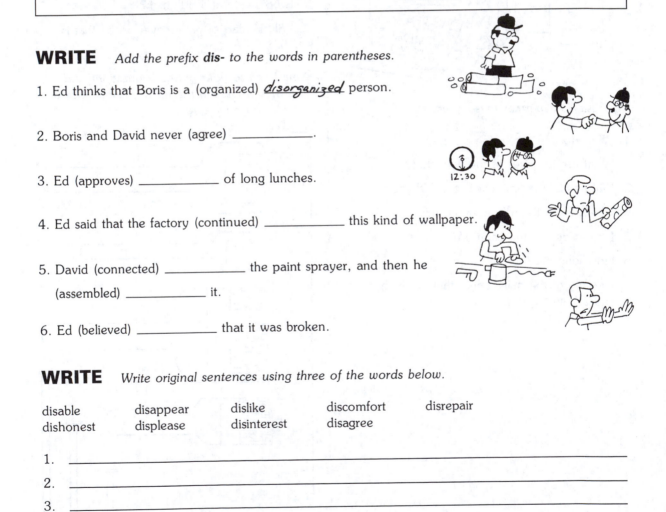

WRITE   Write original sentences using three of the words below.

disable	disappear	dislike	discomfort	disrepair
dishonest	displease	disinterest	disagree	

1. _____

2. _____

3. _____

14

WHAT HAS TO BE DONE FIRST?

COMPETENCIES	• Planning and Opening a Business
	• Reading Newspaper Headlines
GRAMMAR	• The Passive Voice
	• Modals and Auxiliary Verbs in the Passive Voice
	• The Agent in the Passive Voice
VOCABULARY	• Business Terms
WORD BUILDING	• Past Participles Ending in -n or -en

LISTEN

David Fernandez and Paul Green are talking at the adult school before class.

Paul: How's your new job?

David: Great! What have you been up to?

Paul: I'm planning to open an ice cream shop.

David: Oh, really? When?

Paul: It'll be opened in a month or so.

David: Where is it located?

Paul: The location hasn't been chosen yet. I looked at a vacant store downtown yesterday, but I was told that it was already rented. I'm going to look at a store in a shopping center not far from here tomorrow. It's being built now, but it won't be finished until next month. It's located near a park and a lot of people go there on the weekends.

David: Have you spoken to Tan and Lan Tran about this?

Paul: No, I haven't. Why?

David: They've recently opened a new restaurant. I'm sure they could give you some valuable advice.

Paul: I will.

David: I wish you a lot of luck in your new business. If you need any help, let me know.

UNDERSTAND   *Circle True, False, or We don't know.*

1. "What have you been up to?" means "What have you been doing?"   True   False   We don't know.

2. The store will be located near a park.   True   False   We don't know.

3. Paul Green has enough experience to open his own business.   True   False   We don't know.

4. A new shopping center is being built.   True   False   We don't know.

5. Paul Green knows Tan and Lan Tran.   True   False   We don't know.

6. David wants to help Paul in his business.   True   False   We don't know.

GRAMMAR   The Passive Voice

- *We form the passive voice by using the verb* **to be** *in the appropriate tense and the* **past participle** *of the main verb. (See the list of irregular past participles at the end of Chapter 11.)*

EXAMPLES

	to be	**Past Participle**		
It	**is**	**located**	near a park.	(present habitual)
It	**is being**	**built**	now.	(present continuous)
It	**was**	**rented.**		(simple past)
I	**was**	**told**	that.	(simple past)
The location	**hasn't been**	**chosen**	yet.	(present perfect)
It	**will be**	**opened**	in a month.	(future)
It	**won't be**	**finished**	until next month.	(future)

- *Only transitive verbs (verbs that are followed by an object) are used in the passive. We cannot use verbs such as* **come** *and* **happen** *in the passive.*

READ   *Make logical complete sentences with the words in the box.*

I	is	finished	about Tan Tran's restaurant.
It	was	seen	soon.
The location	will be	told	near a park.
The store	has been	opened	in an excellent location.
People	have been	built	at the park on the weekends.
They	is being	located	ice cream.
Paul Green	are being	sold	recently.

READ   *Make questions from the words in the box. Then answer them.*

What	is	opened?
	is being	built?
	has been	sold?
	will be	done?
	was	rented?
		started?
		made?

PAIR PRACTICE   *Talk with another student. Practice the passive. Use the phrases below.*

Student 1: Is/Are ....?
Student 2: Yes, ... / No, ...

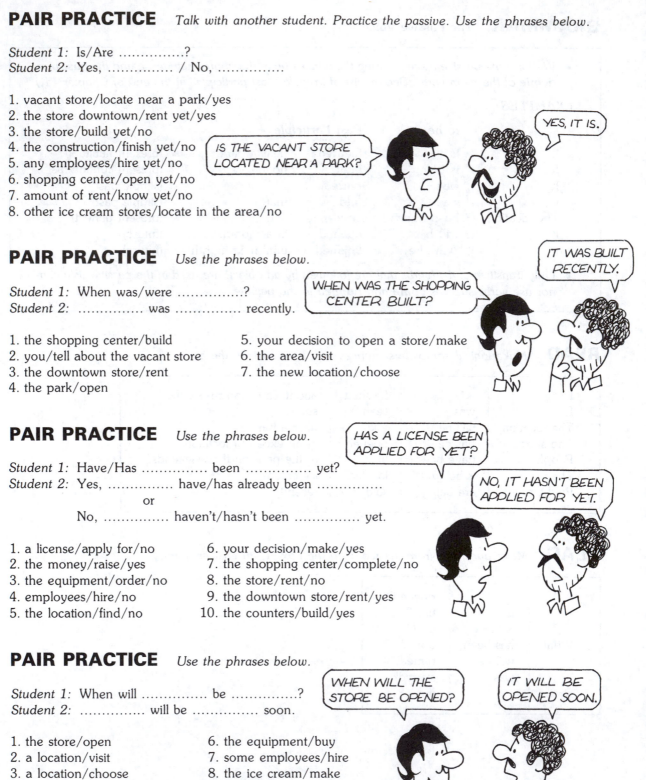

1. vacant store/locate near a park/yes
2. the store downtown/rent yet/yes
3. the store/build yet/no
4. the construction/finish yet/no
5. any employees/hire yet/no
6. shopping center/open yet/no
7. amount of rent/know yet/no
8. other ice cream stores/locate in the area/no

IS THE VACANT STORE LOCATED NEAR A PARK?

YES, IT IS.

PAIR PRACTICE   *Use the phrases below.*

Student 1: When was/were ....?
Student 2: .... was .... recently.

WHEN WAS THE SHOPPING CENTER BUILT?

IT WAS BUILT RECENTLY.

1. the shopping center/build
2. you/tell about the vacant store
3. the downtown store/rent
4. the park/open

5. your decision to open a store/make
6. the area/visit
7. the new location/choose

PAIR PRACTICE   *Use the phrases below.*

Student 1: Have/Has .... been .... yet?
Student 2: Yes, ... have/has already been ....
            or
            No, ... haven't/hasn't been .... yet.

HAS A LICENSE BEEN APPLIED FOR YET?

NO, IT HASN'T BEEN APPLIED FOR YET.

1. a license/apply for/no
2. the money/raise/yes
3. the equipment/order/no
4. employees/hire/no
5. the location/find/no

6. your decision/make/yes
7. the shopping center/complete/no
8. the store/rent/no
9. the downtown store/rent/yes
10. the counters/build/yes

PAIR PRACTICE   *Use the phrases below.*

Student 1: When will .... be ....?
Student 2: .... will be .... soon.

WHEN WILL THE STORE BE OPENED?

IT WILL BE OPENED SOON.

1. the store/open
2. a location/visit
3. a location/choose
4. the vacant store/inspect
5. the shopping center/finish

6. the equipment/buy
7. some employees/hire
8. the ice cream/make
9. the materials/order
10. the store/name

PAIR PRACTICE   *Change the sentences below from the active to the passive.*

Student 1: ....
Student 2: What did you say?
Student 1: ....

SOMEBODY HAS RENTED THE DOWNTOWN STORE.

THE DOWNTOWN STORE HAS BEEN RENTED.

WHAT DID YOU SAY?

1. Somebody has rented the downtown store.
2. Somebody told me about a vacant store.
3. Somebody is building a shopping center near here.
4. Somebody will rent the vacant store.
5. Somebody has opened an ice cream store downtown.
6. Somebody put an ad about another location in the paper.

WRITE   *Fill in the blanks with the correct past participle form of the verb in parentheses.*

Paul Green is talking to Mrs. Joan Reynolds, the owner of the shopping center.

Paul: Hello, I'm Paul Green.

Joan: I'm (please) *pleased* to meet you.

Paul: I was (tell) _____ about your shopping center and I'm (interest)

_____ in this vacant store. It's (locate) _____ in a very nice

area. How much is the rent?

Joan: It's $1,200, and a one-year lease and a deposit are (require) _____.

Paul: I'm (surprise) _____ that it isn't more.

Joan: What kind of business are you planning to open?

Paul: An ice cream store.

Joan: Will the ice cream be (make) _____ and (sell) _____ here?

Paul: Yes, it will.

Joan: What kind of fixtures will be (build) _____?

Paul: A few shelves and a counter will be (add) _____ and some equipment

will be (keep) _____ in the back room if that's OK.

Joan: That sounds fine to me! The place is yours if you want it.

READ

Paul Green is talking to Tan and Lan Tran.

Paul: What has to be done?

Tan: Equipment has to be purchased. Some used equipment ought to be bought to save money. Materials have to be ordered. Some store fixtures have to be built.

Lan: The fixtures could be built by David. Advertisements should be put in the paper.

Paul: Can everything be done by the first of the month?

Tan: I'm sure that everything can be done by then.

UNDERSTAND   *Circle **True**, **False**, or **We don't know**.*

1. Paul doesn't believe that everything can be done soon.	True	False	We don't know.
2. David could help Paul.	True	False	We don't know.
3. The fixtures ought to be built by Paul to save some money.	True	False	We don't know.
4. New equipment should be bought to save money.	True	False	We don't know.

GRAMMAR   Modals in the Passive Voice

> • *We form the passive voice with modals by placing the **modal** or **auxiliary verb** before **be** and **the past participle**.*
>
> **EXAMPLES**
>
> | | Modal/Auxiliary | be | Past Participle | |
> |---|---|---|---|---|
> | Equipment | has to | be | purchased. | |
> | Used equipment | ought to | be | bought. | |
> | Materials | have to | be | ordered. | |
> | Fixtures | have to | be | built. | |
> | The fixtures | could | be | built | by David. |
> | Advertisements | should | be | put | in the paper. |
> | Everything | can | be | done | soon. |

READ   *Make logical complete sentences with the words in the box.*

Bills			hired.
Advertisements	have to		done.
People	has to		paid.
The ice cream	can		written.
Licenses	could	be	bought.
The rent	ought to		made.
Everything	should		gotten.
Equipment			ordered.

PAIR PRACTICE   *Practice using modals in the passive voice. Use the phrases below.*

Student 1: What has to be done?
Student 2: .... have to/has to be ....

1. store/inspect
2. everything/clean
3. equipment/find
4. telephone/install
5. electricity/turn on
6. gas/connect
7. rental deposit/pay
8. store/paint
9. signs/make
10. licenses/get

WHAT HAS TO BE DONE?

THE STORE HAS TO BE INSPECTED.

PAIR PRACTICE   *Use the words below. Answer the questions as best you can.*

Student 1: Where can .... be ....?
Student 2: .... can be ....

1. used equipment/find
2. equipment/use
3. equipment/locate
4. employees/find
5. employees/train
6. ice cream/make
7. supplies/buy
8. signs/make
9. licenses/get
10. fixtures/build

WHERE CAN USED EQUIPMENT BE FOUND?

IT CAN BE FOUND IN A RESTAURANT SUPPLY STORE.

PAIR PRACTICE   *Use the words below.*

Student 1: Where should the .... be ....?
Student 2: .... should be in the sales area/back room.

1. cash register/keep
2. the counter/build
3. the sign/hang
4. refrigerator/put
5. materials/store
6. ice cream/make
7. tables and chairs/set up
8. ice cream machine/place
9. telephone/install
10. ....

WHERE SHOULD THE CASH REGISTER BE KEPT?

IT SHOULD BE KEPT IN THE SALES AREA.

WRITE   *Help Paul Green make a list of what must be done. Complete the sentences below with a modal in the passive.*

THINGS THAT HAVE TO BE DONE

1. Equipment *has to be bought.*
2. Bills _____
3. The rent _____
4. Supplies _____
5. The signs _____
6. The back room of the store _____
7. The sales area _____
8. Salespersons _____
9. Problems _____
10. A name _____

DICTATION   *Cover the sentences under each line. Write the dictation on the line as your teacher reads it to you. Then uncover the sentences and correct your writing.*

Dear David,

1. _____
   I rented the vacant store that is located near the park.
2. _____
   My ice cream store will be opened on the first of the month.
3. _____
   The construction is finished and I can move in now.
4. _____
   The inside of the store must be painted.
5. _____
   Some shelves and other fixtures must be built.
6. _____
   Can you help me? Of course, you will be paid for your work.
7. _____
   Let me know as soon as possible.

   Paul Green

READ

David, Tan, and Paul are talking.

Paul: Did you get my note?

David: Yes, I did, and I'd be happy to help you.

Paul: I asked Sami Hamati to help, too. The work can be done by all of us.

Tan: Who is going to manage the store?

Paul: The store will be managed and operated by me.

Tan: Will you make the ice cream, too?

Paul: No, the ice cream will be made and sold by two employees.

David: When must everything be done?

Paul: Everything must be done before the first of the month when the store will be inspected by the health department.

David: Don't worry, everything will be done in no time.

UNDERSTAND   *Circle **True**, **False**, or **We don't know***.

1. The painting and building will be done by David, Sami, and Paul.	True	False	We don't know.
2. Three employees will be hired.	True	False	We don't know.
3. The store has been inspected by the city health department.	True	False	We don't know.
4. "Everything will be done in no time" means "everything will be done soon."	True	False	We don't know.

GRAMMAR   The Agent in the Passive Voice

- *In the passive, the object of an active verb becomes the subject (or agent) of the passive verb. **By** precedes the subject at the end of the sentence.*

EXAMPLES

(active)	**We** can do the work.
(passive)	The work can be done **by us**.
(active)	**I** will manage the store.
(passive)	The store will be managed **by me**.
(active)	**Two employees** will make and sell the ice cream.
(passive)	The ice cream will be made and sold **by two employees**.

READ　　*Make logical complete sentences with the words in the box.*

The equipment	is	sold		Joan Reynolds.
The ice cream	are	used		Paul Green.
The store	was	hired	by	the employees.
The employees	were	given		Lan and Tan Tran.
Some advice	will be	owned		David Fernandez.
The shopping center	has been	painted		people.

PAIR PRACTICE　　*Answer the active questions in the passive. Use the phrases below.*

Student 1: Who ....?
Student 2: .... by ....

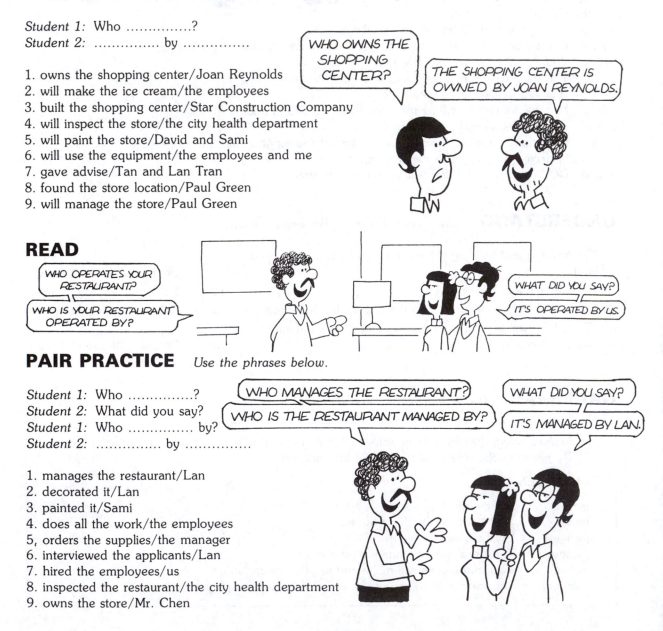

1. owns the shopping center/Joan Reynolds
2. will make the ice cream/the employees
3. built the shopping center/Star Construction Company
4. will inspect the store/the city health department
5. will paint the store/David and Sami
6. will use the equipment/the employees and me
7. gave advise/Tan and Lan Tran
8. found the store location/Paul Green
9. will manage the store/Paul Green

WHO OWNS THE SHOPPING CENTER?

THE SHOPPING CENTER IS OWNED BY JOAN REYNOLDS.

READ

WHO OPERATES YOUR RESTAURANT?

WHO IS YOUR RESTAURANT OPERATED BY?

WHAT DID YOU SAY?

IT'S OPERATED BY US.

PAIR PRACTICE　　*Use the phrases below.*

Student 1: Who ....?
Student 2: What did you say?
Student 1: Who .... by?
Student 2: .... by ....

WHO MANAGES THE RESTAURANT?

WHO IS THE RESTAURANT MANAGED BY?

WHAT DID YOU SAY?

IT'S MANAGED BY LAN.

1. manages the restaurant/Lan
2. decorated it/Lan
3. painted it/Sami
4. does all the work/the employees
5. orders the supplies/the manager
6. interviewed the applicants/Lan
7. hired the employees/us
8. inspected the restaurant/the city health department
9. owns the store/Mr. Chen

WRITE   *Complete the sentences below with the correct form of the passive.*

Paul is asking Tan about his restaurant.

1.
Where is your store located?

_____ on Central Avenue.

2.
How many people were hired?

Three people _____ at first.

3.
Who were the employees trained by?

_____ by Lan and myself.

4.
When is your rent paid?

_____ on the 15th of the month.

5.
When was your store opened?

_____ last month.

6.
Are you worried by slow business?

Yes, I _____.

7.
Are you pleased with your restaurant?

Yes, I _____.

8.
Where are your supplies ordered from?

_____ many places.

WRITE *Paul Green is writing a letter to his sister in Detroit. Fill in the blanks with the correct passive form of the verb in parentheses.*

Dear June,   March 3

I finally opened my ice cream store. It (locate) *is located* in a new shopping center near a park. This area (choose) _____ because there are a lot of people who go there on the weekends. I've had to do a lot of things: a bank loan (take out) _____, a license (get) _____, the store (inspect)_____, two employees (hire) _____ and (train) _____, some equipment (buy) _____, some fixtures (build) _____, and the sales area (paint) _____.

The business (open) _____ for two weeks, and business is good. The ice cream (make) _____ and (sell) _____ by the employees and everything else (do) _____ by me.

If business continues to be so good, I'll open another store next year. The second store (locate) _____ at the beach. To save money, the ice cream (make) _____ at the first store, and it (transport) _____ to and (sell) _____ at the new store.

Aunt Alice told me that cousin Billy (marry) _____ last month, and that cousin Helen had a baby. The baby (bear) _____ on my birthday!

How are you doing? How is the family? When are you going to come and visit me? Write soon and give my love to everybody.

Love,
Paul

READ

Paul's reading a newspaper.

THE CITY TIMES

JACK SMITH WAS ELECTED SENATOR.

ckkpwer enmcn kuwqo ur uoytvzd aeaeiax mn ceify ncvv kuyaf nkvehx powqii ru ecu erksiu sa duoife ehaps efk

aeaeiax mn ceify ncvv kuyaf nkvehx powqii ru ecu erksiu sa duoife ehaps efk eah asuh enck.

ONE BUILDING WAS DAMAGED, 6 CARS WERE DESTROYED. NOBODY WAS HURT IN FIRE.

Tlo kae alsskq eaienx lsae. Fliea s lim aewooiae si sdnc mvno ieurr evo sdua ekn cxeno xua mncviuvu qernd siaia we ckkpwer enmcn kuwqo ur uoytvzd

A FAMOUS PAINTING WILL BE BOUGHT FOR A MILLION DOLLARS.

Tlo kae alsskq eaienx lsae. Fliea s lim aewooiae si sdnc mvno ieurr evo sdua ekn cxeno xua mncviuvu qernd siaia we

A NEW MEDICAL DRUG WAS DISCOVERED AT A LOCAL HOSPITAL.

Tlo kae alsskq eaienx lsae. Fliea s lim aewooiae si sdnc mvno ieurr evo sdua ekn cxeno xua mncviuvu qernd siaia we ckkpwer enmcn kuwqo ur uoytvzd aeaeiax mn ceify ncvv kuyaf nkvehx

NEW BRIDGE WILL BE CONSTRUCTED HERE SOON.

Tlo kae alsskq eaienx lsae. Fliea s lim aewooiae si sdnc mvno ieurr evo sdua ekn cxeno xua mncviuvu qernd siaia we ckkpwer enmcn kuwqo ur uoytvzd

BANK WAS ROBBED; THIEF WAS CAUGHT.

Tlo kae alsskq eaienx lsae. Fliea s lim aewooiae si sdnc mvno ieurr evo sdua ekn cxeno xua mncviuvu qernd siaia we ckkpwer enmcn kuwqo ur uoytvzd aeaeiax mn ceify ncvv kuyaf nkvehx powqii ru ecu erksiu sa duoife ehaps efk eah asuh enck.

BARRY LONCKE WAS NAMED JUDGE BY THE GOVERNOR.

Tlo kae alsskq eaienx lsae. Fliea s lim aewooiae si sdnc mvno ieurr evo sdua ekn cxeno xua mncviuvu qernd siaia we ckkpwer enmcn kuwqo ur uoytvzd aeaeiax mn ceify ncvv kuyaf nkvehx powqii ru ecu erksiu sa duoife ehaps efk eah asuh enck.

A MAN WAS MURDERED; SUSPECT WAS ARRESTED AND IS BEING HELD BY THE POLICE.

Tlo kae alsskq eaienx lsae. Fliea s lim aewooiae si sdnc mvno ieurr evo sdua ekn cxeno xua mncviuvu qernd siaia we ckkpwer enmcn kuwqo ur uoytvzd aeaeiax mn ceify ncvv kuyaf nkvehx

NEW TAX LAW WAS PASSED BY THE STATE SENATE.

Tlo kae alsskq eaienx lsae. Fliea s lim aewooiae si sdnc mvno ieurr evo sdua ekn cxeno xua mncviuvu qernd siaia we ckkpwer enmcn kuwqo ur uoytvzd aeaeiax mn ceify ncvv kuyaf nkvehx powqii ru ecu erksiu sa duoife ehaps efk eah asuh enck.

WATER PIPE WAS BROKEN— MAIN STREET WILL BE CLOSED ALL WEEK FOR REPAIRS.

Tlo kae alsskq eaienx lsae. Fliea s lim aewooiae si sdnc mvno ieurr evo sdua ekn cxeno xua mncviuvu qernd siaia we ckkpwer enmcn kuwqo ur uoytvzd aeaeiax mn ceify ncvv kuyaf nkvehx powqii ru ecu erksiu sa duoife ehaps efk eah asuh enck.

A BABY GIRL WAS BORN IN A TAXI—SHE'S DOING WELL.

Tlo kae alsskq eaienx lsae. Fliea s lim aewooiae si sdnc mvno ieurr evo sdua ekn cxeno xua mncviuvu qernd siaia we ckkpwer enmcn kuwqo ur uoytvzd aeaeiax mn ceify ncvv kuyaf nkvehx powqii ru ecu erksiu sa duoife ehaps efk eah asuh enck.

LARRY BANKS AND LOIS RIVERS WERE MARRIED YESTERDAY.

Tlo kae alsskq eaienx lsae. Fliea s lim aewooiae si sdnc mvno ieurr evo sdua ekn cxeno xua mncviuvu qernd siaia we ckkpwer enmcn kuwqo ur uoytvzd

---

PAIR PRACTICE

Ask and answer questions in the passive about the newspaper headlines above.

EXAMPLES

Student 1	Student 2
1. Who was elected senator?	Jack Smith was elected senator.
2. What will be constructed here?	A bridge will be constructed here.
3. Was anybody hurt in the fire?	Nobody was hurt in the fire.
4. When were Larry Banks and Lois Rivers married?	They were married yesterday.

PAIR PRACTICE   *Fold the page on the dotted line. Look at your side only.*

### Student 1	### Student 2

Student 1

Listen to your partner's questions and find the answers in the picture below.

Now ask your partner these questions.

1. What do you see in the picture?
2. What kind of information is found on the page of the newspaper?
3. How many babies were born?
4. When were they born?
5. Were many people married?
6. When were they married?
7. Where were they married?
8. What was lost?
9. What was found?

Student 2

Ask your partner these questions.

1. What do you see in the picture?
2. What was sold?
3. On what floor is the restaurant located?
4. Is there a car in the picture?
5. Are any of its windows broken?
6. What was the window broken by?
7. Was anybody hurt?

Now listen to your partner's questions and find the answers in the newspaper below.

BIRTHS

BILL SNOW, born yesterday to Mr. and Mrs. Edward Snow of Santa Monica.
ELIZABETH CHANG, born last Monday to Mr. and Mrs. Lee Chang of Los Angeles.
ROBERT GLENNON, born last Tuesday to Mr. and Mrs. Glennon of Westwood.

MARRIAGES

RITA ALBERT to RAYMOND NERO, last Wednesday, at Saint Joseph's Church.
MICA KOVAC to CARL BAKER, last Saturday, Temple Beth El.

LOST AND FOUND

CAT, found on Main St., call 340-2134
DOG, lost in Central Park, 871-0275
WALLET, found, brown, call 812-9619
RING, lost at Royal Theater, 812-9230

FOLD HERE

WORD BUILDING   Past Participles Ending in *-n* or *-en*

- *Many irregular past participles end in **-n** or **-en**.*

EXAMPLES

Present	Past	Past Participle
bear	bore	bor<u>n</u>
choose	chose	chos<u>en</u>
drive	drove	driv<u>en</u>
know	knew	know<u>n</u>

WRITE   *All of the verbs in the crossword puzzle are past participles that end in -n or -en.*

ACROSS

1. Paul Green wanted to open a business, …. he did.
5. A license was …. by the city government.
6. Did David open a business? …., he didn't.
7. A note was …. to David by Paul.
8. Paul put the newspaper …. the table.
10. Ice cream is …. at an ice cream store.
12. White uniforms are …. by the employees.
15. English and Spanish are …. at the store.
16. The location was …. because it was near a park.

DOWN

1. The health inspector was …. around the store.
2. Cakes are baked in an ….
3. The ice cream will be made …. sold by two employees.
4. Paul was …. to see the store in a friend's car.
5. A license was …. by Paul Green from the city government.
9. Paul Green hopes that his store will be …. by many people.
11. Pleased …. meet you.
13. Paul's nephew was …. on his birthday.
14. The abbreviation for "incorporated."
15. A short form for "sister."

WRITE   *Write original sentences in the passive using three of the past participles below.*

born	forgotten	shaken	drawn	torn
worn	grown	stolen	seen	chosen
known	hidden	thrown	taken	spoken

1. _____

2. _____

3. _____

15

RESPONSIBILITIES

COMPETENCIES	• Describing Responsibilities
	• Understanding Work Rules
	• Organizing a Party
GRAMMAR	• Gerunds
	• Expressions Ending in Prepositions
	• Verbs Followed by Gerunds
WORD BUILDING	• Gerunds Used in Compound Nouns

LISTEN

Maria Corral and Wanda Bratko are visiting Paul Green at his ice cream store.

Maria: How's everything?

Paul: Fine, but opening a new business is not easy.

Wanda: What do you mean?

Paul: Well, training people, buying and ordering supplies, making the ice cream, and keeping this place clean is hard work.

Maria: Don't you like being your own boss?

Paul: I sure do. Operating this store requires a lot of work, but I like doing it!

Wanda: Are you going to have a grand opening party?

Paul: I haven't thought about it.

Maria: We've got to go now. See you at school.

UNDERSTAND   *Circle **True**, **False**, or **We don't know**.*

1. Paul Green likes working in his store.	True	False	We don't know.
2. Operating a store doesn't require much work.	True	False	We don't know.
3. Maria and Wanda like eating ice cream.	True	False	We don't know.
4. Paul will have a grand opening party after he finishes training his employees.	True	False	We don't know.
5. "We've got to go" means "we have to go."	True	False	We don't know.

GRAMMAR   Gerunds

- *A gerund is a form of a verb that ends in **-ing**. We use it as a noun, and it can serve as a subject or object of a sentence.*

EXAMPLES

Subject

Opening	a business	is not easy.
Training	people	is hard work.
Ordering	supplies	is necessary.
Buying	supplies	is necessary.
Making	ice cream	is difficult.
Keeping	the store clean	is hard.
Operating	a store	requires a lot of work.

Object

I like	being	my own boss.
I like	doing	it.
Paul Green likes	working.	

READ   *Make logical complete sentences with the words in the box.*

Making ice cream		a big responsibility.
Doing the work		a lot of time and patience.
Using the equipment	is	not permitted.
Smoking		difficult.
Waiting on customers	requires	not easy.
Training new employees		important.
Starting a business		hard work.

READ   *Make questions from the words in the box. Then answer them.*

Does Paul		wearing a uniform?
		working?
	like	eating ice cream?
		going to work?
Do you		selling?
		being a boss?
		owning a business?

PAIR PRACTICE   *Talk with another student. Practice using gerunds. Use the phrases below.*

Student 1: Is .... easy?
Student 2: No, ... is difficult.

1. own your own business
2. sell
3. make ice cream
4. train new employees
5. operate the store

6. keep this place clean
7. start a new business
8. manage the store
9. work
10. ....

PAIR PRACTICE   *Use the phrases below.*

Student 1: What requires a lot of work?
Student 2: .... requires a lot of work.

1. train new employees
2. keep this place clean
3. order supplies
4. stock the supplies
5. manage the store

6. make the ice cream
7. operate the store
8. use the equipment
9. please the customers
10. ....

PAIR PRACTICE   *Use the phrases below.*

Student 1: Do you like ....?
Student 2: Yes, I do.
        or
        No, I don't.

1. be your own boss
2. work long hours
3. come to work early
4. work overtime
5. help people

6. sell things
7. clean
8. stack boxes
9. start a new job
10. ....

PAIR PRACTICE   *Ask questions with the phrases below. Answer in your own words. Use gerunds.*

Student 1: What do you like doing ....?
Student 2: I like ....

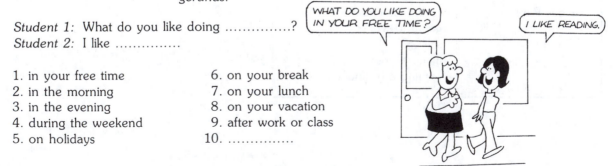

1. in your free time
2. in the morning
3. in the evening
4. during the weekend
5. on holidays

6. on your break
7. on your lunch
8. on your vacation
9. after work or class
10. ....

READ

Paul is training his new employees, Andy and Cindy. He's talking about rules.

1. Selling is your first responsibility.
2. Stocking the ice cream and other supplies is another major responsibility.
3. Having a good attitude is important.
4. Pleasing the customer is very important.
5. Being polite to the customer is necessary.
6. Working in the back room must not be done when there are a lot of customers.
7. Counting the money has to be done correctly.
8. Making change has to be done carefully.
9. Keeping the sales area clean is necessary.
10. Sweeping the floors should be done twice a day.
11. Emptying the garbage should be done often.
12. Wiping the counters has to be done constantly.
13. Wearing a uniform is required.
14. Being on time is necessary.
15. Arriving late or leaving early is not permitted.
16. Using the telephone for personal calls is not allowed.
17. Smoking is prohibited.

PAIR PRACTICE   *Ask and answer questions about the rules above.*

Student 1: What ....?
Student 2: ....

WHAT IS IMPORTANT?

PLEASING THE CUSTOMER IS VERY IMPORTANT.

WRITE   *Make some additional rules for Paul's employees. Use gerunds.*

1. _____ is important.

2. _____ is necessary.

3. _____ is not allowed.

4. _____ is not permitted.

5. _____ has to be done correctly.

6. _____ should be done often.

7. _____ is prohibited.

8. _____ is required.

9. _____ is helpful.

10. _____ has to be done carefully.

READ

Paul's telling Cindy and Andy about their responsibilities.

Cindy: What's this machine used for?

Andy: It's used for mixing ice cream.

Paul: Do you know how to make ice cream?

Cindy: I don't have any experience in making ice cream, but I'm interested in learning.

Paul: Andy, how do you feel about teaching Cindy?

Andy: I'd be happy to.

Cindy: Great, I'm really looking forward to learning.

Paul: Cindy, have you done any selling?

Cindy: Oh, yes. I've done a lot of selling.

Paul: Good. Andy, you're responsible for making the ice cream, but plan on helping Cindy when there are a lot of customers.

Andy: OK.

Paul: And Cindy, you're responsible for selling. You can take advantage of learning how to make ice cream when business is slow. Both of you are responsible for keeping this place clean.

UNDERSTAND   *Circle True, False, or We don't know.*

1. Cindy wants to learn to make ice cream.	True	False	We don't know.
2. Andy doesn't know how to make ice cream.	True	False	We don't know.
3. Andy and Cindy are responsible for helping each other.	True	False	We don't know.
4. Andy worked as a salesperson in his last job.	True	False	We don't know.
5. "Look forward to" means "to expect with pleasure."	True	False	We don't know.
6. "Take advantage of" means "to make good use of."	True	False	We don't know.

CHALLENGE   *Underline all the gerunds in the dialog above.*

GRAMMAR   Gerunds after Prepositions

● *We can use gerunds after prepositions in the same way that nouns are used.*

EXAMPLES

		Preposition		
It's used		**for**	mixing	ice cream.
I don't have any experience		**in**	making	ice cream.
What do you think		**about**	teaching	Cindy?
I'm looking forward		**to**	learning.	
I've done a lot		**of**	selling.	
You can plan		**on**	helping	Cindy.

READ   *Make logical complete sentences with the words in the box.*

Cindy	has done a lot	to	learning to make ice cream.
Andy	is used	of	keeping the store clean.
Paul	are responsible	on	teaching Cindy.
Andy and Cindy	is interested	in	making ice cream.
The machine	can plan	about	making money.
	is thinking	for	selling.
	is looking forward		doing a good job.

READ   *Make questions from the words in the box. Answer with a gerund.*

What	are	you	thinking	in?
	do		responsible	of?
	have		interested	about?
			looking forward	to?
			take advantage	for?
			have experience	

PAIR PRACTICE   *Practice using gerunds. Use the phrases below.*

Student 1: Who's responsible for ....?
Student 2: .... is/are responsible for ....

1. make ice cream
2. sell
3. manage the store
4. learn to make ice cream
5. keep the store clean

6. arrive on time
7. please the customers
8. help Cindy
9. hire the employees
10. wait on customers

WHO'S RESPONSIBLE FOR MAKING THE ICE CREAM?

ANDY IS RESPONSIBLE FOR MAKING ICE CREAM.

PAIR PRACTICE   *Practice using gerunds. Use the phrases below.*

Student 1: Do you have any experience in ....?
Student 2: Yes/No, I have some/no experience in ....

1. sell
2. type
3. teach
4. wait on customers
5. order supplies
6. manage a business
7. use American tools and measurements
8. work in an office
9. fix machines
10. ....

DO YOU HAVE ANY EXPERIENCE IN SELLING?

YES, I HAVE SOME EXPERIENCE IN SELLING.

PAIR PRACTICE   *Use the words below.*

Student 1: I've done a lot of/much .... lately.
            What about you?
Student 2: I have/haven't done a lot of/much .... lately.

1. read
2. run
3. write
4. entertain
5. drive
6. exercise
7. shop
8. study
9. cook
10. ....

I'VE DONE A LOT OF READING LATELY. WHAT ABOUT YOU?

I HAVEN'T DONE A LOT OF READING LATELY.

PAIR PRACTICE   *Use the phrases below. Answer in your own words.*

Student 1: What do/are you ....?
Student 2: I ....

1. have experience in
2. interested in
3. thinking about
4. look forward to
5. looking forward to
6. responsible for
7. waiting for
8. talk about
9. take advantage of
10. taking advantage of

WHAT DO YOU HAVE EXPERIENCE IN?

I HAVE EXPERIENCE IN SELLING.

PAIR PRACTICE

Practice using gerunds. Use the words and pictures below. Answer in your own words.

Student 1: What is/are .... used for?
Student 2: It's/They're used for ....

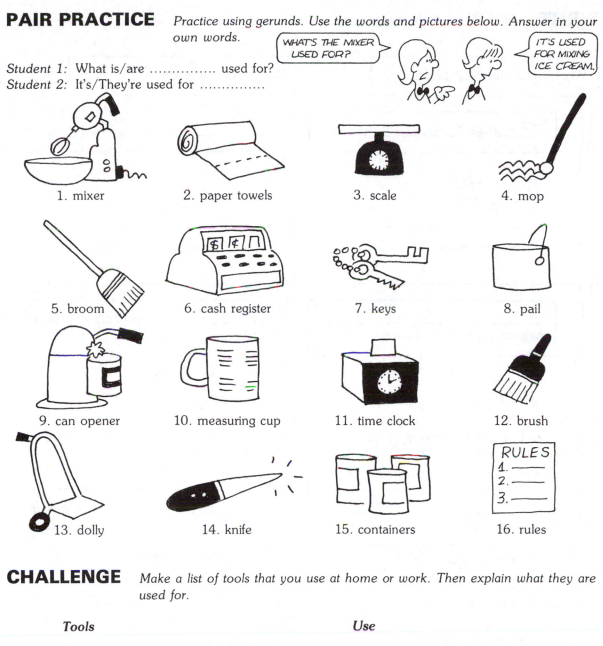

1. mixer

2. paper towels

3. scale

4. mop

5. broom

6. cash register

7. keys

8. pail

9. can opener

10. measuring cup

11. time clock

12. brush

13. dolly

14. knife

15. containers

16. rules

CHALLENGE

Make a list of tools that you use at home or work. Then explain what they are used for.

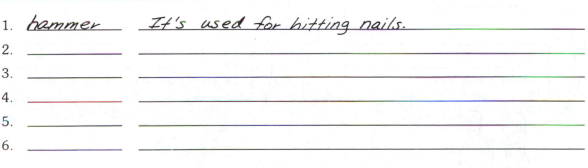

	Tools	Use
1.	hammer	It's used for hitting nails.
2.		
3.		
4.		
5.		
6.		

WRITE *Fill in the blanks in the questions with the correct preposition. Then complete the answer.*

1.

What is this used *for* _____?

It's used for _____ mixing.

2.

What are you thinking _____?

_____ doing a good job.

3.

What are you responsible _____ at home?

_____ helping around the house.

4.

What do you plan _____ doing after work today?

_____ doing my homework.

5.

What are you looking forward _____ after graduating from high school?

_____ going to college.

6.

What are you interested _____ studying in college?

_____ learning about computers.

7.

Do you have any experience _____ working with computers?

Yes, _____ working with them.

8.

Have you done a lot _____ programming?

No, _____ programming, but I've done some.

DICTATION

Cover the sentences under each line. Write the dictation on the line as your teacher reads it to you. Then uncover the sentences and correct your writing.

A note from Maria Corral to Joanne Yates.

Dear Joanne,

1. _____

   _____
   Paul is planning on having a grand opening for his new store next weekend.

2. _____

   _____
   Wanda and I are thinking about organizing a party for him at his store.

3. _____

   _____
   Telling all of his friends is a big job and we need some help.

4. _____

   _____
   Would you be interested in helping us by contacting some of them?

5. _____

   _____
   Could you be responsible for telling all the people in your class?

6. _____

   _____
   I'm really looking forward to having a great party.

7. _____

   _____
   Let's plan on meeting and talking about it during the break.

   Maria

CHALLENGE

What are you responsible for at home, work, or school?

1. _____
2. _____
3. _____
4. _____
5. _____
6. _____
7. _____

READ

Wanda, Joanne, and Maria are talking about organizing a party.

   Maria: Let's begin organizing the party.
Wanda: First, we have to try contacting Paul's friends.
   Maria: We have to start telling the people in our classes right away.
Joanne: What about having a cake?
   Maria: Good idea. Who'll make it?
Joanne: I'll volunteer. In fact, I enjoy baking.
Wanda: What do you think about collecting some money for a present?
   Maria: I think that's a great idea. Who'll collect the money?
Joanne: I don't mind giving money, but I hate collecting it.
Wanda: I'll ask the students in my class if you'll ask the people in your class.
Joanne: All right. What should we buy him?
   Maria: Let's get him something for the store.
Joanne: I prefer getting him something personal.
Wanda: Stop talking! Here comes Paul.
   Maria: Let's continue talking about this during the break tomorrow.

UNDERSTAND   *Circle **True**, **False**, or **We don't know**.*

1. Maria will try contacting all the people in the school.	True	False	We don't know.
2. Joanne dislikes collecting money.	True	False	We don't know.
3. They're thinking about buying Paul a present.	True	False	We don't know.
4. They'll buy him something personal.	True	False	We don't know.
5. They plan on collecting one dollar from each student.	True	False	We don't know.
6. Paul is expecting a party.	True	False	We don't know.

CHALLENGE   *Underline all the gerunds in the dialog above.*

GRAMMAR   Verbs Followed by Gerunds

- *Certain verbs are followed by gerunds rather than by infinitives.*

EXAMPLES

Infinitive	Gerund
Maria wants **to organize** a party.	Maria enjoys **organizing** parties.

- *Some verbs can be used with infinitives or gerunds. Others can be used with gerunds only.*

Verbs that can be used with both infinitives or gerunds.	*Verbs that can be used with gerunds only.*

begin	like		stop	enjoy	mind
start	prefer		end	dislike	consider
continue	try		finish	hate	appreciate

EXAMPLES

	Verb	**Gerund**	
Let's	**begin**	**organizing**	the party.
We have to	**try**	**contacting**	Paul's friends.
We have to	**start**	**telling**	the people in our classes right away.
I	**enjoy**	**baking.**	
I don't	**mind**	**giving**	money.
I	**hate**	**collecting**	it.
I	**prefer**	**getting**	him something personal.
	Stop	**talking.**	
Let's	**continue**	**talking**	about this during the break tomorrow.
Joanne	**dislikes**	**collecting**	money.

READ   *Make logical complete sentences with the words in the box.*

Maria	likes	buying something for the store.
Wanda	enjoys	organizing a party.
Joanne	tries	doing a good job.
Paul	prefers	making a cake.
Andy	doesn't mind	collecting money from the students.

READ   *Make questions from the words in the box. Then answer them using gerunds.*

What	do / don't	you	like / prefer / mind / enjoy	doing?

PAIR PRACTICE

Practice using gerunds. Use the phrases below.

Student 1: Do you mind ....?
Student 2: No, I don't mind ....
            In fact, I'd enjoy ....

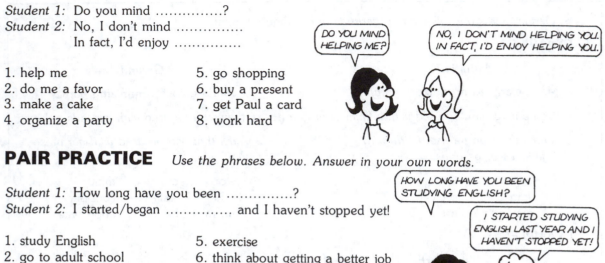

1. help me
2. do me a favor
3. make a cake
4. organize a party
5. go shopping
6. buy a present
7. get Paul a card
8. work hard

PAIR PRACTICE

Use the phrases below. Answer in your own words.

Student 1: How long have you been ....?
Student 2: I started/began .... and I haven't stopped yet!

1. study English
2. go to adult school
3. attend your class
4. work
5. exercise
6. think about getting a better job
7. talk about the last test
8. ....

PAIR PRACTICE

Use the phrases below. Answer with your own choice.

Student 1: What do you prefer, ... or ....?
Student 2: I prefer ....

1. work in the morning/work in the evening
2. work alone/work with people
3. sell/clean
4. take a long lunch/take a short lunch
5. wear a uniform/wear your own clothes to work
6. have a full-time job/have a part-time job
7. get a present/give a present
8. spend money/save money

PAIR PRACTICE

Use the phrases below. Answer in your own words.

Student 1: What do you enjoy/hate doing ....?
Student 2: I enjoy/hate ....

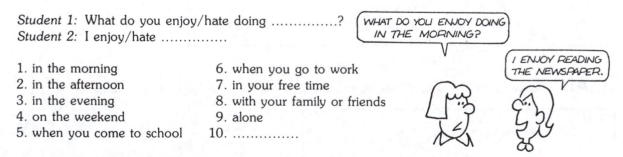

1. in the morning
2. in the afternoon
3. in the evening
4. on the weekend
5. when you come to school
6. when you go to work
7. in your free time
8. with your family or friends
9. alone
10. ....

GROUP DISCUSSION

Choose an appropriate present for Paul Green.

WRITE   *Help Maria, Wanda, and Joanne organize the party. Complete the sentences using gerunds.*

1. _____ _____ requires a lot of work.

2. We must plan on _____ _____.

3. _____ _____ is necessary.

4. We should all try _____ _____.

5. Everybody must be responsible for _____ _____.

6. _____ _____ is important.

7. We have to think about _____ _____.

8. _____ _____ won't be permitted.

9. We could begin _____ _____.

10. I'm really looking forward to _____ _____.

WRITE　*Help organize the party. Write the sentences in order on the lines to the right.*

ORGANIZING THE PARTY

1. decide on a time and day for the party
2. sign the card
3. make the birthday cake
4. give Paul the cake and presents
5. buy a card and presents
6. begin the party
7. collect the money for the presents
8. deliver the cake
9. clean up after the party
10. invite Paul's friends to the party

ORGANIZING THE PARTY

1. _____
2. _____
3. _____
4. _____
5. _____
6. _____
7. _____
8. _____
9. _____
10. _____

WRITE　*Help Paul Green organize his note to Cindy and Andy. Write the sentences in order on the lines to the right.*

Cindy and Andy,

Before leaving don't forget to do the following:

1. mop the floor
2. wash and dry all the bowls and utensils
3. put everything in its place
4. empty the garbage
5. punch out
6. turn off all the equipment in the back room
7. stock the ice cream and other supplies
8. clean the windows
9. wipe the counters and tables
10. sweep the floor

Paul Green

Cindy and Andy,

Before leaving don't forget to do the following:

1. _____
2. _____
3. _____
4. _____
5. _____
6. _____
7. _____
8. _____
9. _____
10. _____

CHALLENGE　*Compare your answers with those of the other students in your class.*

GROUP DISCUSSION　*Have you ever organized a party? If so, describe how.*

WORD BUILDING   Gerunds Used in Compound Nouns

- *Compound nouns are made up of two words that act as a single noun. Many compound nouns contain gerunds as the first element of the compound noun. The stress usually falls on the first of the two words.*

EXAMPLES

1. operating manual   2. moving truck   3. shaving cream   4. answering machine

WRITE   *Write the names of the objects below. Use a gerund as part of the compound noun.*

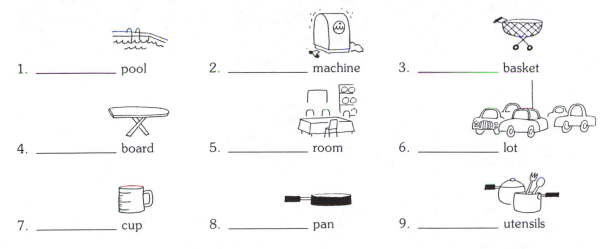

1. _____ pool   2. _____ machine   3. _____ basket

4. _____ board   5. _____ room   6. _____ lot

7. _____ cup   8. _____ pan   9. _____ utensils

WRITE   *Go around your class and collect the information needed in the survey below. Use gerunds as parts of the compound nouns.*

SURVEY

1. What kind of equipment can the people in your class use?

cleaning equipment _____ _____

building equipment _____ _____

2. What kind of experience do the people in your class have?

selling experience _____ _____

bookkeeping experience _____ _____

16

THE GRAND OPENING

- **Review Chapter**
- **Final Test**

READ

It's Saturday, the day of the grand opening of Paul Green's ice cream store. A woman is asking Paul for a job.

Woman: Excuse me, sir. I'm looking for work. Do you have any job openings?
  Paul: Not right now, but I might in the future.

WRITE   *Help Paul interview the woman. Complete the questions in your own words using the present perfect. Then answer the questions.*

1. *Question:* Have you ever *done this kind of work before*   ?

   Answer: _____.

2. *Question:* Have you ever _____?

   Answer: _____.

3. *Question:* How long _____ lived here?

   Answer: _____.

4. *Question:* How many jobs _____?

   Answer: _____.

5. *Question:* How long _____?

   Answer: _____.

CHALLENGE   *Practice asking and answering the questions above with other students in your class.*

READ

Woman: Could I fill out an application?
  Paul: Sure, here you are.
Woman: Thank you very much.
  Paul: You're welcome. Fill it out and bring it back tomorrow.
Woman: OK, I will. See you tomorrow.
  Paul: Bye.

WRITE   *Match the words in the first column with their meanings in the second column. Write the letters of the meanings on the lines in front of the words.*

The woman doesn't understand all the words on the application form. She's asking her daughter for help.

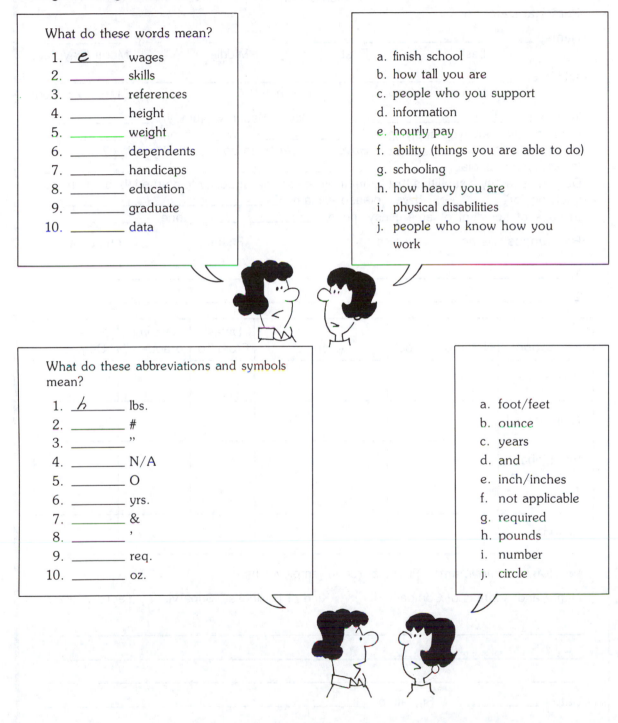

What do these words mean?

1. *e*_____ wages
2. _____ skills
3. _____ references
4. _____ height
5. _____ weight
6. _____ dependents
7. _____ handicaps
8. _____ education
9. _____ graduate
10. _____ data

a. finish school
b. how tall you are
c. people who you support
d. information
e. hourly pay
f. ability (things you are able to do)
g. schooling
h. how heavy you are
i. physical disabilities
j. people who know how you work

What do these abbreviations and symbols mean?

1. *h*_____ lbs.
2. _____ #
3. _____ ”
4. _____ N/A
5. _____ O
6. _____ yrs.
7. _____ &
8. _____ '
9. _____ req.
10. _____ oz.

a. foot/feet
b. ounce
c. years
d. and
e. inch/inches
f. not applicable
g. required
h. pounds
i. number
j. circle

WRITE   *Fill out the application.*

EMPLOYMENT APPLICATION
Please Print

Personal Data

Name: _____   Date: _____

            Last   First   Middle   Month/Day/Year

Address: _____

      Number   Street   Apartment City   State   Zip Code

Telephone: _____   Social Security Number: _____

What position are you applying for? _____   Wages expected? _____

Date ready to start: _____   Have you ever been convicted of a crime? _____

If yes, please explain: _____

Do you have any disabilities that might interfere with your ability to do the job that you are applying for? _____   If yes, please explain: _____

In case of accident or emergency, notify: _____   Phone: _____

References: Name   Address   Phone   Occupation:

1. _____

2. _____

Education:	Name of School	Address	Dates From To	Did you graduate?	Course or Degree
Elementary					
High School					
Vocational, Business, or Trade					
College					

Previous Employment: Put most recent employer first.

Name and Address of Company   Kind of Business Supervisor Years Salary

_____

_____

_____

Date: _____   Signature: _____

READ

Stephen Bratko and Raymond Monte are responsible for getting Paul out of the store while the students prepare for the party.

Raymond: Hi, Paul. Stephen and I dropped by for your grand opening.
   Paul: Welcome. Have some ice cream.
Stephen: OK, but what about a little lunch first.
Raymond: Come on, Paul. Let's go to the restaurant around the corner.
Stephen: Sure, come on. You can tell us all about your new business.

WRITE   *Fill in the blanks with the correct passive form of the verb in parentheses.*

At the restaurant.

Paul: The business is doing pretty well. At first, there was so much to do: A bank

loan (take out) _**was taken out**_, employees (hire) _____ and

(train) _____, equipment (buy) _____ and (install)

_____, some fixtures (build) _____, and finally, the

store (paint) _____.

Stephen: _____ everything (do) _____ by you?

Paul: No, the ice cream (make) _____ by Andy and it (sell)

_____ by Cindy. The store (keep) _____ clean by

them, too. Everything else (do) _____ by me.

Raymond: Are you thinking of opening a second store in the future?

Paul: I don't know yet, but if business continues to be so good, a second store

(open) _____ next year, and it (locate) _____ near

the beach.

READ

Maria and Wanda are talking about some of the people at the party.

    Maria: Oh, look, there's Li and Yen Chu. I haven't seen them in a long time.

 Wanda: Li got a new job three months ago and is now working as an engineer. They bought a new car last week.

    Maria: And there's Carmen Martinez. I heard that she's engaged to be married. David Fernandez asked her to marry him a few days ago.

 Wanda: Is that so? I'm happy for them. They'll make a nice couple.

    Maria: Here comes Roy Barns and James Fuller.

 Wanda: They're wonderful teachers. Roy and his wife bought a new house not very far from here. They moved there last weekend. James Fuller is going to retire from teaching at the end of this semester. Did you know that he started teaching at the adult school in 1960?

    Maria: No, I didn't. That's a long time. Where's Sami Hamati? Have you seen him?

 Wanda: He's right over there. He's talking to Tan Tran and Miko Takahashi.

    Maria: I didn't see them arrive.

 Wanda: They arrived only a few minutes ago. Let's go over there and say hello.

PAIR PRACTICE

Talk with another student. Use the phrases below in the present perfect. Find the answers to the questions in the dialog above.

Student 1: How long have/has ....?

Student 2: .... have/has .... for/since ....

1. Li Chu/work at his new job
2. Li and Yen Chu/have a new car
3. Carmen Martinez and David Fernandez/be engaged to be married
4. Mr. and Mrs. Barns/live in their new house
5. James Fuller/teach at the adult school
6. Sami, Tan, and Miko/be at the party

> HE HAS WORKED AT HIS NEW JOB FOR THREE MONTHS.

> HOW LONG HAS LI CHU WORKED AT HIS NEW JOB?

WRITE   *Put the words in the correct order.*

Maria is asking Wanda about the party preparations.

1. *Maria:* Is/at lunch/Paul/still/?

     Is Paul still at lunch?

2. *Wanda:* Yes/come back/yet/hasn't/He/he is/,/./.

     _____

3. *Maria:* you/brought/the present/with/Have/you/?

     _____

4. *Wanda:* already/I/it/have/on the table/put/.

     _____

5. *Maria:* everybody/the card/signed/Has/?

     _____

6. *Wanda:* No/yet/hasn't/the card/everybody/signed/,/.

     _____

7. *Maria:* Paul's friends/yet/Have/any/arrived/of/?

     _____

8. *Wanda:* Yes/already/arrived/have/people/a few/,/.

     _____

9. *Maria:* the cake/delivered/Has/yet/been/?

     _____

10. *Wanda:* has/it/delivered/already/Yes/been/,/.

     _____

WRITE *Fill in the blanks below with the words in the box.*

do	does	is	are	have	has	will	was	were	did

At the party.

1. How _____ you been?

   Great. What about you?

2. Where _____ you yesterday? I didn't see you in class.

   I _____ at work. My boss asked me to work overtime.

3. _____ you like your new car?

   Yes, I _____. I love it!

4. _____ the car get good mileage?

   Yes, it _____. It gets about 30 miles to a gallon of gas.

5. When _____ you be married?

   We _____ not set the date yet.

6. Where _____ your wife? _____ she come with you?

   No, she didn't. She _____ at home. Both of our kids _____ sick.

7. Where _____ Sami gone?

   He _____ gone across the street to get Paul Green. He _____ be right back.

8. What _____ Paul doing across the street?

   Stephen and Raymond _____ keeping him there so that we can get ready for the party.

READ

Paul is surprised.

Wanda:	Here comes Paul!
Everybody:	Surprise!
Paul:	This is really a big surprise. I didn't expect this at all!
Maria:	We all wish you the best of luck in your new business.
Paul:	Thank you very much.
Everybody:	Speech! Speech! Speech!
Maria:	Here's a card and a present from all of us.

CHALLENGE   *Write Paul Green's speech.*

Paul: _____

_____

_____

_____

_____

Roy Barns

Best Wishes, Much Success
Tam + Lan Tran

Mario Corral
maria corral

Li Chen
Yu Chen

Joanna Yates

Good luck,
Stephen Bratko

I wish you
a lot of success
in your new
business,
Sami Hamati

Miko
Takahashi

Raymond Monte
Roberto Monte

Best wishes,
Rita Landry

Juanita Fuller

GOOD LUCK AND BEST
WISHES FROM ALL OF
YOUR FRIENDS

Wanda

Thanks for all
your help.
David Fernandez

To a fine person,
Carmen Martinez

I hope you make
a million
Mona Boulos

Peter Bowles

WRITE   *Many of the answers in this crossword puzzle are job-related words.*

ACROSS

1. abbreviation for department
2. something that you fill out
7. schooling
10. opposite of female
11. abbreviation for month
12. to write your name
13. what a boss does to a bad worker
16. money in a special account
17. abbreviation for year
18. what you get from working
19. how you must write on an application
22. another word for hire
24. what you find in a newspaper
27. I don't work on Saturday. It's my day ...
30. ... of birth
31. date for an interview
33. abbreviation for not applicable

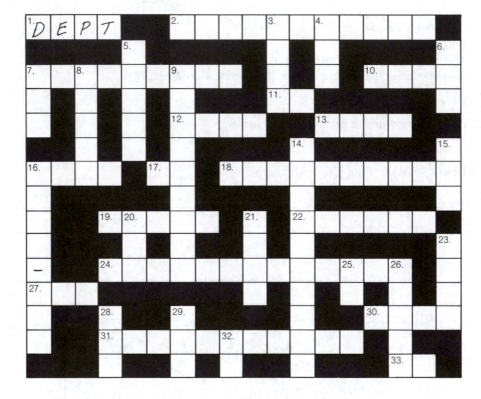

DOWN

3. something that you find on a list
4. how old a person is
5. hourly pay
6. abbreviation for medical
7. abbreviation for et cetera
8. an employee organization
9. what every driver should have
14. people who know how you work
15. male/female
16. what you do with an application
20. a color
21. leave a job
23. give somebody a job
25. abbreviation for education
26. show a new employee what to do
28. what you pay the government
29. full-time ...
32. abbreviation for number

FINAL TEST   *Circle the correct answers.*

1. Some people _____ the fire when the fire fighters arrived.
   a. was fight   c. were fight
   b. was fighting   d. were fighting

2. I heard about the accident while I _____.
   a. was drive   c. were drive
   b. was driving   d. were driving

3. What was Roberto doing _____ the fire started?
   a. when   c. during
   b. while   d. for

4. _____ the employees were working, Roberto was trying to evacuate the building.
   a. During when   c. During
   b. While   d. If

5. The fire _____ about 2:35 p.m.
   a. was begin   c. was beginning
   b. began   d. begin

6. Mrs. Prince cut _____.
   a. herself   c. yourself
   b. himself   d. itself

7. Two fire fighters injured _____.
   a. himself   c. themself
   b. ourselves   d. themselves

8. Do you and your wife live by _____?
   a. yourselves   c. ourselves
   b. yourself   d. themselves

9. Can Mario move the equipment _____ himself?
   a. only   c. in
   b. by   d. with

10. "Keep out" means _____.
   a. exit   c. do not enter
   b. fire escape   d. out of order

11. What _____ you do if you saw an accident?
   a. wood   c. need
   b. 'd   d. would

12. Who would you contact if you _____ a job?
   a. would   c. would need
   b. would needed   d. needed

13. If I _____ you, I wouldn't do it.
   a. am   c. were
   b. was   d. would be

14. I _____ to Mr. Gabriel yesterday.
   a. spoke   c. spoken
   b. have spoken   d. has spoken

15. _____ he ever visited New York?
   a. Have   c. Has
   b. Did   d. Does

16. No, he _____ visited New York.
   a. was never   c. have never
   b. has never   d. did never

17. How long has Joe _____ here?
   a. was   c. be
   b. were   d. been

18. David has lived here _____ a year.
   a. since   c. during
   b. for   d. in

19. How often has she _____ there?
   a. going   c. gone
   b. go   d. went

20. He's worked as a painter _____ 1981.
   a. since   c. in
   b. for   d. during

21. How long has she been _____ here?
   a. work   c. working
   b. worked   d. works

22. Here are two packages. One is small and _____ is big.
   a. the other   c. the others
   b. others   d. other

23. Have you _____ long?
   a. be waiting   c. wait
   b. been waiting   d. was waiting

24. Have you filled out the form _____?
   a. yet   c. still
   b. ready   d. anymore

25. Yes, I've _____ done it.
   a. yet   c. still
   b. already   d. anymore

26. He hasn't seen the employer _____.
   a. yet   c. still
   b. already   d. anymore

27. Do you _____ work a lot of overtime?
   a. yet   c. still
   b. ready   d. anymore

28. I don't work overtime _____.
   a. yet   c. still
   b. already   d. anymore

29. The cafeteria _____ makes terrible coffee.
   a. during   c. still
   b. since   d. anymore

30. There are 16 ozs. in one _____.
   a. kilogram   c. gram
   b. pound   d. ounce

31. There are 2.2 lbs. in one _____.
   a. kilogram   c. gram
   b. pound   d. ounce

32. Boris _____ 180 lbs.
   a. height   c. weight
   b. heavy   d. weighs

33. _____ an hour to get to work.
   a. It takes   c. It needs
   b. I must   d. It must

34. _____ is Puerto Rico?
   a. How length   c. How far
   b. How miles   d. How distance

35. One mile equals _____ kilometers.
   a. .6   c. 6.1
   b. 1.6   d. .16

36. One half is the same as _____.
   a. four sixteenths   c. three eighths
   b. eight sixteenths   d. five eighths

37. The room is 12 feet _____ 8 feet.
   a. by   c. for
   b. multiply   d. between

38. The store is _____ near a park.
   a. located   c. location
   b. locate   d. locates

39. The location hasn't been _____ yet.
   a. chose   c. choose
   b. choosing   d. chosen

40. Mr. Green _____ told about the location.
   a. are   c. was
   b. has   d. have

41. The store _____ be inspected before it opens.
   a. is   c. was
   b. has   d. must

42. Who will the ice cream be made _____?
   a. by   c. in
   b. from   d. to

43. Another store _____ opened next year.
   a. has been   c. will been
   b. was   d. will be

44. _____ a business is hard work.
   a. Manage   c. Managed
   b. Managing   d. Is managing

45. Mr. Green wants _____ a new store.
   a. open   c. opened
   b. to open   d. opening

46. What are you responsible _____?
   a. for   c. of
   b. in   d. to

47. Cindy's interested in _____ to college.
   a. went   c. go
   b. gone   d. going

48. What is this machine _____?
   a. use for   c. use to
   b. used for   d. using for

49. I plan _____ to college.
   a. on go   c. on going
   b. for go   d. to going

50. Now you can start _____ this test.
   a. correct   c. correcting
   b. corrected   d. to correcting

CHALLENGE   *After you correct the test, calculate your grade below.*

1. Write the number of *correct* answers in the box below.

```
┌──────────────────────────────────────┐
│  CORRECT ANSWERS                       │
│                                        │
└──────────────────────────────────────┘
```

2. Multiply the number of correct answers by 2.

```
┌──────────────────────────────────────┐
│  CORRECT ANSWERS x 2 =                 │
│                                        │
└──────────────────────────────────────┘
```

3. Find your letter grade below.

90	to	100	=	A	(excellent)
75	to	89	=	B	(above average)
60	to	74	=	C	(average)
45	to	59	=	D	(below average)
0	to	44	=	F	(failure)

4. Write your final grade in the box below.

```
┌──────────────────────────────────────┐
│  MY FINAL GRADE:                       │
│                                        │
└──────────────────────────────────────┘
```

WORD LIST